Vatican II
Forty
Personal
Stories

WILLIAM MADGES and MICHAEL J. DALEY
editors

TWENTY-THIRD PUBLICATIONS
185 WILLOW STREET • PO BOX 180 • MYSTIC, CT 06355
TEL: 1-800-321-0411 • FAX: 1-800-572-0788
Bayard E-MAIL: ttpubs@aol.com • www.twentythirdpublications.com

Twenty-Third Publications
A Division of Bayard
185 Willow Street
P.O. Box 180
Mystic, CT 06355
(860) 536-2611
(800) 321-0411
www.twentythirdpublications.com

ISBN:1-58595-238-9
Library of Congress Catalog Card Number: 2002109053
Printed in the U.S.A.

Dedication

To our families
June, Cara, Brendan
Marsha, Katie, and Sarah

And to our former theology teachers at Xavier University

Acknowledgments

We would like to express our thanks to the forty contributors who agreed to share their personal reflections about the Second Vatican Council and its significance for their work and ministry. In addition, we would like to recognize publicly Dan Connors of Twenty-Third Publications for guiding this project and Darleen Frickman of Xavier University for assisting in the preparation of the final manuscript. Finally, we wish to thank our spouses, June Pfaff Daley and Marsha Erickson, for their personal support and encouragement during this project.

Table of Contents

Glossary

Aggiornamento—Italian for "bringing up to date"; speaks to church renewal and adaptation; as phrased by John XXIII: "opening up of windows."

Aula—Latin for "hall." The nave of St. Peter's Basilica served as the meeting place where the Council's proceedings were held.

Constitutions—Vatican II issued four of these documents: two dogmatic constitutions (Church and Revelation), one constitution (Liturgy), and one pastoral constitution (Church in the Modern World). One of the most formal expressions of an ecumenical council, they usually describe or define doctrinal matters, but as the term "pastoral" suggests in the Pastoral Constitution on the Church (*Gaudium et Spes*) they can also speak of the application of doctrinal beliefs and moral principles to specific situations.

Declarations—Vatican II issued three of these documents (Education, Religious Freedom, and Non-Christian Religions). They summarize and articulate (often showing significant development) the church's current teaching on the subject at hand.

Decrees—Vatican II issued nine of these documents (Eastern Catholic Churches, Ecumenism, Priestly Formation, Laity, Religious Life, Office of Bishops, Missionary Activity, Social Communications, and Priesthood). Like constitutions, these documents can contain doctrinal matter. Similar to declarations they contain more specific recommendations and suggestions of reform pertaining to the topics under discussion.

Encyclical—Latin for "circular letter." Formal letter, written by the pope, which addresses doctrinal, moral, and/or disciplinary matters.

Osservatore Romano—first published on July 1, 1861, it serves as the semi-official newspaper of the Vatican.

Papabili—used as a reference to those who are considered papal front-runners before and/or during a papal election.

Pensioni—lodgings, dwellings, hotels.

Peritus, periti—Latin for "expert" or "advisor," theological advisors. Bishops were able to appoint their own theological advisors and to bring them to the council.

Secretariats—some originated as preparatory bodies (Promoting Christian Unity and Social Communications), others (Dialogue with Non-Christians, Dialogue with Non-Believers) came about as fruits of the council. Served to promote conversation and be a resource concerning their respective topic. Their work found its way into some council documents. After the council some became offices of the Roman Curia.

Secretary General—did preliminary and organizational work for the council. Kept the council's proceedings orderly and timely. Appointed by John XXIII, Archbishop Pericle Felici served this role.

Theological Commission—one of the council's ten preparatory commissions. Headed by Cardinal Alfredo Ottaviani and closely connected with the Holy Office, it saw itself as the guardian of orthodoxy throughout the council as all doctrinal matters passed through it.

Introduction

All is Story

Life is all about the story we tell ourselves and others. If we want to make a point with our children, we can repeat a rule or we can tell a story. The story is often more effective. If we want our students to remember an event, we can give the date and relate the facts about the event. Or we can tell a story that captures something of the essence of the event. The effect of telling the story is usually lasting and substantial.

Yet, in the context in which we find ourselves today, the story and its telling are in crisis. Which leads us to a story. In his book *Leadership is an Art*, Max DePree tells of the struggle between the campfire and the light bulb.[1] A friend of his had been doing some work in Nigeria in the sixties. Electricity was working its way into the villages. In the hut of each family was a single outlet. As evening came, after all the work was done, families would gather in their huts and look up at their light bulb. They were proud and excited to have such a tangible symbol of technology in their very own homes.

In the middle of the village, where the tribal fire burned, the chief and tribal elders gathered. Except no one came. It appeared that the allure of the light bulb was keeping the villagers in their huts. There, with nothing to read, families sat mesmerized by the light. "Progress," they said. All the while the village storytellers waited by the fire to pass on the tribe's history and traditions. Unfortunately, a few light bulbs were beating hundreds of years of community.

So it is with us as Catholics. We are our stories. Catholics have never been "Dragnet" Christians. We are not like Detective Joe Friday, people who want "just the facts." We possess a religious sensibility that anticipates the flowering of them. Christian faith began by telling a story: the life, death, and resurrection of Jesus

1

of Nazareth. Since that time Catholics have done their utmost embellishing and adding to this foundational story.

A story is not a story, though, unless it is told. But the story must also be told well. "*Bad*" stories—stories about power, intrigue, or deception—can become "good" *stories*, if they are told well. Likewise, we have heard good stories told so poorly that their potential is lost. So the challenge becomes one of telling our good stories well. That is when the "Wow!" happens, when the possibility of transformation appears. The question we ask then is, what stories are we telling?

Now more than ever, one chapter in the church's story that must be told involves an event that took place close to four decades ago: the Second Vatican Council. Along with its sixteen documents, the council produced some wonderful stories. Stories that, if we are not vigilant in preserving and telling, will be lost. With this in mind, what we seek to do in this book is to introduce the reader to some of the council's stories and their various characters (and there *were* some characters).

Thus, we have adopted a narrative, or storytelling, approach to the Second Vatican Council. Due to the good will of numerous individuals (some of whom were participants at the council itself; all of whom live in its shadow), we have collected forty stories that describe how Catholics and others responded to the council and its teachings. The significance of this collection becomes all the more clear when one recognizes that many of those who experienced the council first-hand are moving into, or are already in, their senior years. These stories must be told!

Related to this invitation to storytelling, we believe the book can meet the needs of a variety of different audiences. For general readers, the book can serve as an introduction to the state of the church today as reflected through the teachings of Vatican II. For college students, the book can be used in connection with another text about Catholicism or the council to give students a variety of perspectives on Vatican II's meaning and its effects. For adult education classes and faith-sharing groups, the book can provide stories that connect with their own lives and encourage them to tell their own stories about what it means to be church.

In general, we think the book will appeal to people who seek to have their perspectives broadened or their spirits affirmed by opening themselves to these stories of Vatican II.

Part One

The Council in Context

Introduction: What Story Will We Tell?[1]

Michael J. Daley

Whenever I think of Vatican II, of all the possible images that come to mind, a small, thick, paperback book enters my head. On the cover of it, in front of a red background, is a gold medal engraved with the faces of Popes John XXIII and Paul VI, *the* fathers of the council.[2] The title of that now classic book is *The Documents of Vatican II*. As the title suggests, it contains the sixteen documents of the Second Vatican Council—from church to liturgy, revelation to ecumenism, laity to missions.

As we continue to move further and further away from the actual, historical event itself, which consisted of four sessions beginning on October 9, 1962 and ending on December 8, 1965, a new understanding and image of the council is emerging. It is one that speaks to the *process* of Vatican II—the story, if you will, not only then but now—rather than the product. Lawrence Cardinal Shehan, archbishop of Baltimore during the council, captured it well when, writing in the introduction to the above mentioned text, he said, "The Council has ended; the Council has just begun."

The Process Begins

If asked for one of the more important dates in the history of the church I would be willing to bet that few, if any persons, would offer January 25, 1959. And yet it was on that day that John XXIII, having been pope for only ninety days, announced his decision to convoke a new council. This announcement, as indicated by Etienne Fouilloux in *History of Vatican II*, occasioned on the part of many a two-fold surprise: 1) that a reigning pope would admit the need to update the church; and 2) that he would choose a council as the way to do so rather than papal fiat.[3] So began the surprising and irreversible undertaking that his predecessors had resisted.

Although it was called "A Gesture of Serene Boldness" by the French newspaper *La Croix*, historian Giuseppe Alberigo relates that Pope John XXIII's announcement of a council before a small gathering of cardinals was met with "impressive, devout silence."[4] While the response of the public to the prospect of a new council was one of open-mindedness and expectation,[5] the response of the college of cardinals was one of "bewilderment and worry."[6]

This sentiment is best conveyed through one of the council's many anecdotes. Trying his best to explain what *aggiornamento* meant to a group of bishops, Pope John XXIII sensed his words about church renewal and responding to the "signs of the times" were falling on deaf ears. To better illustrate what "bringing up to date" entailed, John XXIII went to the nearest window, opened it, and said, "The church needs to let in some fresh air." Referring both to personal, interior renewal of self and adaptation of the church's teachings and structures to modern times, *aggiornamento* quickly became part of the Catholic vocabulary. Its familiarity by all was secured due to its frequent usage by Pope John XXIII and eventual acceptance by the majority of the close to 2,500 bishops at Vatican II.

Adding to the mood of reservation and resistance from some, and hope and confidence from others, was the ambiguity surrounding the character of the council. In his book *Pope John XXIII: Shepherd of the Modern World*, Peter Hebblethwaite conveys this sense in a conversation at the last and decisive meeting of the Central Commission, whose task it was to prepare the documents for the council's discussion. Some time prior to the meeting, John XXIII had taken out a ruler and measured a page from a preliminary draft and said: "Seven inches of condemnations and one of praise: is that the way to talk to the modern world?" (These words would soon be echoed by him again in his opening address to the council when he said "Nowadays, however, the Spouse of Christ prefers to make use of the medicine of mercy rather than that of severity. She considers that she meets the needs of the present day by demonstrating the validity of her teaching rather than by condemnation."[7]) Cardinal Giovanni Battista Montini, the then archbishop of Milan and future Pope Paul VI, went to that final meeting of the Central Commission and said that mercy, charity, and Christian witness—not anathemas and condemnations—were the way to reach the modern world. Realizing that Cardinal Montini spoke with the authority of the pope, Cardinal Alfredo Ottaviani, one of the council's more conservative voices and Secretary of the Sacred Congregation of the Holy Office (today called the Congregation for the Doctrine of the Faith), was heard to murmur: "I pray to God that I may die before the end of the Council—in that way I can die a Catholic."[8] As evidenced in Cardinal Ottaviani's words, "conservatives" at the council thought that to approach the modern world without condemnation meant to abandon traditional Catholic beliefs and practices.

Initially many people sought to understand the reason for the calling of the council by referring to previous ones, specifically the Council of Trent (1545-1563) and Vatican I (1869-1870). Yet, as Alberigo makes clear, there was neither a similar historical situation nor any of the traditional reasons—"doctrinal errors or disciplinary divisions"—for calling a council.[9] Still, many thought Vatican II would be a completion of Vatican I, which began on December 8, 1869 and was suspended on October 20, 1870. This council, in its constitution *Pastor Aeternus,* declared the dogma of papal infallibility. In response to these tendencies, John stressed that the orientation of the upcoming council would be pastoral, rather than doctrinal. He also emphasized its ecumenical character, foreseeing it as a "new Pentecost."

The next major step toward Vatican II began on Pentecost Day, May 17, 1959, with the establishment of the Antepreparatory Commission.[10] The main tasks of this commission would center around a universal consultation of the episcopate, creation of an outline of subjects to be discussed at the council, and suggestions regarding the membership of the preparatory groups. This herculean task was entrusted to Cardinal Domenico Tardini, Pope John's Secretary of State. Unfortunately, he did not live to see the fruits of his labors; he died on July 30, 1961.

Fr. Francis X. Murphy, C.Ss.R., the long-suspected but now revealed "Xavier Rynne" of conciliar fame (see page 10), says that "in organizing the council, Tardini followed the pattern of curial congregations or offices, gradually employing their prelates and advisors—conservatives to a man—in proposing some seventy schemata for debate and excluding forward-looking cardinals and theologians. Thus the preparatory stages revealed a fundamental split in the church's thinking between the static, juridical theology of the curia and the mindset of prelates who accepted Pope John's challenge to consider the church as the people of God rather than the political entity suggested by the traditional phrase of a 'perfect society.'"[11]

According to Fouilloux, the Episcopal responses, or *votas,* to this invitation of the Antepreparatory Commission followed three major lines of thought.[12] The first group expressed "intransigence." Here definitions and condemnations prevailed, and Mariological declarations were championed at the expense of ecumenism. The second group of responses favored adaptation in diverse areas. This response presaged the final concerns of Vatican II: Episcopal collegiality, liturgical renewal, and greater lay participation. Alongside these two lines of thought was the Roman viewpoint to the upcoming council, which was gradually shifting from an initial "contempt" or "indifference" to a more measured response of "distrustful cooptation."

The Speech Heard Round the World

In his opening speech, on October 11, 1962, Pope John XXIII gave the council fathers a personal and collective spiritual challenge to engage in the process of *aggiornamento* rather than take refuge in negative readings of the state of the church and the world. In these now memorable words, Pope John said:

> In the daily exercise of our pastoral office, we sometimes have to listen, much to our regret, to voices of persons who, though burning with zeal, are not endowed with too much sense of discretion or measure. In these modern times they can see nothing but prevarication and ruin. They say that our era, in comparison with past eras, is getting worse, and they behave as though they have learned nothing from history, which is, none the less, the teacher of life. They behave as though at the time of former Councils everything was a full triumph for the Christian idea and life and for proper Christian liberty.

> We feel we must disagree with these prophets of gloom, who are always forecasting disaster, as though the end of the world were at hand.

> In the present order of things, Divine Providence is leading us to a new order of human relations which, by men's own efforts and even beyond their very expectations, are directed toward the fulfillment of God's superior and inscrutable designs. And everything, even human differences, leads to the greater good of the Church.[13]

For Pope John, then, the council's agenda wasn't to be focused on retrieving or restoring some golden age of the church, as if there ever was one, but instead on bringing about a renewal in dialogue with the modern world.[14] As John was very apt to say, "The substance of the ancient doctrine of the deposit of faith is one thing, and the way in which it is presented is another."

The question still remained as to how to use the prepared schemas, written by the largely Roman and curial-controlled preparatory commissions. That question was answered in large measure on October 13, the first working session of the council. Supported by Cardinal Frings of Germany, Cardinal Liénart of France asked for and was granted a postponement of several days for the bishops to consult with members of their national or regional conferences as to whom to elect to the council's commissions. This was in response to the basically predetermined curia-approved members of the various commissions, which likely would have led to the adoption of the schemas already prepared. Without this intervention, many argue that Vatican II would have become a charade rather than a council.[15]

As evidenced in the preparation for the council and its subsequent unfolding, there could be said to have been two different and, at times, competing understandings about the purpose and goal of the council. This is seen in two of the council's more dramatic personages. Pope John's vision was open, conciliatory, pastoral, and oriented toward the future. Cardinal Ottaviani's vision was more defensive, doctrinal, and oriented toward the past. The motto on his episcopal coat of arms was, after all, *Semper Idem*, "Always the same."[16]

Which understanding of Vatican II carries us into the future will be determined by what stories we tell. Have you heard the one about...?

Francis Xavier Murphy, C.Ss.R.

A. k. a. Xavier Rynne

Francis Xavier Murphy was born in the Bronx, New York, on June 26, 1914. He progressed through the usual stages of education and was ordained a Redemptorist priest on June 23, 1940. Over the next 60 years he marked out a distinguished career as theologian, professor, and journalist. Fr. Murphy served as chaplain to the Catholic midshipmen of the U.S. Naval Academy, and he worked with Catholic War Relief Services in Italy and Germany. He joined the U.S. Army and served in Korea, Germany, and France from 1951 to 1958. After completing military service, Fr. Murphy accepted a university position at the Academia Alphonsiana in Rome, where he taught patristic and moral theology from 1959 to 1975. Among some of the many books he published during this time were A Monument to St. Jerome *(1953),* Peter Speaks Through Leo *(1954), and* Pope John XXIII *(1958).*

During the Second Vatican Council, Fr. Murphy gathered information about, as well as reported his personal observations concerning, the course of the debates about the subject matter of the various conciliar documents. In addition, he documented the church politics engaged in both behind the scenes and during the debates on the floor of the council. His detailed reports appeared first pseudonymously in The New Yorker *magazine. These reports, augmented with additional material, were eventually published in four book-length volumes, each devoted to one of the four sessions of the council.[17]*

For his scholarly and other accomplishments, he was recognized with honors from the Aspen Institute, the Folger Shakespeare Library, and the Woodrow Wilson International Center for Scholars. Fr. Murphy died on April 11, 2002.

Reporting the Secrets of the Council[18]

I was teaching at the Redemptorist Academia Alfonsiana, on the Faculty of Moral Theology, during the preparations for Vatican II as well as throughout the council. Never one to shrink from politics at any level, I began compiling notes about the intrigues and secretive manipulations by a number of prominent prelates as the agenda for the council was being formulated. I pulled these notes together into an article and submitted them to John Chapin, a literary agent. He in turn put me in touch with Robert Giroux, Vice President and Senior Editor of Farrar, Straus & Cudahy. He liked my piece and thought it worthy of publication. When he asked me where I'd like to have it placed, I replied, without the slightest hesitation, "In *The New Yorker*." Somewhat taken aback, Bob said, "Oh Father, I think there's too much religion for *The New Yorker*." I stuck to my guns and after some discussion Bob agreed to send it to Bill Shawn, the editor of *The New Yorker*.

Two days later Bob called me with the good news that my piece had been accepted. Going over the manuscript in preparation for its final submission, Bob suddenly said, "And what name are you going to use for the author? Since you are involved with the papal curia, it might be dangerous." Although the article contained nothing heretical or unorthodox, its revelations of the gossip and activities of the curia might infuriate members of that group. "They might report you to the Holy Office and have you relieved of your professorship," he said. All of a sudden the name Xavier Rynne (my middle name and my mother's maiden name) popped into my mind. "Excellent," Bob said. And that was the name I used.

The article, a "Letter from Vatican City," was published in *The New Yorker* at the very start of the first session of the council. A long and apparently authentic account of names and activities, guesswork and facts about the preparations for the council, it sent shock waves through the assemblage of cardinals, bishops, and priests. Many were outraged, and some frankly appalled. A surprising number became hell-bent on pursuing the whereabouts of Xavier Rynne, an effort that, fortunately, except for a few close calls, was unsuccessful for the duration of the council. "Who the hell is Xavier Rynne?" became a persistent question throughout the council and for many years after the deliberations ended.

Although the conciliar debate resulting in the church's historic self-critique was supposed to be conducted under the rule of secrecy, the fanfare with which the council opened and the gravity of the matters under consideration proved too great a burden for the traditional Vatican organs of information.

Meanwhile, thanks to Xavier Rynne, a rare spotlight had been focused on the Vatican's entrenched inner circle. The prelates and clerics of the Roman curia, who determine church policies from the top, were thus exposed to conciliar criticism, much to the chagrin of their suppositious leader, Cardinal Alfredo Ottaviani of the *ancien* Holy Office (formerly known as the Inquisition), who considered himself the paragon of orthodoxy.

From its inauguration, the council had proven a startling event, providing journalists and TV and radio commentators by the hundreds with hard news: Pope John referring to some of his counselors as "prophets of doom"; Cardinal Liénart and Cardinal Frings upsetting the first meeting by demanding a free election of the commissions that would produce the council's documents; the frequent skirmishes between curial cardinals and their opponents; the gracious confrontations of adversary prelates and *periti* in the *Bar Jonah* and the *Bar Rabbas*. (These were the coffee, snack, and toilet facilities provided by Pope John in the sacristy and interior vestibule. "If we do not let them smoke somewhere," he is reported to have advised, "they'll be hiding their cigarettes under their miters.")

Over the course of the next three years, the council's annual two-month sessions were reported in extraordinary detail through twelve subsequent *New Yorker* articles by the stealthy Xavier Rynne. Each article created a firestorm of controversy within the assemblage. But, for all the hue and cry, the speculations and interrogations, no one seemed capable of identifying the author of the missives.

It was only at a clerical gathering in Baltimore some twenty years later that I admitted authorship to the departing Apostolic Nuncio, Pio Laghi. Asked why, after all these years of pseudonymity, I was coming up out of the catacombs, I replied, "If I died tomorrow the Jesuits would claim him [Rynne] and the Redemptorists would be delighted to be rid of him."

Nonetheless, as I had been writing articles for *America, Catholic World, The New York Times, Boston Globe, Los Angeles Times, Baltimore Sun*, and other journals, suspicion soon fell on me. In particular, the professors at the Jesuit-run Biblicum questioned me strenuously and often. However, by the assiduous use of casuistry, I managed to preserve my anonymity, although some of my closer friends and an occasional sharp critic were certain that I was their man.

I had been appointed a *peritus* through the good graces of the Redemptorist bishop of Monterey-Fresno, Aloysius Willinger, a close friend of Cardinal

Cicognani, the Vatican Secretary of State. Shortly after the arrival of the first *New Yorker* article in Rome, he questioned me as to the authorship, concluding with the observation that there were many expressions that sounded like mine. That evening he had Archbishop Egidio Vagnozzi and a few younger bishops to dinner and, finding them ignorant of the Rynne article, took great glee in disabusing them of their ignorance.

About a month later I learned that I was going to be called to the Holy Office to be put under an extremely rare oath of secrecy, under pain of excommunication. When I inquired as to the subject matter for the oath, I was told I would be informed after I arrived at the Holy Office. I replied that I simply refused to take a blind oath. The next morning I sought out both Cardinal Spellman and the English Cardinal John Heenan, suggesting that if I were not back in the conciliar hall by noon, they should send somebody after me.

I arrived at the Holy Office and awaited the arrival of Archbishop Pietro Parente, Assessor of the Congregation, who entered promptly at ten o'clock. He was accompanied by two monsignori, one of whom was Henry Cosgrove, an acquaintance of mine from Brooklyn.

"Kneel down," said the archbishop in Italian, "and we will take the oath of secrecy."

"Not until I know why," was my caustic response.

"I will tell you after the oath."

"No, Monsignor. I am not taking an oath about something of which I do not know the substance."

"You will be told. . ."

"No, Monsignor," I interrupted. "And what are these two gentlemen doing here?"

"One is my secretary, the other a translator."

"It is obvious that I need no translator. Henry," I said, turning to the American monsignor, "you can be my secretary."

With the archbishop's temper rapidly rising, I asked if he wanted to interrogate me regarding the magazine with little pieces of paper he had tucked under his arm. On his acquiescence, I took an oath about what I might know regarding that particular magazine. He began reading me a series of quotations, and for each I agreed that they were written by one Xavier Rynne, but carefully added that I was Fr. Francis Murphy. Then he came to a defamatory passage about himself, describing his expulsion from Rome some twenty years earlier by Pope Pius XI. "*Listen*," he said, "*you understand that Pius XI was a little sick in the head.*"

"Henry," I shouted to my newly-acquired secretary, "write that down!"

Suddenly realizing the significance of what he had just said, the archbishop bolted out of the room. The three of us stood silently, not knowing exactly what to do. Finally, I whispered the closing prayer of the oath, dismissed the monsignori, and walked quietly back to my quarters. I never heard from the archbishop again.

Monika K. Hellwig

Monika K. Hellwig was born in Breslau, Germany, on December 10, 1929. After earning degrees at the University of Liverpool (England), she came to the United States, where she completed the M.A. in 1956 and the Ph.D. in 1968, both at the Catholic University of America. In addition to visiting professorships at a number of colleges and universities, Hellwig taught at Georgetown University for about 30 years, completing her tenure there as the Landegger Professor of Theology (1990-1996). Since 1996 she has been the Executive Director of the Association of Catholic Colleges and Universities of the United States.

Dr. Hellwig has served on the editorial board of prominent theological journals, such as Theological Studies *and the* Journal of Ecumenical Studies. *In addition, she has been a member of national committees established by the U.S. Catholic Conference and has held the office of President of the Catholic Theological Society of America (1986-87). She has published more than 100 articles and more than 20 books. Some of her more important publications include* Understanding Catholicism *(1981),* Jesus, the Compassion of God *(1983), and* The Modern Catholic Encyclopedia *(1994), which she co-edited with Michael Glazier. In recognition of her outstanding contributions to Catholic theology, Hellwig has been awarded more than twenty honorary doctorates.*

> *During the Second Vatican Council she was in Rome, first to ghost-write a book for a Vatican official, then as part of a retreat team for Movemento Mondo Migliore, and finally as a broadcaster for the English language program of Vatican Radio while making abstracts of the council documents.*

Vatican II: The Glorious Years

Those of us who had the privilege of being in Rome during the Second Vatican Council are not likely ever to forget the intellectual excitement of those times. Every autumn of those four years the streets in the neighborhood of St. Peter's and around the pontifical universities bustled. There was talk about what was happening in the *aula* and about what was happening behind the scenes. The debates spilled into restaurants and bars. There was speculation about the strategy sessions going on behind doors in *pensioni* and religious houses. Sometimes the debates spilled into the streets with bishops and long robed cardinals striding along engaged in discussion with their own *periti* or trying to shake off importunate journalists or petitioners.

The four sessions took place always and only in the autumn, when the weather in Rome was gracious and it was good to be out of doors. Even before the bishops arrived from all over the world, lectures and press conferences by the *periti* would be announced. This would be a little before the beginning of the academic year at the Roman universities, and some world-renowned speakers would be billed. Much as the organizers would try to limit attendance to those with press credentials, those of us who were in Rome on other pursuits would crowd the halls, thirsty for the kind of theology and scripture scholarship to be had so freely at that time.

Once the sessions began, the *Osservatore Romano* would report daily. Of course the editors observed scrupulously the rule that the actual speeches should not be reported because it was not to be known which participant bishops were taking which positions in the discussions. No documents were actually published until the end of the second session. Until they were passed, the matter of the discussions was to be kept *segreto* (secret). *Osservatore Romano,* therefore, gave on the front page only the list of speakers in the order in which they had spoken on the previous day. From the second session onward, however, one could read the entire texts of the speeches without attribution towards the back of the paper. The speeches were printed in the same order as the list of speakers on the front page. This material, after all, was *segreto*, or at most *segretissimo*, by no means classified as *segretissimo segretissimo* (!) And so we who read Italian were getting day by day the most wonderful theological education. The speeches, but for rare exceptions, were assuredly written not by the bishops but by their *periti*, and many bishops had picked their *periti* among top rank scholars.

Between the first and second sessions of the council, Pope John XXIII died, a truly saintly and pastoral pope. A man of great common sense and shrewdness, he was the visionary, prophetic leader who had launched the council with such great expressed hopes for a new Pentecost of the Holy Spirit. He died saying that he offered his life for the continuation of the council. We all held our breath over the coming election of the next pope as the rumors flew around Rome. There had been much calculation as to who were the *papabili* and which among them was the front-runner. Everyone had both hopes and fears concerning the impact that a change in the papacy would have on the council and its outcome. It was very well known that there were curial cardinals who, along with their permanent staffs, had been and remained utterly opposed to the very idea of the council. They were convinced that they were running the church very efficiently so that no changes were needed. Moreover, they knew that the German bishops and those of Asia and Africa were a great threat to this excellent established order of the church, properly governed out of Rome to preserve changeless uniformity even in small matters. Already they were saying, "I told you so," and "Look at the disturbance they have caused." A refrain one could pick up sometimes in the street was, "Fifty years, fifty years, it will take us fifty years to get the church back in order after this council." Looking back now, after forty years since the opening, the refrain sounds more ominous in light of recent developments than it did then when we laughed at it as a huge joke.

In the event, it was Montini of Milan who was elected, and it was assumed that he would move in the same direction as Pope John XXIII. Indeed it was Montini who had made a very strong speech on collegiality in the church during the first session. On the day after his election he announced publicly that the main business of his pontificate would be the continuation of the council. Moreover, his inaugural encyclical opened some of those windows of which John XXIII had spoken in initiating preparations for the council: "I want to open the windows of the church and let some fresh air in." It was rumored in Rome that Pope Paul VI, having had experience of the kinds of tricks played on popes by some gentlemen of the curia, and having been a papal speech writer himself under Pope Pius XII, was taking no chances with his inaugural encyclical. He wrote it word for word himself and, so I was assured by one in a position to know, stood at the presses all night to make sure that what was printed was what he had actually written and not someone else's "correction" of his text.

Unfortunately in the general excitement of the council, this encyclical, *Ecclesiam suam,* did not attract, then or since then, the attention it should have received. Presenting the church as essentially a process of dialogue, the encyclical opened possibilities for great progress in ecumenism (which some in the curia have diligently tried to close since then). Pope Paul VI certainly began his pontificate with a very dynamic, forward-looking concept of the church, with imagery that effectively complements the imagery used in *Lumen Gentium,* the "Dogmatic Constitution on the Church," already then under discussion, though not promulgated until the end of the third session.

Meanwhile, the council went on. In the second session *Sacrosanctum Concilium,* the "Constitution on the Sacred Liturgy," was promulgated along with two lesser documents. There had, of course, been a ferment of liturgical scholarship both in Europe and in America. In the fifties, some of us in the United States who were fortunate had been attending summer sessions at the Catholic University of America and at the University of Notre Dame. Many of the great European scholars in scripture, patristics, and liturgy were lecturing there, along with towering American scholars such as Godfrey Diekmann. The passing and promulgation of *Sacrosanctum Concilium* seemed like a vindication of our professors, almost all of whom had at some time suffered from curial disapproval and sanctions. The passing of this document initiated years of wonderfully happy rediscovery and retrieval of the spirit of the liturgy, all now firmly legitimated. However, it was not in Rome, but later upon return to the U.S. and to the graduate programs in theology at the Catholic University of America that I actually experienced this excitement of rediscovery with like-minded congregations of worshipers.

One by one the great Vatican II documents opened vistas of possibilities for Catholics around the world. There was the battle led by Cardinal Suenens over the placement of chapters in *Lumen Gentium.* Symbolically this was an important issue: was the church to be described primarily as the people of God, or primarily as a hierarchic structure? Clearly the stance of a powerful group of curial cardinals and bishops was that this was not even a question. In their view the church was essentially a hierarchic structure, to be maintained with an unswerving fidelity that was equated with unqualified changelessness. Therefore there was no question that after an introductory chapter, more homiletic than consequential, the next step was to set out the centralized hierarchic structure of the church.

Against this Suenens pressed for a second chapter on the people of God as describing the true nature of the church. This in turn had consequences for the large document on the church in the modern world, *Gaudium et Spes,* and for the documents on the role of the laity, on revelation, on ecumenism, and more.

Because of the press conferences and public lectures of the *periti,* these discussions conveyed to us who were living in Rome at the time a real ferment of hope for a renewed church. We began to share the vision of a church immediately relevant to the real problems and challenges of the world of the twentieth century. We began to see the integration of what we had studied with what was actually happening. We began to have hope of wide-awake Catholic communities in lively participatory liturgies. And we began to realize in a whole new way that not only the hierarchy and clergy, but we ourselves, the laity, were this church that was being talked about. Already at this time in the sixties, this was perceived as especially good news for women, though in the council itself the women were totally excluded, even such as economist Barbara Ward, who had contributed massively to the preparatory work for *Gaudium et Spes.*

When the council ended, it was on a great surge of hope and new energy. The liturgy was to be thoroughly renewed for intelligibility, more biblical content, and more active participation by the congregation. There was to be a substantial reform of the curia. There were to be regular means for the exercise of episcopal collegiality to express the voices of the local churches. There was to be a whole new approach to and emphasis on ecumenism. The church was to engage the reality of the modern world on a note of hope and collaboration, not with a predetermined stance of rejection and condemnation. And this engagement was largely to be in fields where the combined expertise of the laity was to play the key role, with room for multiple initiatives. Post-conciliar commissions were to be put in place to make sure it all happened. What was perhaps not well enough thought out was the extent to which the huge, complex, change-resistant Roman curia was in the strategic position to control whether or not it all happened.

Soon after the council, I traveled in Switzerland, Germany, and Britain, and then returned to the U.S. to complete doctoral studies at the Catholic University of America. Implementation of the liturgical changes was, of course, piecemeal as directives came out from the post-conciliar committee, and patchy as parish clergy responded with varying degrees of enthusiasm or lack of it. Slowly parish councils came into being, implementing at the grassroots level the principle of collegiality introduced by the council with references to the bishops of the local churches. In fact, as the years wore on, it could be observed that the principle of collegiality was implemented rather better within the local churches than at the global level, where the curia remained implacably opposed to it.

Within the graduate department of Religion and Religious Education (then part of the Graduate School of Arts and Sciences) scripture, theology, and liturgy had truly come alive. Immense enthusiasm and creativity was expended on the preparation and celebration of the regular eucharistic liturgies, as well as on paraliturgical occasions, and eventually community penance celebrations. It constituted a training ground for many who would later be lay ministers in the parishes, and gave them an experience of Christian community that carried over into religious education, musical and liturgical ministries, publishing, and other fields. In those days everything was still possible and, at least on the university campus, enthusiasm was not spontaneously met with suspicion.

It was not only in liturgical celebration but also in the classroom that profound change and renewal were taking place. In the fifties at the Catholic University of America (as was probably the case elsewhere on Catholic campuses) the Index of Forbidden Books loomed so large that a considerable collection of modern philosophy and theology was literally padlocked in cages in the library. The zeal of the librarians was such that even Romano Guardini's *The Lord* (in its English translation) was locked away because scripture quotations had been taken from a better translation, which was therefore closer to the German but which had not been officially approved for use by American Catholics. After the Second Vatican Council many of the books in the cages had been liberated and had migrated onto the graduate reading lists, where they were absorbed with recognition and appreciation. We were making a transition from dogmatic theology to systematic theology, from explanation of established positions assumed to be formulated in unchangeable ways to a mode of inquiry that began with existential questions and explored the tradition for resources to answer those questions. We were reading and discussing across Christian denominational boundaries, and going further afield to learn from Jewish authors, eventually moving into the whole sweep of human religious traditions.

Lay students in those days were flocking to the graduate religious studies and theological programs both during the academic year and during the summers, when many of them were using their vacation time from full-time jobs to pursue these studies with a passion. Some certainly hoped to be active in various church ministries, but many were simply in pursuit of knowledge and understanding of this remarkable rebirth of the church that had happened with Vatican II. Most significant was the number of women, both religious and lay, with this thirst for deeper understanding of theology and of the Catholic tradition. Combined with the Sister Formation movement that had been so widespread in the fifties, boosted by the personal urging of Pope Pius XII, this new enthusiasm on the part of women for biblical, theological, and liturgical studies contributed to a certain gap between an increasingly educated body of Catholic women and a commonly much less educated parish clergy. Typically at public theological lectures and at seminars and institutes on theological and church topics, the clergy were absent and the women turned out in force.

Of course, it was not long before the reaction set in. The changes were so swift and so central that many in the church, both lay and clerical, feared that everything was falling apart. It must indeed be acknowledged that with less rigid catechetical instruction, younger Catholics seemed to know less about the traditional teachings. With a more personal approach to morality and church law, many followed their own conscience on matters such as birth control, and took ritual laws like Sunday eucharistic attendance much more lightly. With a new understanding of sacramentality, few could make sense of the sacrament of penance in the way we had been practicing it. On the other hand, those who longed for a more meaningful celebration within a context of spiritual direction were hard put to find such a confessor among the parish clergy. Many simply drifted away. Meanwhile, slowly, we rediscovered the Rite of Christian Initiation of Adults, which put new demands both on the clergy and on the parish communities—demands for which not all of them were ready either intellectually or in terms of lived Christian community.

It cannot be denied that the aftermath of Vatican II left us with great inspiration and hope, but also with great confusion and tension that constantly has threatened to polarize the community. In the midst of that confusion the social justice concerns of *Gaudium et Spes* came to the forefront among some clergy and theologians in Latin America and elsewhere, and in a whole new way in the U.S. Catholic Bishops' Conference. The Catholic Church has become a political force on behalf of the poor and excluded, and it is increasingly a force to be reckoned with. But precisely where the bishops' conference has become very forward looking, pro-active, and ready to undertake radical social justice initiatives, the Catholic community in the pews has largely been unwilling to follow, holding instead the values and opinions of the general American population.

Have we realized the potential created by the Second Vatican Council? Yes, in some aspects and to some degree. We shall not be able to reenact that council and try over again. But how about Vatican III soon?

Lisa Sowle Cahill

Lisa Sowle was born in Philadelphia in 1948. After attending elementary and secondary schools in Virginia and Washington, D.C., she studied at the University of Portland and Santa Clara University, where she received her undergraduate degree in 1970. She earned the M.A. and Ph.D. degrees from the Divinity School of the University of Chicago in 1973 and 1976.

Ms. Sowle married Larry Cahill, an attorney, in 1973, and they became the parents of five children, three of whom are adopted from Thailand. Currently Dr. Sowle Cahill is the J. Donald Monan Professor of Theology at Boston College, where she has taught since 1976. She has been a visiting professor at Georgetown University and Yale University. In addition, she has received eight honorary degrees. Dr. Sowle Cahill has held leadership positions in important professional organizations, such as president of the Catholic Theological Society of America and president of the Society of Christian Ethics. She has published widely on bioethics, reproductive issues, and social ethics. Among her books are Love Your Enemies: Discipleship, Pacifism, and Just War Theory *(1994),* Sex, Gender, and Christian Ethics *(1996), and* Family: A Christian Social Perspective *(2000).*

Dr. Sowle Cahill has frequently been called upon as a theological consultant. For example, she was a consultant to the U.S. Catholic bishops in preparation for the 1987 Synod on the Laity as well as a consultant subsequently on a variety of marriage and family life issues. She has been a member of the Catholic Health Association Theology and Ethics Advisory Committee, the National Advisory Board for Ethics in Reproduction, and the March of Dimes National Bioethics Committee. Dr. Sowle Cahill continues to serve on the Advisory Board of the Cardinal Bernardin Center at the Catholic Theological Union in Chicago.

The Council as Seen from a Catholic Girls' School

I attended the Sisters of Mercy Holy Trinity High School in Washington, D.C., from 1962 to 1966, years roughly coinciding with the Second Vatican Council. One of my most vivid memories is listening with rapt attention as my senior year theology teacher conveyed to us the contents and significance of the almost-daily bulletins from Rome, extensively covered by both religious and secular news media. Granting that my memory forty years later is highly selective and occasionally inventive, and that many events and details are recollected as having a significance that they could only have acquired later, I still look back on those years as emblematic of the situation of Catholic women "then" and "now," and the changes that both connect and disconnect the past and the present.

My childhood in the 1950s and early '60s is suffused with memories of Catholic piety and practices that were at once parochial, romantic, prayerful, stifling, uplifting, fear-inducing, identity-forming, spiritual, hopeful, and sexist. I can remember my dad's love for the sisters who taught him in grade school in Michigan and, by his account, consistently outsmarted his shenanigans. I can remember my dad taking us into church on All Souls' Day, so that we might offer magical prayers that would suddenly (and on that day only) release my grandparents from the torments of purgatory. I can remember having holy water fonts full of (diluted) Lourdes water in our bedrooms. I remember being in Rome, about nine years old, pressed in throngs of people in St. Peter's, who craned for a glimpse of Pius XII being carried about on a gilt chair. I can remember Mass in

Latin and CYO dances. I can remember parading with the other eighth-grade girls, dressed in white, to crown the Virgin Mary.

I can remember the class being called up to sister's desk one by one after we had taken a career aptitude test, and her strained smile as she read off the testing service's first career choice for me ("priest or minister"), and quickly moved on to the second ("volunteer or social worker"). I can remember my convert mother's stiffness in and around Catholic religious services, the baby brother who lived a few hours (my parents had been advised by doctors to use birth control), and my mother's increasing hostility toward Catholic moral teachings and trappings of just about any sort. But I also remember that she kept in her room a crucifix and a small bust of Mary handed down from her own "fallen away" mother.

All this is background to my personal experience of the Second Vatican Council, refracted through my Catholic girls' school experience. It is often said that single-sex education is a good seedbed for the self-confidence of young women, and I believe that was generally true in the case of myself and most of my schoolmates at Holy Trinity. It was a small school; most members of our graduating class of about 25 are still in touch. My teachers reflected in microcosm many blessings, tensions, and revolutions in Catholic women's experience of the time. Sisters Perpetua and Joseph taught us math and science, respectively; some of us may have had difficulties with the subject matter, but we never believed it due to a design flaw in the female brain. Sr. Mary Nivard took an interest in me when I was a shy freshman, and left a pastel statue of the Virgin Mary in my locker. I heard she now works in AIDS ministry. Sr. Mary Frederick, our lively English and drama teacher, later married a young priest assigned to the adjoining parish. They are both active in CORPUS, an association of former priests and activists for change in church rules mandating clerical celibacy. A few years ago, after I had given a lecture on feminist theology in a series sponsored by the Mercy sisters and Jesuit Spring Hill College in Mobile, Sr. Rosalie, who taught Spanish and was from Alabama, wrote to me to tell me she is proud of my work. I understand she now works with the sick and dying.

Our theology instructor in senior year was Lucy Denise, a young lay woman studying for a master's degree in theology from a Catholic women's college, Dumbarton Oaks. Although I think few of us were even aware of the term "feminism," Miss Denise provided an alternative to the reigning expectations for girls like us. Engaged to be married and a paragon of style in the eyes of her fascinated charges, she sought an advanced degree in an area of study considered almost exclusively a male preserve. Her enthusiasm for the council and a message of lay empowerment fairly flowed from her coverage of the "Pastoral Constitution on the Church in the Modern World" (*Gaudium et Spes*). Miss Denise's very presence signified the seismic shifts that were taking place not far below the surface of the Catholic culture of the day.

I appreciate the paradoxical complexity that probably accompanies every paradigm shift when I recall that in my senior year I lived in an Opus Dei residence for women, recommended by my high school principal to my parents, whom an employment change took out of state. In 1965, Opus Dei piety did not seem closed, elitist, or bizarre; a lot of Catholics acted as if they belonged to a secret society.

The experience of Vatican II was definitive for my self-consciousness as a Catholic and especially as a Catholic woman. The Catholicism of the '50s could be narrow and superstitious, but it imbued me with a sense of the transcendent and of the presence of God in everyday life that carried many of my generation through the turmoil of change and its aftermath, steeped in a tradition that has always remained a home, even if not always a peaceful or comfortable one. As a woman who grew up largely before the council, I remain indelibly marked by the role expectations that went with the territory (wife and mother, and in a prescribed mode). Yet I have benefited from and thrived in the liberation of Catholic women now praised, if within limits, by the pope himself. My vocations as wife, mother, theologian, and professor are combined and intertwined in ways that were barely even conceivable before 1962. The reconstitution of women's place in Catholic life, theology, and liturgy is unfolding, increasingly carried forward by the experience, practices, and voices of women themselves.

Joan Chittister, O.S.B.

Joan Chittister was born on April 26, 1936. She earned a master's degree in Communication Arts in 1968 from the University of Notre Dame and a doctorate from Penn State University three years later. As a member of the Benedictine order she has held many important leadership positions. The respect she has elicited from her peers is reflected in the fact that she served as prioress of the Benedictine Sisters of Erie (Pennsylvania) from 1978 to 1990, as president of the Conference of American Benedictine Prioresses from 1974 to 1990, and as president of the Leadership Conference of Women Religious from 1976-77.

Chittister is a recognized expert in Christian spirituality with an international reputation. She has been a keynote speaker from Pasadena, California to Washington, D.C., from Cambridge, England, to Rome, Italy. She has published more than two dozen books. Among her more recent titles are Illuminated Life: Monastic Wisdom for Seekers of Light *(2000),* Living Well: Scriptural Reflections for Every Day *(1999), and* Heart of Flesh: A Feminist Spirituality for Women and Men *(1998).*

Among her current commitments, Sr. Chittister serves on the board of directors of Emmaus Ministries, the National Catholic Reporter, *and the* International Peace Council, *which draws upon the wisdom of the world's religions to resolve conflicts around the world. Sr. Chittister is also the executive director of Benetvision, a Research and Resource Center for Contemporary Spirituality.*

The Struggle Between Confusion and Expectation: The Legacy of Vatican II

As Vatican II ended, I was just about to begin doctoral studies in communication theory and social psychology. I didn't know a lot about either subject at the time, but, with one foot in a religious life spawned by the Council of Trent and the other in a religious life awash in Vatican II, I knew that anthropologists and social psychologists were missing the academic news of the century. Right in front of their eyes, a subculture was about to unleash its own cultural transformation—by design, with impunity, and *in toto*. It was a human undertaking of massive proportions. It added a great deal to religious life, but it exacted a cost as well. Or, as Robert Hooker put it over two centuries ago, "Change is not made without inconvenience, even from worse to better."[19]

For those who have never experienced the maelstrom of massive social change, have never lived in the vortex of an institutional storm, have never spent their adult life at the ground zero of organizational meltdown, it may come as a shock to realize that "change" and "renewal" are not the same things. Though Vatican II called the religious orders of the church to "renewal," it took a great deal of "change" to tap into the marrow of the process. And it is change that can both obstruct and impersonate renewal. In the end, it has been an unending struggle to reconcile the two. The fact is that it is not possible to have renewal without change, but it certainly is possible to have change without renewal.

The changes in religious life that had been spurred by Vatican II brought personal maturity, new creativity, and transition from the mindset of one century to another. They also brought high expectations, personal confusion, spiritual dis-ease, and lack of clarity of purpose.

Maturity, long denied to women religious in the name of obedience, came with relief, but not without some angst for women whose entire personal lives had been choreographed by people euphemistically called "superiors." Finally, faced with making decisions common to teenagers—with whom to travel, where to go, what to do, when to be back—women religious integrated the two disconnected dimensions of their lives: the personal and the professional. Having been for long years highly developed professionally, they were now able to grow into the kind of adulthood that went with it. They began to make ministry decisions based on personal interests, public needs, and particular talents rather than simply on the institutional identities of the congregations to which they belonged. They began to take public positions in non-church institutions—as administrators of welfare centers or soup kitchens or women's shelters, for instance—in order to serve humankind in general, not simply the descendants of the Catholic immigrant population that had prompted their congregation's historic move to this country in the first place. They made public statements, in the manner of any concerned citizen. They took public interest in public situations. They marched in Selma and were arrested in anti-war demonstrations. They moved beyond the denomination to the universal. They grew up and they grew into the world around them. They became a bridge between the strictly spiritual life and an avowedly secular one. They became voices of the gospel in the public arena.

But they also did more than serve established institutions around them. They began to create new ones. They closed old academies to open education centers for the poor. They phased out orphanages to open hospitality houses for the destitute. They formed civil rights groups and began peace and justice centers. It was a heady time. Creativity, the right to have new ideas, to suggest new approaches to old problems, to make life new—exhilarating as the possibility may have been—was, at the same time, awkward, even frightening for some. Individual religious—whole congregations—quavered between these realities, fixated on the danger of leaning too far, too long, in either one direction or another if the best elements of the past were to be preserved and the most imperative dimensions of the future were to be addressed. Congregations moved in small steps to deal with cosmic questions: they left schools one person at a time, they experimented with schedules one tiny house at a time, they launched new inroads with the new poor, one small soup kitchen at a time, while the rest of the congregation tried to go on attending to the internal questions of new prayer styles, new schedules, new clothes. And one at a time they had to struggle with it. A woman at a parish church with me broke into tears over a run in her hose. Another one got angry because, after 50 years in a convent, she didn't know how to style her hair anymore. A novice set her jaw and said, "I can't wait around here any longer for this to change." Young nuns left religious life in large numbers, disillusioned by the slowness of the small changes and the amount of personal energy that had to be expended over what were to them minuscule issues in apparent danger of never being resolved.

Social transition from the mentality of past centuries to integration into this one—in dress, in ministry, in life-style, in personal interactions—took a heavy toll. What was really true and permanent, stable and real, if things once defined as permanent, invariable, and of the essence of religious life were no longer immutable? The major restructurings Vatican II required in the name of "fidelity to the charism of the founder, the signs of the times, and the needs of the members" broke the hardened shell of religious life into shattered glass.

For many, as a result, religious life as they had lived it was forever over, and with that realization came deep personal despair and a kind of institutional depression. For others, religious life as they envisioned it had only just begun, and with that realization came high energy and new commitment to the worthy, the noble, the necessary.

The teeter-totter on which these two elements balance has not completely stabilized yet, a good thirty years after the fact. Nor perhaps should it if the ancient values on which religious life have been based are to fuel the new directions in which it must develop if it is to have anywhere near the social impact of its origins. If the ancient takes over again, religious will be nothing but museum pieces in a surging new world, the dinosaur survivors of a life that is fascinating but irrelevant. If the tradition is lost completely, religious will be nothing but social service workers who make their work their lives. The tension between the two is clearly the very lifeblood of renewal. It was not easy to come by.

The maturity, creativity, and social transition of religious of the period were easy to see. More difficult to understand, on the other hand, were the doldrums into which what seemed to be such positive activity was to cast religious life in general. After years of membership loss, especially among the newer, younger members of congregations who were disaffected by the control and routinization of a life they had expected to find charismatic or prophetic, even fewer women entered a developing Vatican II religious life, whatever its fledgling directions and its real but tentative developments. The question in the face of the new creativity, the clear maturity, and the necessary social transition was why? The answers may well be many. But there are at least two, which, in the climate of the time, may well deserve consideration. In the first place, the Catholic population itself, whatever its deepest attitudes toward Vatican I religious life, was not prepared for the changes sparked by Vatican II. In the second place, religious communities themselves, though awash in change, had yet to be able to ground change in renewal.

Vatican II was an event whose hour did not really come. Most pastors, formed in another council themselves, gave few homilies on the subject and provided even fewer programs. Lay people were left to cope with change altar rail by altar rail, hymn by hymn, liturgy by liturgy. There were few explanations given, little theology taught. Parishes simply implemented new formulas, accepted nuns in new habits—grudgingly in many places—said prayers in new translations, and watched in sullen sadness or deep resentment as the church as they had known it faded into oblivion.

Of all the church, the people most mobilized for change were women religious.

Mandated to hold renewal chapters and write renewal constitutions, groups retrained their entire memberships in the theology of Vatican II in anticipation of what would of necessity be a community project. Change was impossible without the support of the entire group. Groups suspended their Vatican I constitutions and instituted experimentation in every area of religious life. The work moved quickly, but almost entirely internally. There was very little consciousness of the confusion it generated among a laity that had no idea whatsoever why the changes in process were historically sound, let alone necessary, and even less rehearsal for it.

It was an exciting time. It was also a dangerous time, a time of great personal tension and deep spiritual struggle. Religious themselves asked, Why stay when life here was just like life anywhere else? Why give up so much for nothing? Lay women and religious themselves asked, Why give yourself to a life so unlike any other if, in the end, they were all the same? No "higher" vocations? No hundredfold? No privilege or special treatment or public status? It was a question that begged for answers. It was the renewal question that no amount of change could supply.

The truth is that religious had been formed in the spirituality of the virgins and martyrs, of sacrifice and perseverance—virtues men had traditionally required of women—when what Vatican II called for was the spirituality of priests and prophets, of community-building and witness. It was, then, on the deepening, the broadening, of both personal development and spirituality that the transition to Vatican II religious life really depended. To bring the church into the modern world, it would take a spirituality far beyond docility and childlike obedience. It would take women committed to risk and with courage for the unknown. But prophecy and risk are not the hallmarks of large groups. It was not large groups who started religious life, and it is not large groups that will renew it now. Religious life must travel light into the future, burdened by nothing of its successes of the past, held down by none of its past goals but fresh in direction, vital in its meanings for the people of today.

A movement that loses its radical creative edge, loses its vision and its reason for existence. A movement that is only radical can lose both its popular base and its stabilizing foundation. The continuing task of Vatican II is to sharpen the edge of religious life again. What religious did for past generations, they must now do for those forgotten peoples of our own generation. A whole new global population must be carried beyond the limitations of their lives, become visible to those who see them not, be heard by those who are deaf to their tears.

The truth is that out of this conflict between creativity and spiritual confusion has come something far more dynamic than either. The image of a religious life steeped in the prophetic dimensions of its founders and at the same time deeply immersed in the life of the spirit, the search for the holy, and the spiritual wisdom of the past is becoming ever more apparent. Lay people by the thousands are attaching themselves to the prayer life and ministry of women religious, who have found their old identity again in new ways. Associate, oblate, and lay membership programs are thriving. Women's centers and retreat programs are developing out of women's congregations all over the country. Women are entering religious life again: older now, yes, but totally committed in whole new ways to doing the new things that the new suffering need; they are being educated, formed, and directed by women's congregations everywhere. More than that, religious communities are beginning to realize that everyone who comes to a religious community does not want to stay forever, a principle of membership understood and integrated by Buddhist monasteries for thousands of years. Now, temporary membership is a developing dimension of religious life in a culture where few expect to do anything forever anymore.

Conformity is no longer the major religious virtue, togetherness masking as community, and the fear of change is no longer the agenda of religious life. Renewal of spirit, openness to new needs and depth, if not necessarily length, of personal commitment has become the new norm. "Why did you come here?" I asked a new applicant. "Because this is the only group of women I have been able to find that cares about exactly what I do—community, the Gospel of Jesus, and a commitment to peace and justice," she said simply. Interestingly enough, I couldn't help but think that her answer sounded to me exactly like what Vatican II wanted from religious, too: that they would examine their life from the perspective of the "charism of the founder, the needs of society, and the gifts of their members." But if that's the case, religious life is not only new again, it is also a long way from being over.

Michael Novak

Michael Novak was born in Johnstown, Pennsylvania. He studied at the Catholic University of America and Harvard University, where he earned an M.A. Degree in history and philosophy of religion (1966). He has taught at Stanford University, SUNY Old Westbury, Syracuse University, and the University of Notre Dame. In 1978 he joined the American Enterprise Institute as a resident scholar.

Mr. Novak currently holds the George Frederick Jewett Chair in Religion and Public Policy at the American Enterprise Institute in Washington, D.C., where he also serves as director of Social and Political Studies. Mr. Novak has served as Ambassador of the U.S. Delegation to the U.N. Human Rights Commission (1981-2), as head of the U.S. Delegation to the Conference on Security and Cooperation in Europe (1986), and as a member of the Presidential Task Force on Project Economic Justice (1985).

Mr. Novak has written more than 20 books, including The Spirit of Democratic Capitalism *(1982),* Will It Liberate? Questions About Liberation Theology *(1986), and* The Catholic Ethic and the Spirit of Capitalism *(1993). He was co-founder of the publications* This World, Crisis, *and* First Things.

Mr. Novak has received more than a dozen honorary degrees and numerous awards, including the George Washington Honor Medal from the Freedom Foundation (1984), the International Award from the Institution for World Capitalism (1994), and the Templeton Prize for Progress in Religion, which was awarded in 1994 at Buckingham Palace in London.

The Rescue of Vatican II[20]

We come now to an aspect of church history that has been lost sight of since the council. Journalistically (I later worked for *Time* magazine, during the third session of the council), it was much easier to portray the sheer novelty of the council than to portray its continuities with the past. The news business is in the business of *news*—novelty—and the public does not go to the press for solid scholarship. In a delicious irony the media bring us the opposite of "nonhistorical orthodoxy," nonorthodox novelty. Important realities are often distorted, and history itself is significantly falsified. For instance, the era before the council was more like a golden age in Catholic history than like the dark age described to an eager press by the post-conciliar "progressives." There were many glaring deficiencies in it, and yet it was in many respects healthier and more faithful to the gospels than much that came later in the name of "progress" and "openness."

Once the passions of those participating in the council rose, the victorious majority (the "progressives") acquired a vested interest both in stressing new beginnings and in discrediting the leadership and the ways of the past. That emphasis shifted the balance of power in the church into their hands. To them accrued the glory of all things promising, new, and not-yet-tried; to their foes accrued the blame for everything wrong. The more power wrested from the "old guard," the more massive the power acquired by the reformers. The more the past was discredited, the greater the slack cut for new initiatives and new directions. The politics of the post-conciliar church in the United States and some parts of northern Europe became an unfair fight.

Within a decade of the end of the council, every major institution in the American church and in many others was dominated by the progressives, under the sway of "the spirit of Vatican II." That spirit sometimes soared far beyond the actual, hard-won documents and decisions of Vatican II. Some seized the right to go *far* beyond those. It was as though some took the church to be dis-incarnate, detached from flesh and history—detached, that is, from Rome and the Vatican, and so far as possible from any concrete local authority. Detached, too, from past tradition and the painful lessons of the past. It was as though the world (or at least the history of the church) were now to be divided into only two periods, pre-Vatican II and post-Vatican II. Everything "pre" was then pretty much dismissed, so far as its *authority* mattered. For the most extreme, to be a Catholic now meant to believe more or less anything one wished to believe, or at least in the sense in which one personally interpreted it. One could be a Catholic "in spirit." One could take Catholic to mean the "culture" in which one was born, rather than to mean a creed making objective and rigorous demands. One could imagine Rome as a distant and irrelevant anachronism, embarrassment, even adversary. Rome as "them."

It is not too much to say that John Paul II rescued Vatican II from disaster. His total awareness of the presence of the Holy Spirit at the council, the new Pentecost, suffused his every action as archbishop, then cardinal, of Krakow and later as Universal Pastor of the Church. He brought back a sense of incarnation, concreteness, discipline, and practicality, and he has been an indefatigable theoretician. He has given a thorough and authoritative interpretation of Vatican II.

Bishop Wojtyla wrote even before the Second Vatican Council assembled that the most important word for the council to tell the world concerns Everyman's answer to the question: Who am I? Who are we? What is the meaning and sense of the human project? In formulating this answer, three terms seemed to him crucial: *freedom*, the *person*, and *community*. These three are tied together by the active energy that drives through all of them: love of the truth about man. Freedom is for truth, and is built up, constituted, by fidelity to truth. The search for truth is communal, not only personal, and it requires for its exercise the open society—open in its polity, its economy, and its culture. It is the vocation of the church to keep this vision before the human race, in part by living out this vision in advance of the human race, through its own constant repentance, reform, and starting again.

All these points Vatican II wrestled with, for instance in its debates about the meaning of the liturgy (public worship) of the church, its most vital, inmost source of connection with God's action in the world, for this connection is at once communal, personal, and free. And then wrestled with them again in its discussion of the meaning of the church. *Person, community,* and *freedom* were important red threads coursing through all its debates. They were woven into worldly contexts in the later debates in later sessions, first raised in this second session, in such documents as those on "Religious Liberty" and, as it was at first called, "The Church in the Modern World." In both these documents, Wojtyla played leadership roles in committee, not always in the very front rank, but by making intellectual contributions at crucial intersections.

Although he was only forty-two when the council opened, Wojtyla made eight oral interventions in the council hall, a rather high number, and often spoke in the name of large groups of bishops from Eastern Europe. (Altogether he made 22 interventions, oral and written.) He was an unusually active member of various official drafting groups for *Gaudium et Spes*, and even a chief author of what was called the "Polish draft." His voice was crucial to the passage of the document on religious liberty and to the deepening of its philosophical and theological dimension, in line with the necessities of the non-free nations behind the Iron Curtain. No one, perhaps, was more influential in persuading the Americans and Europeans that their own views on liberty needed to be deepened, in order to account for questions arising from other cultures. In later memoirs about the council, such world-class theologians as Yves Congar and Henri de Lubac praised Wojtyla's acumen in committee work as well as his magnetic presence.

All in all, the council met for four sessions across four consecutive autumns from 1962 through 1965. It reached agreement on sixteen major documents. All these were published in official form in the languages of the nations and have been subjected to a stupendous amount of commentary. Still, it is rare how few Catholics, even well-educated ones, have actually spent time reading the documents themselves. (Those most fond of the "spirit" of Vatican II seldom sent students to study the "letter.") These "Declarations," "Decrees," and "Constitutions" are for the most part splendidly poised and balanced, and quite nourishing to the inquiring soul. They were written as if with devotional purposes in mind, to move the heart as well as intellect.

John Catoir

Father John Catoir is the founder and president of St. Jude Media Ministries, a national organization that uses radio and TV to reach out to millions of Americans.

Born in New York City in 1931, Catoir graduated from Fordham University's School of Business in 1953. After two years in the Army, he entered the seminary and was ordained a priest for the Diocese of Paterson, New Jersey, in 1960. He received his doctorate in canon law in 1964, and served as judicial vicar until the priests of his diocese elected him clergy personnel director in 1973. In 1978 he became the director of the Christophers, a Catholic multi-media organization based in

Manhattan. He hosted a nationally syndicated TV series called "Christopher Closeup," for over 17 years.

From 1997 to 2000, Catoir was executive director of New Jersey's most comprehensive poverty program, called Eva's Village. This ministry feeds 700 free meals a day to the poor; it also runs separate drug and alcohol rehabilitation centers for men and women.

Fr. Catoir was the president of three national organizations: the Catholic Press Association (1988-1990), the Association of Catholic TV and Radio Syndicators (1983-1985), and the National Association of Church Personnel Administrators (1975-1977). He has written 15 books and is a syndicated columnist for Catholic News Service.

In 1993, Catoir received the St. Francis de Sales Award for outstanding contributions to Catholic journalism, the highest award of the Catholic Press Association.

Cardinal Suenens Predicted a Third Vatican Council

Leon-Joseph Cardinal Suenens was one of the four moderators of Vatican Council II, appointed by Pope John XXIII. In his book *Memories and Hopes*,[21] he mentions me as his "occasional" secretary. I was honored to have traveled with him many times back and forth across the ocean during the 1980s and early '90s. The Cardinal told me of his efforts during the council to get the bishops to empower the "sleeping giant" of the laity. He was convinced that the age of the laity had arrived. This idea met with fierce resistance.

Cardinal Suenens led the charge of the reformers against the traditionalists headed by Cardinal Ottaviani. Cardinal Suenens told me that he met Cardinal Ottaviani in a Vatican elevator after the council. The battle was over, or so it seemed. They both smiled and exchanged polite greetings. No other words were spoken. The reformers may have prevailed at the council, but their hopes have not yet been fully realized.

The following retrospect may be helpful in understanding the history of the two Vatican Councils.

Pope Pius IX (1846-1878) was elected as a moderate progressive, against the reactionary Cardinal Lambruschini. His pontificate, the longest in history, soon became an imperial one. He centralized authority, and his encyclical *Quanta cura* (1864), with its "Syllabus of Errors," dealt a fatal blow to the nineteenth-century rationalist movement. He summoned the First Vatican Council (the twentieth general council, 1869-1870) to declare the infallible authority of the pope in matters of faith and morals. He wanted to cancel all conciliarist interpretations of papal authority. This awakened storms of protest. There was a great deal of unfinished business.

Eighty-eight years later, on October 28, 1958, Angelo Giuseppe Roncalli, the aging cardinal of Venice, was elected pope on the twelfth ballot. He was obviously a compromise candidate, chosen in his old age so as to have a short reign. He chose the name John XXIII. Within three months, on January 25, 1959, he captured the attention and the imagination of the world by calling the Second Vatican Council. He said it was in response to an inspiration of the Holy Spirit. His leadership met with strong opposition within the Holy See, but he stood his ground. His optimism was contagious. He disagreed with "those prophets of gloom, who are always forecasting disaster, as though the end of the world were at hand." In contrast to them, John believed that: "In the present order of things, Divine Providence is leading us to a new order of human relations which, by men's own efforts and even beyond their very expectations, are directed toward the fulfillment of God's superior and inscrutable designs."[22]

John XXIII died in 1963, and Pope Paul VI was elected to finish the work of the council. Paul asked Cardinal Suenens to memorialize Pope John at the opening of the second session of the council. The Cardinal told me it was an honor he would never forget. In his eulogy, Suenens declared:

> John XXIII was the pope of dialogue, and this has special reference to the men of our time. . . . The words of John awakened a response.
>
> Men recognized his voice, a voice speaking to them of God, but also of human brotherhood, of the re-establishment of social justice, of a peace to be established throughout the whole world.
>
> They heard a challenge addressed to their better selves, and they raised their eyes towards this man whose goodness made them think of God. For men, whether they know it or not, are always in search of God, and it is the reflection of God that they sought in the countenance of this old man who loved them with the very love of Christ.[23]

Cardinal Suenens told me that for Pope John the council was not merely a meeting of the bishops with the pope, a horizontal coming together. It was, first and above all, a collective gathering of the whole episcopal college with the Holy Spirit. It was a vertical coming together, with an openness to an immense outpouring of the Holy Spirit.

Paul VI (1963-1978) continued the work of the council, raising the hopes of progressives by his willingness to listen. They thought that henceforth church leaders would be willing to discuss problems more openly before arriving at unilateral decisions. However, when Paul VI issued his encyclical *Humanae Vitae* in 1968, condemning artificial contraception, he ignored the advice of his own consultants. Thousands of priests resigned in protest, and a multitude of laity left the church. I asked Suenens if Paul VI really believed in collegiality, a concept he formally approved. He said that Pope Paul was a holy man, but his many years as an official of the Roman curia shaped his thinking. He was by training a product of the curia.

When Paul VI died in August of 1978, John Paul I was elected on the first day of balloting. This is a rarity in the history of the church. The cardinals said they wanted a pope who had no past connections with the curia. John Paul I, who was dubbed "the Smiling Pope" in contrast to his predecessor, who was always frowning, immediately took steps to shed the traditional pomp of his papal coronation. He even held press conferences. His sudden death on September 28, 1978, however, shocked the whole world and disappointed millions of Catholics.

Karol Wojtyla of Krakow, Poland, was elected shortly after, and he chose the name of John Paul II. However, he soon began calling himself a restorative pope, indicating his view that the Second Vatican Council had gone too far. It wasn't long before he became a great disappointment to many progressives. Many bishops thought that he paid only lip service to the idea of collegiality. Within the Holy See there was a common opinion that the word "collegiality" should only apply when there was a true ecumenical council. The many synods called by John Paul II were an exercise in Vatican control.

This pope was the first non-Italian to be named pope since Pope Hadrian VI in 1523. He was not, however, an outsider. His ideas were more in line with the curia than anyone expected. Nevertheless he won world-wide acclaim for his part in bringing about the collapse of Soviet communism.

I once asked Cardinal Suenens what he thought of Pope John Paul II. He replied, "In the middle of a storm, one does not comment on the cleanliness of the captain's uniform." When I asked him about the future of the church,

Suenens was optimistic. He predicted, "There will be a Third Vatican Council in the twenty-first century because so much more needs to be done to realize our goals, and complete the work of renewal. We still have to awaken fully the sleeping giant of the laity."

Cardinal Suenens's own efforts to awaken the laity are reflected in the FIAT movement that he inspired. He asked me to head it up in the United States and Canada. The idea is based on the centrality of evangelization in the life of the church. Suenens wanted the laity to take more responsibility in spreading the faith. "We can no longer depend on a handful of missionaries to pass the faith along to the next generation." Perhaps evangelization will be a theme in the next ecumenical council.

Suenens asked the laity to turn to Mary for guidance. Her words, "Fiat mihi"— "Be it done unto me according to your word" (Luke 1:38), were spoken to the Angel Gabriel. This disposition is a spiritual model for all Christians. Mary taught us how to interact with the Holy Spirit. The cardinal often called Mary the secret of Pentecost. She was with the twelve frightened apostles when the Spirit descended. She taught them how to pray and be open to the Spirit. The apostles emerged from that room, awakened and emboldened to carry the Good News to the four corners of the world. Based on this model, Cardinal Suenens envisioned a network of prayer meetings where the laity would imitate Mary, invoking the Holy Spirit for strength to go forth and make Christ known and loved.

This dream of his remains to be realized through the FIAT movement, which is alive and well, having chapters in 80 countries worldwide. The headquarters of the movement is in Brussels, Belgium, under the supervision of Cardinal Danneels.

Part Two

Vatican II and the Liturgy

Liturgy: The Church Praying is the Church Believing

Michael J. Daley

As I entered the church, I remember it being very quiet, almost silent. This was a place where, if your child cried, you took him or her out with you. Things were very serious. Statues and candles abounded. Combined with the stations of the cross, the ornate reredos behind the altar, and the like, one's senses were challenged, perhaps somewhat distracted. The women, of course, were veiled (St. Paul would have been proud). The men, for the most part, were nicely dressed. An air of formality, as well as transcendence, pervaded the place. When the opening song began, there was no singing. It was more like liturgical muzak with sounds coming from the organ.

After the initial greeting, the priest conducted the Mass in Latin, with his back to the people. His movements were very measured with a concern for the rubrics. Even when he had to face the people, he was instructed not to make eye contact with them. The rationale was that you didn't want to disrupt anyone's prayer. The server, his constant companion, was busy genuflecting and ringing bells. It was, however, hard to hear either the priest or the server. The best one could do was follow along in one's missal and hope to keep up.

The sermon had no reference to the scripture of the day. Its theme was one of suffering. The world, according to the priest, was full of temptation. It was both to be avoided and converted at the same time. Limbo was spoken of. It was real to him and to these people. At communion one encountered the solid, imposing rail that separated the lay people from the sanctuary. The Eucharist was given to you there, on your tongue, with the server holding the paten ever so attentively.

As Mass ended and I was walking out, I said to myself, "Thank God for Vatican II!" The unfortunate thing, however, was that I had just been with a group of people who cursed Vatican II. This was a story not of yesteryear, but from last week. What was it about Vatican II and the change in the liturgy that so offended these people? Why was their pain my joy?

The Cart Before the Horse

Of all the conciliar decisions that have most affected people, it could be argued that the ones instigated by "The Constitution on the Sacred Liturgy" (*Sacrosanctum Concilium*) have had the most concrete and, in some circles, contentious results. As Mark Massa notes in his book *Catholics and American Culture*, "perhaps more dramatically than any other decree issuing from the council, the decree on church worship touched the 'folks in the pews' in immediate and understandable ways...."[1] A great liturgical scholar, Austrian Jesuit Josef Jungmann, said that it was this constitution "more than anywhere else that the *aggiornamento* which John XXIII had demanded of the Council assumed visible and incisive forms."[2]

Put into its proper context, however, the changes evidenced in the decree weren't anything revolutionary, but more the seeds of years of liturgical scholarship beginning to bear fruit.[3] Many place the beginnings of the liturgical movement at the feet of Dom Prosper Guéranger who, in 1833, reestablished the Benedictine Order in France at the Abbey of Solesmes. There he devoted the resources of the abbey to the study of the church's liturgical traditions. The abbey's influence eventually spread to other monastic centers in Europe, most notably Maria Laach (Germany), where historical scholarship was combined with a desire for translating liturgical reforms to a more general audience.

Godfrey Diekmann, O.S.B., long-time editor of *Worship* magazine and one of the architects of the council's document on the liturgy, further pinpoints the movement's development to August of 1924. It was then at Maria Laach, through the initiative of Father Lambert Beaudin, that the first dialogue Mass was celebrated. Diekmann says "people gathered around the altar and everyone played a part. The worshippers realized that day that the roles in ritual were meant to be distributed. They discovered that the laity had a role in worship and in the church. ... Rome was very, very nervous about it for quite some time. But the church has never been the same since."[4] Diekmann's own monastery, St. John's Abbey in Collegeville, Minnesota, became a leader in the American liturgical reform movement under the direction of Virgil Michel. In 1926 he began The Liturgical Press and published the first issue of *Orate Fratres* (today known as *Worship*), a periodical devoted to liturgical practice and pastoral ministry.

Since the early twentieth century, there was hesitant but encouraging papal approval of the initiatives of the liturgical reformers. One increasing concern on the part of the popes was that the laity were being relegated to observers during the Mass. This prompted Pius XII, in 1947, to issue *Mediator Dei*. This encyclical was devoted entirely to liturgical matters. For those who previously had been resistant to the liturgical movement, it gave encouragement; for those who had long labored in the forefront of the movement, it gave cautious support.

As the council approached, then, much of the legwork had already been done. The challenge was to make the council fathers aware of these developments and see the benefits of renewing the liturgy.

The Council's First and Foundational Document

Many consider *Sacrosanctum Concilium*, the first document promulgated by the council, on December 4, 1963, to be Vatican II's most important one. Diekmann, speaking shortly after the council to an international group of theologians gathered at the University of Notre Dame to examine its significance and progress, saw its choice as the first matter to be discussed as "felicitous." He went on to remark that "[i]t was not the theological construct of the post-Constantine or post-Tridentine eras, but the living Church describing her self-discovery in liturgical action that to a very large extent determined the ecclesiology basic to all subsequent documents, including the great *Constitution on the Church*."[5]

Echoed in the refrain of the document's words "full, conscious, and active participation" (no. 14), the image of church as the people of God emerged. This image stressed over and above the long-standing hierarchical understanding of church, that we are first and foremost a community of disciples charged by baptism to participate in Jesus' threefold office of priest, prophet, and king. In more general and musical terms, as has been illustrated by Kenneth E. Untener, Bishop of Saginaw, Michigan, the concert of the priest became the sing-along of the people.[6]

Perhaps just as challenging, if not more so, than the call to a participatory liturgy and church, was the council's admission of change. If anything illustrated the church's absolute and timeless traditions, it was the Latin Mass. Since the Council of Trent (1545-1563), it had experienced little change and acquired a uniformity that it had not possessed in the past. With this in mind, the constitution realized the need for revision:

The rite of the Mass is to be revised in such a way that the intrinsic nature and purpose of its several parts, as well as the connection between them, may be more clearly shown, and that devout and active participation by the faithful may be more easily achieved.

To this end, the rites are to be simplified, due care being taken to preserve their substance. Duplications made with the passage of time are to be omitted, as are less useful additions. Other parts which were lost through the vicissitudes of history are to be restored according to the ancient tradition of the holy Fathers, as may seem appropriate or necessary.[7]

The impression that the church had always done things the same way was broken. This admission was carried throughout the other documents as well. Commenting on this circumstance, Diekmann concluded that "[o]ne of the great achievements of the Council is its demolition of the image of the monolithic Church, of the *de facto* canonization of uniformity in the name of unity.... And because this canonization of uniformity had obtained so triumphantly in the liturgy, and for so long, its firm rejection in the liturgy Constitution set a liberating precedent for the following documents."[8]

With the desire that the liturgy truly be experienced as "supremely effective in enabling the faithful to express in their lives and portray to others the mystery of Christ and the real nature of the true church" (no. 2) and "the summit toward which the activity of the church is directed" (no. 10), the council fathers engaged in a process of making the liturgy more intelligible, relevant, and participatory for all. Physically, the priest turned around to face the people, and with him the altar was placed closer to the people. In many places the communion rail was taken down. Lay people were allowed to enter the sanctuary and exercise the ministerial roles of lector, server, and, eventually, extraordinary minister of communion (no. 29). The vernacular, the language of the people, became the order of the day, replacing Latin (nos. 36.2, 54). Commenting on Latin's supposed unifying aspect for the church, more than one person has observed that you could go anywhere in the world and not understand the Mass. In defense of the staunch supporters at the council who desired to retain Latin, however, it must be admitted that Latin served as a powerful symbol uniting the church in all times and places.

Theologically, for a people who had been used to so emphasizing the presence of Christ in the Eucharist, "the Sacrifice of the Mass," it was both inviting and challenging to allow them to see that Christ was also present in the minister, the other sacraments, the proclaimed word, and the gathered community (no. 7). The constitution further instructed that liturgical studies be promoted in seminaries and other institutions of learning (nos. 15-19). Having long played second fiddle to the Eucharist, the document said, "it is essential to promote that warm and lively appreciation of sacred scripture to which the venerable tradition of both eastern and western rites gives testimony" (no. 24). Admitting the true catholicity of the church, the constitution called for adaptation of the liturgy to various traditions and backgrounds of people (no. 37). Additionally, the catechumenate, also known as the Rite of Christian Initiation of Adults (RCIA), was restored, and the council fathers expressed the desire to revise the rites for the celebration of the other sacraments (nos. 66-82); the divine office (nos. 83-101); the liturgical year (nos. 102-111); sacred music (nos. 112-121); and church architecture (nos. 122-130). An adage that guided the council fathers through these changes could be well summarized in a statement attributed to Cardinal Montini, the future Pope Paul VI, who during the debate on liturgy remarked: "The liturgy is for men, not men for the liturgy."[9]

Looking back at the council and the succeeding years of the council's liturgical implementation, long-time Catholic journalist Arthur Jones asks people to "look for a moment at what didn't happen in the 1960s. Millions of Catholics did not abandon the church. Even in the earliest post-Vatican II days, for all the public tumult, millions upon millions of American Catholics still went to Mass on Sunday, and now they heard it on a repeated basis in a language they could understand. Not only that, the scripture readings and prayers were heard to be relevant to the struggles in the street, in the home, in the soul."[10]

As I said earlier, "Thank God for Vatican II."

Bill Huebsch

Bill Huebsch was born in 1951 and raised on a family farm near Perham, Minnesota. He and his family were from Perham, but they belonged to St. Lawrence Parish. It was at the parish church that major moments in his life were celebrated. It was there that he learned the prayers at the foot of the altar, there that he memorized the answers in the Baltimore Catechism, and there that he first heard about a great council of the church that would be held in Rome, beginning in 1962.

Huebsch began his years at Crosier Seminary prep school just as Vatican II was winding down. Later he earned a B.A. in religious studies at the University of North Dakota, and, in 1981, an M.T.S. from the Catholic Theological Union of Chicago. He spent five years each on the diocesan staff in Crookston and New Ulm in Minnesota, and many years on the pastoral staff of St. Stephen's parish in suburban Minneapolis. For the past half decade he has worked in Catholic publishing, first as vice-president at Tabor (RCL) Publishing in Texas, and currently as an editorial advisor to Benziger in Los Angeles.

In 1990 Huebsch established The Vatican II Project, which contributes to the effort being made within the church to keep alive the spirit and energy of Vatican II.

His current teaching commitments also take him to college campuses, parishes, and conferences around the world. He has published ten books in recent years, along with numerous booklets, articles, and screenplays. One of his books, A Spirituality of Wholeness: the New Look at Grace *(1988), was named in* U.S. Catholic *among the top seven most influential books on spirituality for today's world. His most recent book is* The General Directory for Catechesis in Plain English *(2001).*

The Church on the Eve of Vatican II[11]

I was raised in the 1950s. We were American Catholics. We were from the immigrant working class of the nineteenth and early twentieth century. We never had a lot of money or prestige or social power. But none of that really mattered then because our faith—the center of our lives—was *certain* for us. The Protestants may have had the presidency. They had Billy Graham and Norman Vincent Peale. But we were Catholics; we had the Mass. On our altars, Christ became *real*. We were certain. Presidents and preachers be damned. No one could top the Mass!

So when Vatican II reformed the Mass, a sea change occurred in Catholic self-understanding. The council unwittingly tinkered with far more than the liturgy of the church when it did its work. It also tinkered with a huge, collective, unconscious Catholic memory that prevailed in the church on the eve of the council.

This is a memory of dark, heavy church aromas—incense lurking about the pews and beeswax candles burning silently at the tabernacle, leaving ages of sulfur behind them. A memory of sacristies, redolent with the fragrance of spilled wines and the after-shave lotions of the priests. So many priests then. Altar servers playing with fire, lighting candles and charcoal, fumbling with the chains of the thurible, tripping on the hem of life.

It's a memory of faithful masses, kneeling in the pews: patient, silent, waiting. Genuflection was serious. Doubles during Benediction of the Blessed Sacrament. God was watching. This was *His* place (and there was no doubt about God's gender then). The high ceilings and unseen crosses at the tops of the steeples made God larger than life, than the very life created by God.

It's a memory of Benediction: a brief ceremony of songs, poems, and silence accentuated with incense, holy water, and gold monstrances. The monstrance: the most holy object at the parish church, the place where the priest put the host, larger than the ones you received, white, crisp, the Body of Christ. Round like the moon, rising above the kneeling congregation, "exposed" for all to gaze upon in absolute reverence. The Body of Christ was "exposed" in benediction, a vaguely, deeply sensual act. I think I remember being taught that you weren't even supposed to *move* while it was visible. Catholics fell to their knees to adore the sacred sacrament. The heart and soul of being Catholic was believing that this, indeed, is the true and absolute flesh and blood of God's own Son. As the *Tantum Ergo* came to a close, a clear and palpable sense of blessing descended on the congregation: Blessed be God. Blessed be His Holy Name. Blessed be Jesus Christ, true God and true Man…blessings, praises. A sweet beatitudinal sense of well-being and honor fell upon everyone.

And, of course, it's a memory of Latin. Memorized by priest and altar server alike, it added a surreal dimension to all the devotions. God, we might have believed, understood our prayers better when they were uttered in Latin. *Introibo ad altare Dei. Ad deum qui laetificat juventutem meam.* [I will go to the altar of God. To God who gladdens my youth.] Could that have been true? Did God understand Latin better?

It's a memory of Gregorian chant being sung *to us* by distant choirs huddled in lofts at the back of the church. We didn't want to sing. We wanted to be *sung to by the choir.* Protestants sing; Catholics listen. That's how it'd been since the sixteenth century.

Attending Mass and contributing money were the measures of being a good Catholic. The money we gave was spent for buildings, by and large: bricks and mortar. The buildings were ours; pastors would come and go, traveling missionaries would come through town, leaning out of pulpits, spinning stories about the horrors of life on the other side of the world, but the *building* was our foundation. It belonged to us. We built it.

It's a memory of Catholic devotional life. You could spot a Catholic car from 50 feet because there was a statue of a saint, normally Christopher, on the dashboard. Devotion to the saints and devotions in general were what we did. We used the saints to find lost things (St. Anthony), to bless farm fields (St. Isidore), and to protect us from harm (all the rest).

I knew a woman once who believed firmly in spontaneous combustion, not of her or of anyone she knew, but of her house. She was convinced that at any time her attic might burst into flames! Because of this fear, she developed a staunch devotion to St. Florian, patron against home fires, and she gradually filled her attic with St. Florian medals and holy cards. She would occasionally go up there, sprinkle the place with holy water, and read a prayer to St. Florian who, apparently, helped her, since the attic survived. During these little prayer services in the attic this same woman would, of all things, *light a candle!* Florian protected her from all harm.

It's a memory of Mary. Mary, of course, was more. She wasn't "just another saint." She was the Saint of the saints, the leader. She offered Catholics a sort of female version of the deity, a place near God where power and glory were apportioned almost equally. After all, what decent fellow would not want his own mother to have as much glory as himself? There's really no basis for comparison among the holy men and women of the church: Mary was The Greatest, The Queen. "Holy Mary," we prayed. "Mother of God, pray for us sinners (she wasn't one herself, after all) now and at the hour of our death."

We knew she would if we asked sweetly. What a blessing to have Mary praying for you. Devotion to Mary, alone among devotions, sometimes even rivaled the

Mass for its place in our Catholic lives. It was, after all, something we could do without a priest. When someone died, the first thing a family did was to pray a rosary. When bad weather blew in from the West, Catholics headed to their basements, rosary cases and blankets in hand, to sit among the vegetables in the root cellar and pray to Mary for protection.

She wasn't our only source of blessing, of course. There was also a jar of holy water standing on the banister in most Catholic houses with which we blessed ourselves and our homes. Every night after our bedtime prayers, Catholic moms moved quietly through their houses with the holy water jar, blessing each child and, finally, herself and Dad. What a lovely gesture, what a loving, gentle way to enter sleep. Each year we waited in the car after the Easter Vigil, the memories of those solemn ceremonies still fresh while the Easter bunny was on his way, as Mom obtained a new supply from the parish crock. The parish moms seemed to like this moment in the year, standing among the lilies with each other, dressed in pink and yellow spring dresses, putting all their hopes for the blessing of their families into mayonnaise jars.

Catholic boys, the pre-seminarian ones, kept extensive holy card collections like others did baseball cards, except our cards were blessed, powerful in some important, invisible way. They had pictures of the saints on them, but they also had "ejaculations." Holy card ejaculations were brief prayers one memorized and, periodically, spontaneously uttered. "All for the honor and glory of God and for the poor souls in purgatory!"

These holy cards were icons of our Catholic devotional identity. They carried an energy all their own, and those prayers printed on them merited indulgences for the user. Catholics could build up an "account" of these indulgences counted as "days off in purgatory," 500 days for this, 1,000 days for that. It was all rather like a frequent flier club for Catholic souls who were willing to sacrifice themselves for God. There were *Catholic* holy cards and *Catholic* indulgences. No one else had them.

It would be inaccurate to paint too romantic a view of life in the church on the eve of the council. There were also terribly fierce, inflexible rules that, when enforced, caused great harm. Families expelled their own children for marrying improperly, for divorcing, and for failing to follow the rules exactly. "Fallen away" Catholics were treated harshly and excluded from Catholic circles, left to roam among Protestants. And Protestants were considered apostates and heretics, people who had left the one true church and who now would not see heaven. The unbaptized of the world, including all the Jews, Buddhists, and others, were simply targets for conversion to Catholicism. Their failure to convert sentenced them to Limbo, at best, and to Hell, at worst.

The huge, collective Catholic consciousness that existed on the eve of Vatican II consisted of an odd mixture of love and fear. It was both sublime and harsh. It was Benediction and Bingo.

Then, rather suddenly it seemed, Pope John XXIII was elected to the papacy. He was funny! He was plump! He was welcoming to Protestants and Jews. He was absolutely extraordinary! We'd never seen a Catholic, much less a pope, like him. And soon thereafter, Vatican II got underway leading us to a Catholic Church we'd never seen before either.

Owen Campion

Owen Campion was born in Nashville, Tennessee, on April 24, 1940, and was educated there through the secondary level. He received his bachelor's degree in United States history and psychology from St. Bernard College, Cullman, Alabama, and his graduate theological training at St. Mary's Seminary and University in Baltimore, Maryland.

On May 21, 1966, he was ordained a priest of the Diocese of Nashville. After five years in pastoral ministry, he became editor-in-chief of The Tennessee Register, *the Catholic weekly newspaper then serving all Catholics in Tennessee. He held this position until 1988, when he became associate publisher of* Our Sunday Visitor.

From 1981 to 1984, Monsignor Campion served as treasurer of the Catholic Press Association of the United States and Canada, and from 1984 to 1986 he was president of the Association. In 1989, the Holy See named Campion its ecclesiastical adviser to the International Catholic Union of the Press (UCIP, using the initials of its French name). He served the maximum number of terms in this capacity, leaving it in 1998. The International Union named Campion a member for life of its governing council in 2001.

In 1988, the Catholic Press Association conferred upon Campion the St. Francis de Sales Award, for contributions to Catholic communications. The University of Dayton presented him with its Daniel J. Kane Award in 1997, also for contributions to Catholic communications.

Human Experience and Liturgy

I was a freshman in college when the recently elected Pope John XXIII announced that he wished to convene another ecumenical council. At the time of his announcement, very few persons alive had memories of such a council, the First Vatican Council having closed about ninety years before.

The processes of councils were unknown. Even more unknown was the pope's reason for summoning a new council. It was said, accurately or not, that John XXIII wanted "to open the windows" of the church. However, no one knew what this meant. My recollections of the council center not upon its birth, but upon the fact of the council itself, and its aftermath.

By the time the council actually convened, I was a graduate student in theology, preparing for the priesthood. Certainly the Catholic academic world was attuned to developments at the council. The Catholic press reported it extensively, and no other Catholic event since the time has generated as much coverage in the commercial media.

Coincidentally, for me the council occurred when profound, and at times deeply divisive, conditions were happening in American society. I was a son of the South, descended from generations of Southerners, and I was very much familiar with the attitudes and realities in Southern life surrounding race. Earlier, I had been in the first secondary school class in Tennessee to be desegregated. I remembered the energetic, and not uncommonly angry, discussions that had accompanied racial integration. Over the years, those discussions had led to a great national effort, historically now called the Civil Rights Movement, and a counter-effort with considerable strength itself.

President John F. Kennedy had been assassinated, and dark rumors of conspiracy and disloyalty were in the air. It is true that many Americans learned from the president's murder how far hatred could go.

The Vietnam War was beginning to take its toll in lives. It also was taking a toll on the collective American mind and heart.

The days were stormy in many respects.

From this perspective, I heard with the strictest attention and the greatest delight the council's expressions of the church and of where the church stood in the entire human experience.

The great "Constitution on the Church" and on the "Church in the Modern World" created within me a peace and furthermore an enthusiasm. I saw the church, described in the eloquent words of the council, and in definitions drawing so heavily from the Scriptures and the most majestic sources of Christian theology, as possessing the answer even to the most troubling of human problems and worries.

It was a feeling that has remained with me for thirty-five years of priestly service. Most of my priesthood has been spent in the Catholic press, and every day for almost a generation and a half I have been expected to look at problems, great or small, confronted at the very moment by people with a thought toward relief. My excitement about the church, realized years ago as I read about the council, has never failed me.

Because of this excitement, I have never felt overwhelmed or defeated even as causes in which I believe, such as human rights, perennially seem here and there to meet their match. My hope for a world of human opportunity and dignity, with God and under God, is as vivid as ever. I thank the council.

In another personal sense, but equally as compelling, the council's steps to reform the Roman liturgy greatly have benefited me.

Here I must be clear. I loved the drama and elegance of the older liturgy, when it was done well, of course. But, the reformed liturgy has allowed me greater personal participation in the formal worship and a much greater insight into the realities behind the symbols.

As time has passed, and as my opportunities and responsibilities have broadened, I have on many occasions been in the company of Catholics from cultures quite distant and different from my own. For my perception, the use of the vernacular, a reform advocated by the council, has very strongly reminded me of the universality of the church and of the gospel that the church proclaims. It is more than the mere mechanism of language. It is that, through the use of languages and gestures most profoundly rising from the heart, the church is enabling people, through formal, public liturgy, to express to God their deepest beliefs and thoughts. Nothing could be more universal, and indeed more Catholic, than the enablement of this expression.

The council produced a new day for the church through so many statements and reforms. It also prepared for the church three marvelous pastoral leaders at the highest level, Popes Paul VI, John Paul I, and John Paul II.

Paul VI probably is best recalled for his many efforts to put into practice the mind of the council. These efforts deserve to be recalled. For me, in my vision of the church and humanity, an equally great contribution by Paul VI to the human experience was his sense of human dignity, individually and collectively. He splendidly guided the church through the demise and aftermath of colonization and through the anxiety of nuclear war. Even in his controversial encyclical, *Humanae Vitae*, he taught the world the great Christian understanding of human relationships and of human cooperation in the divine act of creation.

While destined to guide the church for only a month, Pope John Paul I gave the world a full picture of joy and hope when life stands on the gospel.

And of course, Pope John Paul II, for a generation, has become the boldest and most frequent advocate for human rights and for theism itself.

Would I wish to have lived in any other period of time? God has always been with us, and God was with those who preceded us. I would not have feared in other times. But I thank God that I have lived in the era of the Second Vatican Council, because the council so magnificently has given me, through the message of the church, a glimpse of the loving God we cannot see.

Joseph H. Champlin

Father Joseph Champlin was born on May 11, 1930, and educated in the public schools of New York State before graduating from Phillips Academy at Andover, Massachusetts, in 1947. After studying at Yale and Notre Dame, he began and continued his journey to the priesthood at seminaries in Rochester, New York. He was ordained for the Diocese of

Syracuse in 1956. During 45 years of priestly ministry, Father Champlin has served as pastor in three parishes within his diocese, but also held the post of associate director for the Liturgy Secretariat, National Conference of Catholic Bishops in Washington, D.C., from 1968-1971.

Father Champlin has traveled more than two million miles here and abroad during these years, lecturing on liturgical and pastoral matters as well as conducting retreats for priests and missions for parishes. He has also written 45 books with over twenty million copies of his publications in print. For many years he wrote a weekly column on the liturgy and worship distributed by the NC News Service. In addition, he has appeared in about a dozen videos and made numerous television appearances. His most popular book, Together for Life *(1970, rev. ed. 1988), continues to be used by two thirds of all couples being married in the Catholic Church.*

Champlin currently serves as rector of the Immaculate Conception Cathedral in Syracuse, New York, and continues to write and lecture around the country. For the past several years he has written a monthly column, "Eucharist and Life," for the periodical Eucharistic Minister.

At the time of the Second Vatican Council, Father Champlin was serving as associate pastor of the cathedral in Syracuse and as secretary for the then recently established diocesan liturgical commission.

Reflections on the "Constitution on the Sacred Liturgy"

My remote preparation for the Second Vatican Council and its "Constitution on the Sacred Liturgy" took place as a youngster during the 1930s in a small southern tier New York State village. My instructors were three maiden aunts who walked a few blocks to daily Mass and prayed that either my brother or I would become priests. The other instructor was my devout single parent mother who, burdened by a divorce, heart disease, and the Depression, drew great strength and wisdom from frequent participation in the Eucharist.

My proximate preparation for the council occurred during the 1940s and '50s in another small village, but now in central New York. My guide was pastor of the local parish in the town where I attended public high school. A musician who taught teenagers to play the pipe organ for daily Masses, Father Harold Quinn loved the liturgy, read everything available about it, and guided me through a tumultuous adolescence to the priesthood. He also changed my life forever by taking me as a seminarian to the Liturgical Conference in Grand Rapids, Michigan. I never missed one of those conferences over the next two decades.

It was at those sessions that I met some great giants in the church and in the field of worship. Two of these individuals, Benedictine Father Godfrey Diekmann and canonist Father Frederick McManus, were to become consultants at the council. I also listened to, spent time with, and was greatly influenced by Monsignor Martin Hellriegel, the visionary pastor of Holy Cross Church in St. Louis.

Those conferences and these people introduced me to the historical perspective of liturgical reform. Maria Laach, Solemnes, and Pius Parsch in Austria, St. John's, St. Meinrad's, and Dom Damasus in New York—all these became familiar names and places.

I also began to understand a nearly century-old pattern of renewal in the liturgy: the double impact of, from the top, official changes, and, from the bottom, advocacy recommendations. Thus, there were Vatican directives like St. Pius X's decree on communion, music, and participation; and there were the unofficial movements urging vernacular in the liturgy, restored Holy Week services, and Mass facing the people. Later, we received the papal documents in the 1940s on the Mystical Body, the liturgy, and biblical studies; at the same time, others from below urged a richer appreciation of baptism, involvement of lay people, and a deeper understanding of the Mass. Just prior to the council, the church issued several small, but radically transforming ritual changes—mitigation of the eucharistic fast, introduction of evening Masses, and several rites in the vernacular.

As we know, these decades of liturgical research, advocacy, and change meant that when Pope John XXIII convened the Second Vatican Council the only topic with significant background material ready was the liturgy. This subject consequently became the first under discussion and the first approved.

Many viewed that timing as distinctly providential. They saw the sequence in this fashion: the bishops having studied, debated, and voted on worship matters, returned home and lived the renewed liturgy for almost a year before returning for the subsequent sessions. They then did discuss the theology of the church, the priesthood, the modern world, but only after having experienced what the church at worship could or should be.

During those 1960s, I was full-time at a busy center city cathedral, but working as the part-time secretary for the recently formed diocesan liturgical commission. That meant writing, lecturing, and meeting about these liturgical renovations. I also witnessed and personally suffered through the complexities and the pain of the change process.

In 1968 another development occurred that also was to change my life forever. Father Frederick McManus invited me to Washington to work as his associate in the liturgy secretariat for the National Conference of Catholic Bishops. This proved to be a radical shift for me. An individual with great love for the liturgy, but without formal education in it, and an experienced parish priest, but with no "office" background, now instantly becomes a national expert, working with highly detailed materials in a complex structural setting.

During the following three years there were, in addition to work with the new liturgical books or directives, several developments flowing out of the liturgy constitution that directly impacted me.

Father McManus asked that I organize a national conference in Chicago for church leaders on the U.S. document *Music in Catholic Worship*, which was then in development, and on the recently approved eucharistic prayers, one of the first fruits of the "Constitution on the Sacred Liturgy." The participants were mostly church musicians and chancery office personnel (there were few trained liturgists on a bishop's staff at that time). As a result of the conference, many of these diocesan officials were anxious to have especially the new eucharistic prayers explained to their clergy. My official status, parish background, and plain talk apparently appealed to them. Invitations to address the clergy multiplied. For the next three years I criss-crossed the country, conducting workshops on all of the current and impending liturgical changes.

During that time, I wrote two books that grew out of the directives from the Second Vatican Council. *Christ Present and Yet to Come* provided guidelines for the priest presider in the revised liturgy. The second, *Together for Life*, offered to clergy and engaged couples a practical vehicle for implementing those many rich options contained in the new *Rite of Marriage*. The success of both texts indicated that they fulfilled a real need.

During those three years, the seeds were being sown and the foundations being established for a semi-official liturgical organization and for centers of graduate liturgical study. The Federation of Diocesan Liturgical Commissions emerged from these efforts, and opportunities for such advanced degrees opened up in places like Catholic University, Notre Dame University, and St. John's in Collegeville.

In 1971, my bishop called me home to become pastor of Holy Family Church in Fulton, New York, a small-size central New York city. I thought this shift would end my lecture journeys, but that did not happen. My position and experience as a pastor added credibility to those lectures in the 1970s and 1980s, while we introduced additional liturgical changes and integrated more fully the spirit and principles of the liturgy constitution.

I knew from my Washington experience that a revised order of penance would soon be released. With this in mind, I converted, aided by a liturgical artist and local contractor, a church room into a reconciliation chapel, one that would accommodate the alternatives of the new ritual (e.g., biblical readings, extension of hands, face to face confessions), yet retain the traditional elements (e.g., privacy, anonymity, kneeling). A local photographer made slides of the room, and I published a lengthy article about the revised rite. Armed with the slides and copies of the essay, I spoke over the next few years to clergy and lay people in about 60 U.S. dioceses, explaining this restored ritual for penance, reconciliation, and confession.

Throughout the last decade, while still speaking and writing about the implementation of the liturgy constitution, I have observed the efforts of two groups at the opposite ends of the liturgical spectrum: those who judge that changes of the Second Vatican Council, including the worship revisions, have gone too far, too fast, and those who judge that they have not gone far or fast enough. In between are those many people, the majority, who have quite warmly welcomed the documents of the Second Vatican Council in general and the "Constitution on the Sacred Liturgy" in particular. This corps of Catholics believes that these documents and their implementation, despite limitations, have significantly enriched the church.

Cyprian Davis, O.S.B.

Cyprian Davis was born September 9, 1930, in Washington, D.C. He attended the public schools in the same city. When he was fifteen, he was received into the Catholic Church. His freshman year of college (1948-49) was at the Catholic University of America. The following year he entered St. Meinrad Seminary, where he received an A.B. degree in 1953. He entered St. Meinrad Archabbey (St. Meinrad Abbey at that time) in 1950 and made the first vows of a Benedictine in 1951. Davis was ordained to the priesthood in 1956 and received an S.T.L. degree from the Catholic University of America the next year. He pursued advanced studies at the Catholic University of Louvain in Belgium, where he received a license in historical sciences in 1963 and a doctorate in historical sciences in 1977.

Currently Davis is professor of church history in the St. Meinrad School of Theology, having joined the faculty in 1963. He is also adjunct professor of history in The Institute of Black Catholic Studies, a summer institute at Xavier University in New Orleans. In addition, Davis serves as archivist for St. Meinrad Archabbey and the Swiss-American Benedictine Congregation, as well as archivist for the National Black Catholic Clergy Caucus, of which he was a founding member.

Davis has written very extensively in the area of monastic history, black Catholic history, and black Catholic spirituality. In 1990 he published The History of Black Catholics in the United States, *which was awarded the John Gilmary Shea Award in 1991. He co-edited* Taking Down Our Harps: Black Catholics in the United States *(1998) with Diana Hayes. At present he is working on the life of Henriette Delille, a woman of color, who founded the Sisters of the Holy Family, and he is co-editing a volume of primary sources from African American Catholic history in the American Catholic Identities Series.*

Davis served on the subcommittee for the preliminary drafts of the U.S. Catholic bishops' pastoral letter "Brothers and Sisters to Us," published in 1979, and the Black Catholic Bishops' pastoral letter "What We

Have Seen and Heard" in 1984. Between the years 1994-2000, he served as visiting lecturer in history and archival management in several Benedictine and Trappist monasteries of monks and nuns in the West African countries of Senegal, Togo, Burkina Faso, Benin, Ivory Coast, and Nigeria.

The Liturgy, Inculturation, and the Renewal of Religious Life

In the summer of 1958, I was sent to the University of Louvain in Belgium to get a degree in history. I had been ordained only two years. I found a home at the Benedictine Abbey of Keisersberg (at that time Mont César). I was one among several young monks from all over Europe who came to study at what was one of the most prestigious Catholic universities in the world. The monks of Mont César were established scholars, men such as Abbot Bernard Capelle, Dom Bernard Botte, Dom Odon Lottin, Dom Hildebrand Bascour, and others.

Shortly after my arrival, Pope Pius XII died on October 9, 1958. His death marked the end of an era. The election of Angelo Roncalli as John XXIII a few weeks later was to have a tremendous impact on us all, collectively and as individuals. This impact, of course, was the Second Vatican Council, which John XXIII announced in the year following. The professors at the University of Louvain would play important roles in this council.

Historically, Louvain had acquired the reputation of being a center for relentless scholarship and "cutting edge" research in theology, scripture, and history. Certain of my fellow students in theology, liturgy, and other sacred sciences had a ringside seat at history-in-the-making because their professors were involved in the preliminary work of the council. One of those involved with the preliminary commissions on the "Constitution on the Sacred Liturgy" was Bernard Botte, a monk of Mont César, one of the foremost scholars in liturgical history, and founder of the Liturgical Institute in Paris. Later, over a glass of wine, he would regale us students, monks, and others with stories about the committee meetings both before and after the council.

I remember the day when John XXIII died, June 3, 1963. The first session of the council had been concluded that winter. The entire world had literally watched at the pope's bedside. A fellow student, a friend, told me that he was so moved by

John's death that he came back to the practice of the faith—he needed to be again one with those who were members of the church that mourned him.

I returned to the United States in August of 1963. Pope Paul VI had been elected a few weeks before. I had been absent from the United States for five years. I had left the country with a view of Catholicism that was somewhat triumphal and narrow. I returned with a heightened sense of the Catholic Church's history, a sense of the breadth of Catholicism, and the richness of its past and its present. It was this view of the church that would enable me to understand and accept the tide of change that would sweep over the ecclesiastical landscape after the council.

Before returning to my monastery, I visited with my parents in Washington. I had arrived just in time to participate in the "March on Washington" and to be present on the Mall when Martin Luther King, Jr. delivered his "I have a dream" speech. During my absence, the Civil Rights Movement had begun a new day for black Americans. While in Europe, I had experienced my own black consciousness. The marchers walked in groups to the Monument Grounds. I marched with the Benedictine monks from St. Anselm's Abbey in Washington. Before the council there would never have been this open display of Catholic priests marching for justice and an end to racial discrimination. The Catholic Church in America was reticent about open participation in protests or "political" movements. The council, on the other hand, reminded us that the church was present in this world and that the church had to speak out against injustice with a prophetic voice.

Today we speak freely about inculturation. It was the council, however, with its teaching on the liturgy and on missions that made it possible for Africans and African Americans to re-introduce the drum and other African musical instruments into the liturgy. Today in almost every African American Catholic parish, the people sing Gospel music, clap their hands, and sometimes dance because of the encouragement given by the council for adaptations in the liturgy by the local church. Perhaps even more telling is the increase of musical compositions by black Catholic composers such as Clarence Rivers, Rawn Harbor, and Grayson Brown.

Returning to St. Meinrad was a return to a monastic community that was in transition. In the next few years there would be dramatic changes in our monastic way of life. The celebration of the liturgy is the center of any Benedictine monastery. It was after the close of the council in 1965 that the implementation of the liturgical decrees was carried out. Since the liturgy has such an important place for Benedictines, any changes are fraught with tension and insecurity. In December of 1964, St. Meinrad was designated as one of the places in the archdiocese for liturgical experimentation. The altar was moved to face the people. The priest-monks began to concelebrate at the conventual Mass. By 1966 the non-ordained monks began receiving communion under both species. At first Vespers for the Feast of All Saints in 1967, the monks of St. Meinrad began cele- brating the Liturgy of the Hours in English. It was a little like a minor earth- quake. The Monastic Breviary, which contained the Divine Office for monks and nuns of the Benedictine Order, had ceased to be used in this monastery where it had been used from its foundation. It had profound implications for our spiri- tual life and our monastic discipline. What is more, it meant that we needed to translate into English many ancient liturgical texts, compose new prayers and antiphons, or rewrite old ones when needed. We needed a new lectionary and a new ordering of scripture readings for the Office of Vigils. Finally, we needed more musical compositions. Thanks to the talents of many monks within our community, and with the collaboration of monks and nuns elsewhere, within a year or so we had created a very beautiful Office.

The conciliar document on the renewal of the religious life called each religious community to return to an understanding of the original charism of one's order or community. For monks, this meant serious research into the Rule of St. Benedict and into the historical development of each monastic house. This resulted in regular meetings and lengthy discussions on how to bring our monas- tic way of life into line with the spirit of the council. Here again there were real tensions and some bitter discussions regarding clerical monasticism and non- clerical monasticism and between professionalism and manual labor. Every monastery knew these tensions. St. Meinrad was no exception.

Life in a monastery is structured by a certain formality. Much of it is based on seniority according to profession. Traditionally, priests and clerics preparing for priesthood took precedence over brothers. In keeping with the demands of the council, this sort of distinction between clerics and lay changed. In 1968 the order of precedence was no longer based on ordination or lack of ordination. From now on the monks would take precedence according to the year of one's profession of vows.

This really meant a shift in the status of brothers. It meant a realization that the monastic charism was the focal point of our life, not priesthood. We no longer considered the Order of St Benedict as a clerical order. There was a corollary. Before the council, only those in solemn vows belonged to the chapter and had the right to elect the abbot. Brothers made perpetual vows, not solemn vows. As a result of the conciliar document on the renewal of the religious life, "all brothers were to be brought into the heart of the religious life." Everyone in the monastery now has solemn vows and a place in chapter meetings. Today every member of the community with solemn vows has the right to elect the abbot.

In the period that followed Vatican Council II many religious communities underwent the struggles of internal division and dissension. This was certainly the experience of my own community, although less so than in other communities. Yet for most the council brought an opportunity for renewal and restoration. It brought about a deepening of faith and a greater understanding of the tradition. Let me close this reflection with the words of a Benedictine monk who left such an important imprint on the liturgical renewal at the Second Vatican Council.

> In spite of the scandals and abuses the church of Christ is the guardian of the deposit of faith. It's the church of the apostles, of the martyrs, and of the saints of all times. During the Council the Holy Spirit visibly inspired in the church the desire to purify itself and to return to its ideal. We should believe that the Spirit is still there, according to Christ's promise, and that he will complete the work he began.[12]

M. Basil Pennington, O.C.S.O.

Father M. Basil Pennington, O.C.S.O., is a Cistercian (Trappist) monk and resigned as Abbot of the Abbey of Our Lady of Holy Spirit in Conyers, Georgia, in 2002. He was born on July 28, 1931, in Brooklyn, New York. After graduating from the seminary there, he joined the monastic community in 1951. After his ordination on December 21, 1957, he studied in Rome, obtaining degrees in theology from the Pontifical University of Thomas Aquinas (1959) and canon law from the Gregorian University (1963).

Fr. Pennington served as a peritus in the Second Vatican Council and collaborated in the preparation of the new Code of Canon Law and the new constitutions of his Order. In 1968 in collaboration with Thomas Merton, he founded Cistercian Publications and fostered the work of translating the Cistercian Fathers into English. Three years later he collaborated in the establishment of the Institute of Cistercian Studies at Western Michigan University, Kalamazoo.

In 1971 in response to Pope Paul VI's request that the Cistercians help the church renew the contemplative dimension of life, Father Pennington began teaching—through retreats and workshops, articles and books— the simple, ancient method of entering into contemplative prayer found in their tradition. It soon became popularly known as Centering Prayer or Prayer in the Heart. He is on the advisory board of Contemplative Outreach, an international lay movement to foster Centering Prayer among the laity. He is also one of the founders and chairman of the Mastery Foundation, an interreligious outreach that seeks to help those in sacred ministry to empower their ministry through Centering Prayer.

Pennington has taught Centering Prayer in over fifteen countries, including China, and has published some 50 books and 1,000 articles in twenty-five languages. His primary books are Centering Prayer: Renewing an Ancient Christian Prayer Form *(1980) and* Lectio Divina: Renewing the Ancient Practice of Praying the Scriptures *(1998).*

Liturgical Moments

It was an unforgettable moment in world history, a moment whose impact only the centuries will fully reveal. The river of white miters flowed steadily out of the Bronze Doors and across the Square toward the great open portals of the largest basilica in Christendom, St. Peter's. At the end was the pontiff, the incarnation of tradition, so it appeared, sitting on his portable throne, riding above the crowd on the shoulders of the handsome men in rose brocade. Tradition was about to blossom forth in an unprecedented way: The Second Vatican Council convoked by Blessed John XXIII.

For so many of us gathered on that day, an ecumenical council was something that sort of descended from heaven, bearer of infallible truth. How often had we heard in the course of our theological training: the Vatican Council [i.e., Vatican

I] said this; Second Lateran declared; Trent anathematized.... And now suddenly here we were in an ecumenical council. Like most of the American contingent, we pretty much expected to simply have a presentation of the schemas that had been prepared by the preparatory commissions, then a great signing, and home we would go. I suspect we were as shocked as anyone when Cardinal Liénart claimed the council for us. Soon enough we began to learn the lessons of incarnation as the negotiations for the council commissions got under way.

The one pre-conciliar schema that survived with any fullness was that on the liturgy. As I look back on the council now, I wonder how much myth has grown up even in my own mind, history embellished to bring out more fully the reality of days and events that were too full of the transcendent to be contained in the narrow confines of definable concepts.

Certainly Father Cyprian Vaggagini has become a mythical master. The story is that after ordination he spent five years studying sacred scripture, then five years studying the fathers of the church. With this background, comparable to that of the great medieval scholastics who studied *sacra pagina* [literally, the sacred page; that is, scripture] for years before beginning their own masterly lectures, Father entered into a five-year study of scholasticism, largely under the tutelage of Thomas Aquinas. Finally came the years of liturgical study that gave birth to his own two-volume work, *Theological Dimension of the Liturgy,* and the subsequent pre-conciliar schema.

In that first session of the council, there was a rather superficial study of the light-weight schema on communications. The Spirit seems to have helped them to realize that it was not the time to say much about a field that was shortly to explode. Fortunately this decree left the way wide open for the church to embrace all the potential that today's developments offer us to fulfill Christ's mandate to bring the Good News to all nations. Sad to say, as with all the inspired documents of the council, the potential has hardly begun to be realized.

Then the real work began with the schema on liturgy. The possibilities were very exciting. Among all those wondrous happenings, there are two that stand out for me personally: one because with all its simplicity it has had a profound effect on my life, the other because of my personal involvement with it and its potential significance.

It was a rather ordinary session and things were going along in a rather ordinary way when a bishop—I don't know just who, one of the multitude (this was one of the profound learning experiences for the bishops, so used to being the center of everything back home: to find themselves just one of the "school boys" seated in the bleachers) stood up and made a very simple, apparently prosaic statement. But it was one of those moments of grace in the council, a moment greeted by a profound and profoundly aware silence. The bishop simply said: When the gospel is proclaimed at the liturgy, Jesus Christ proclaims his Good News.

It seems so obvious. Look what happens at the liturgy. The priest or deacon prays over us: "The Lord be with you." And we pray over him: "And also with you." Then he proclaims: "The Gospel according to...." And what do we respond? "Glory to you, O Lord." And at the end? "Praise to you, Lord Jesus Christ." The priest or deacon has disappeared. It is the Lord. No wonder we stand, as it were, at attention. The Lord himself is speaking to us. Each day at the liturgy I eagerly await this moment when the Lord is going to speak to me and give me a word of life for the day, a word I can bring to others, even as it enlivens my life. In this simple way, my being as a disciple of Jesus Christ has been tremendously and constantly nourished through all the years since that seemingly very ordinary but very special day at the first session.

The second happening came about when the very gentlemanly and gentle bishop from Brooklyn, Charles R. Mulrooney, asked me to help prepare an intervention. His proposal was in effect that national hierarchies should be able to make national or local "feasts," such as Thanksgiving in the United States, to be full-fledged liturgical feasts. As a monk, living the liturgy is a very big part of my life. It had long seemed to me most incongruous that, while we as a community, along with the rest of America, celebrated Thanksgiving abundantly in the refectory, in church, apart from a "votive" Mass of thanksgiving, we were able to give the feast little attention. Indeed, we usually were required to celebrate the office with the somber tones of a ferial day. The bishop's proposal, which was substantially incorporated into the "Constitution on the Sacred Liturgy," while it satisfied a liturgical need, actually had more far-reaching significance. It affirmed that liturgy and life should be closely and coherently one, that liturgical prayer should be an expression of the life of the people. What a people believe and live should guide the way they pray. It was a clear, concrete expression of indigenization. The universal liturgy of the church was to make room to take on the color and spirit of the people who were celebrating it. But perhaps more significant for the future of the church was that this proposal sought to return to the bishops, the national or regional or local hierarchy, their authority to decide a matter that affected their people pastorally.

I do not know how many in the *aula* realized the full implications of what was being proposed by the apparently very quiet and gentle American bishop. Some certainly did, so that, while the idea of allowing space for local feasts was granted, the mode of the proposal, giving authority to the local episcopate, was sidestepped. This remains an area of struggle if not strife, in an ongoing tug of war between Roman authorities and national conferences of bishops in the area of liturgy as well as in many other areas of church life.

Exciting moments, moments of growth, of deeper realization of who we are as church, what it means to be church: the people of God, Christ's people guided by him to express who we are in prayer and praise and bring that Good News to the people among whom we live. Praise and glory to the Assumed Queen of Heaven and Earth!

Part Three

What It Means to Be Church

Formulating a New Understanding of Church

William Madges

I was born during the final third of the pontificate of Pope Pius XII (pope from 1939 to 1958). As I entered Catholic grade school, it was customary for me to be told "The church believes this" and "The church teaches that . . ." Of course, it was clear to me who "the church" was. It was the pope, the bishops, the priests. What they taught is what I must believe. (My instruction in the faith, however, didn't come directly through bishops or the pope, but through the nuns who taught at my school. Their trustworthiness to communicate accurately what "the church" taught was always beyond question for me.) The point is that, although I "belonged" to the church (that is, was baptized, accepted the church's teaching, received the sacraments, etc.), I was not *really* an essential part of the church. The *essential* part of the church was the clergy—in particular, the hierarchy. I was part of what was called "the faithful." Our job, as the name itself suggests, was simply to follow faithfully the guidance and the teaching of the clergy (a.k.a., "the church"). It was not our job to take the initiative in any aspect of the church's life; rather, it was our task to follow the clergy's lead. All that began to change in the wake of the Second Vatican Council.

The nature and structure of the church had been one of the two topics considered at the First Vatican Council (1869-1870), the first Roman Catholic council to be held since the Council of Trent responded to the Protestant Reformation. The council had been called by Pope Pius IX to address some of the pressing challenges posed to the traditional beliefs and practices of the church by the development of modern culture. In particular, the council felt compelled to defend certain basic convictions of Catholic faith: that God exists and can be known by reason, that divine revelation is credible, that faith elevates reason, that faith and reason can never be at odds with each other. The council also felt it was necessary to defend the primacy and authority of the pope.

This defense seemed necessary in light of the developing trends in modern thought and culture. Enlightenment philosophers had, in the words of Immanuel Kant, encouraged people to think for themselves. "Enlightened" individuals should not hold something as true simply because the church or the state taught it. Dramatic discoveries and theories in science also challenged the authority of the church. Charles Lyell's geological discoveries and Charles Darwin's theory of evolution challenged the veracity of traditional and biblical beliefs concerning the age of the world, human origins, and God's providential role in the unfolding of cosmic and human history.

The nineteenth century was also an age of revolution in politics. After the upheavals of the American and French Revolutions, the political scene continued to be unstable. People rebelled against systems of absolute monarchy and governments that ignored their wishes, as evidenced by the political turmoil in Europe in 1830 and 1848. By mid-century Karl Marx had called upon the workers of the world to unite to create a classless society, in which religion would evaporate because the economic and social conditions that brought it into existence would have been transformed. People everywhere wanted greater freedom. Traditional authority in its different forms was under attack.

In response to the revolutionary political changes and the anti-Catholic policies of a number of European governments, many Catholics, including bishops, wanted to see the power of the pope not merely maintained, but increased as a counterbalance to the power of nation states. The Italian occupation of Rome and the attack on the Papal States in the final third of the nineteenth century appeared to severely threaten not only the political, but also the spiritual authority of the pope. It was believed that without the Papal States the pope would no longer have the independence necessary for the exercise of his spiritual authority.

Vatican I was in session when its work was cut short by the invasion of nationalist military forces seeking to unify Italy and by the Franco-Prussian War. The bishops completed only four of the anticipated fifteen chapters of the "Dogmatic Constitution on the Church of Christ" (*Pastor Aeternus*). These four chapters described the establishment of the apostolic primacy of St. Peter, the continuation of Peter's primacy in the Roman pontiffs, the power and nature of the pontiff's primacy, and the infallible teaching authority of the Roman pontiff. In these chapters, the council fathers affirmed that Jesus had placed St. Peter at the head of the other apostles so that the unity of bishops, the apostles' successors, and the unity of faith of all believers might be maintained. They identified the primacy of the pope as the bulwark and firm foundation of the church.[1] Moreover, the bishops affirmed that the pope has full and supreme power of jurisdiction over the entire church, not only in matters that pertain to faith and morals, but also in matters that pertain to the discipline and government of the worldwide church.[2]

With regard to faith and morals, the bishops of Vatican I declared that "when the Roman pontiff speaks *ex cathedra*, that is, when, in the exercise of his office as shepherd and teacher of all Christians, in virtue of his supreme apostolic authority, he defines a doctrine concerning faith or morals to be held by the whole church, he possesses, by the divine assistance promised to him in blessed Peter, that infallibility which the divine Redeemer willed his church to enjoy in defining doctrine concerning faith or morals. Therefore, such definitions of the Roman pontiff are of themselves, and not by the consent of the church, irreformable."[3]

This emphasis upon papal primacy and authority, understandable as it is within the nineteenth-century context, permitted misconceptions about the nature of the church in the decades following Vatican I. It appeared to some that all that really needed to be said about the nature of the church had been contained in what was said about the pope. And the pope's role and authority were described in such a way that the church appeared to be a society of unequals, governed by an absolute papal monarch. In such a perspective, for example, the bishops appear only as deputies or representatives of the pope, rather than as successors of the apostles in their own right. And the laity appear as faithful subjects, but not really active participants in the mission of the church.[4]

When Pope John XXIII, on January 25, 1959, announced his intention of convening an ecumenical council, many concluded that its primary goal would be the completion of Vatican I's work of describing the tasks of the church. Few initially expected that the upcoming council would ultimately situate papal primacy within a much broader and a more biblical understanding of "church" than had been the case in the nineteenth century. A strong and vocal minority of bishops and cardinals consistently supported a scholastic, juridical, and hierarchical definition of the church, in keeping with the lines laid out at Vatican I. The majority, however, argued for a more biblical, inclusive, and pastoral definition. The clash between these two different approaches was evident from the very first session of the council.

The initial draft (schema) of Vatican II's "Dogmatic Constitution on the Church" (*Lumen Gentium*) outlined an understanding of church that was consistent with the then standard emphasis upon the hierarchical and juridical aspects of the church. It had been prepared by the Theological Commission, headed by Cardinal Alfredo Ottaviani.

When first presented to the council fathers toward the end of the first session of the council (December 1-7, 1962), it was roundly criticized. Emile Josef De Smedt, Bishop of Bruges (Belgium), criticized the schema for triumphalism, clericalism, and juridicism. Instead of speaking of the church as the "church militant," with its members lined up in battle array prepared for victory, De Smedt advocated a more pastoral and humble description of the church as Christ's flock. Instead of regarding the church as a pyramid of people, priests, bishops, and pope, De Smedt emphasized that the church was essentially the people of God, who shared the same fundamental rights and obligations of being part of Christ's Mystical Body. Finally, in place of a juridical concept, De Smedt declared that the church should be presented to the world as the "mother" of humankind, who were all brothers and sisters to one another. The initial schema was similarly criticized by others, including Cardinal Döpfner of Munich, Cardinal Frings of Cologne, Cardinal Suenens of Maline-Brussels, Cardinal Bea of the Secretariat for Christian Unity, and Cardinal Montini of Milan (the future Pope Paul VI). But it was also defended by Cardinal Ottaviani, Cardinal Siri of Genoa, Cardinals Bacci and Browne of the curia, and others.[5]

Between the first and second sessions of the council, Pope John XXIII died and Cardinal Montini was elected Pope Paul VI. The intersession was dominated by bitter clashes within the various commissions. As the council made a new beginning in September 1963, it also had an entirely new document on the church to consider.[6] The new draft, however, was subjected to revision, in light of the debates at the second (1963) and the third sessions (1964). Finally, the "Dogmatic Constitution on the Church," in its present form, was overwhelmingly approved on November 21, 1964, by a vote of 2,151 bishops in favor and only five opposed.

The document finally approved in November 1964 was significantly different in content and tone from the original draft of the text that had been prepared two years earlier. The reorientation of the document becomes apparent even in a cursory comparison of the chapters of the draft constitution considered by the bishops during the first session of the council in 1962 and the final constitution approved two years later.

The 1962 draft contained the following chapters: 1) The nature of the church militant; 2) The members of the church militant and of the need for them to be saved; 3) The episcopate as the highest degree of the sacrament of order and of the priesthood; 4) Residential bishops; 5) States of evangelical perfection; 6) The laity; 7) The magisterium of the church; 8) Authority and obedience in the church; 9) The relations between church and state; 10) The necessity of the church to proclaim the Gospel to all peoples everywhere; 11) Ecumenism.[7]

The 1964 approved text contains the following chapters: 1) The mystery of the church; 2) The people of God; 3) The church is hierarchical; 4) The laity; 5) The universal call to holiness; 6) Religious; 7) The pilgrim church; 8) Our lady. The final draft supplements the first draft's juridical and hierarchical emphasis with the inclusion of more pastoral and communitarian elements.[8] The reorientation is well illustrated in three areas: the relationship of clergy and laity within the church, the relationship between the Catholic and other Christian churches and communities, and the relationship of the bishops to the pope.

At least since the time of the Reformation in the sixteenth century, it had been commonplace to think of the church, first and foremost, as the clergy and, in particular, as the hierarchy. Vatican I had further highlighted and emphasized the focal position and authority of the hierarchy, especially the pope. Therefore, it came as no surprise that, in the first draft of the "Dogmatic Constitution on the Church," the role and power of the bishops was presented before the exposition of the role of the laity, and that the issues of authority and obedience receive special emphasis. In the second draft of the constitution, a single chapter was devoted to the people of God and the laity. Cardinal Suenens from Belgium proposed dividing this chapter into two chapters, and he recommended that the separate chapter on the people of God be placed before the respective chapters on the hierarchy and the laity. The final draft of the constitution did exactly that. Moreover, the final document affirms the "priesthood" of all believers, laity as well as clergy. The issue whether the clergy and the laity constituted two separate spiritual estates or only one was a central, divisive issue at the time of the Reformation. Now four centuries later, Vatican II declared that all the baptized, "by regeneration and the anointing of the holy Spirit, are consecrated as a spiritual house and a holy priesthood" (*Lumen Gentium*, no. 10). Although the council continued to distinguish the "common priesthood" of the laity from the "ministerial priesthood" of the clergy, the acknowledgment of the laity's share in Christ's priesthood was a significant reorientation. In addition, the final version of the constitution affirmed that the laity participates not only in Christ's priestly office, but also in his prophetic office.[9] This means that all of the baptized faithful, and not only the hierarchy, can possess a sense of the faith that has been inspired and sustained by God's Spirit. Although the hierarchy possesses the ultimate authority to interpret the meaning of the faith, all of God's people share in the possession of the faith and in helping to penetrate its depths. With confidence, therefore, the constitution declares:

> The whole body of the faithful who have received an anointing which comes from the holy one (see 1 Jn 2:20 and 27) cannot be mistaken in belief. It shows this characteristic through the entire people's supernatural sense of the faith, when, "from the bishops to the last of the faithful," it manifests a universal consensus in matters of faith and morals. By this sense of the faith, aroused and sustained by the Spirit of truth, the people of God, guided by the sacred magisterium which it faithfully obeys, receives not the word of human beings, but truly the word of God (see 1 Th 2:13), "the faith once for all delivered to the saints" (Jude 3). The people unfailingly adheres to this faith, penetrates it more deeply through right judgment, and applies it more fully in daily life.[10]

A second area in which *Lumen Gentium* reoriented Catholic teaching concerns the relationship between the Catholic Church and other Christian communities. Although the constitution re-affirms the traditional teaching that the "one, holy, catholic, and apostolic" church was handed over to Peter and the apostles to be shepherded, *Lumen Gentium* backs away from the simple identification of the Roman Catholic Church with the Mystical Body of Christ, which the original draft of the constitution had endorsed.[11] In its final version, *Lumen Gentium* declares:

> This church, constituted and organized as a society in the present world, subsists in the Catholic Church, which is governed by the successor of Peter and by the bishops in communion with him. Nevertheless, many elements of sanctification and of truth are found outside its visible confines. Since these are gifts belonging to the church of Christ, they are forces impelling towards catholic unity.[12]

Instead of asserting, in an unqualified way, that Christ's church or mystical body is the Catholic Church, the constitution acknowledges that Christ's church subsists—exists or lives—in the Catholic Church and that elements of truth and sanctification can exist outside of its visible structure. This statement was not an endorsement of "indifferentism," the term used in the nineteenth century to characterize the belief that it does not really matter whether one is a Catholic Christian or a Protestant or Orthodox Christian. Vatican II, however, does move away from the nineteenth-century, Catholic position that all elements of truth and sanctification are to be found in the Roman Catholic Church and none is to be found elsewhere. Vatican II affirms that some elements of truth and sanctification are to be found in other Christian churches and elsewhere, while the Roman Catholic Church possesses those elements in their *fullness. Lumen Gentium* offers a more inclusive understanding of church. Thus it asserts that the church "has many reasons for knowing it is joined to the baptized who are honored by the name of Christian, but do not profess the faith in its entirety or have not preserved unity of communion under the successor of Peter."[13] In addition, *Lumen Gentium* affirms that Jews and Muslims have a special relationship to the people of God. In fact, even those who know neither the gospel nor the Christian church, including atheists, can attain salvation. The constitution declares:

> Those who, through no fault of their own, do not know the Gospel of Christ or his church, but who nevertheless seek God with a sincere heart, and, moved by grace, try in their actions to do his will as they know it through the dictates of their conscience—these too may attain eternal salvation. Nor will divine providence deny the assistance necessary for salvation to those who, without any fault of theirs, have not yet arrived at an explicit knowledge of God, and who, not without grace, strive to lead a good life. Whatever of good or truth is found amongst them is considered by the church to be a preparation for the Gospel and given by him who enlightens all men and women that they may at length have life.[14]

The third area of significant reorientation has to do with the relationship of the bishops to the pope. Here too *Lumen Gentium* exhibits both continuity with past declarations about the nature of the church and new emphases as well. Thus, for example, the constitution reiterates the teaching of Vatican I concerning the primacy of the pope and his infallible teaching authority (*Lumen Gentium*, nos. 18 and 25). On the other hand, it also emphasizes the principle of collegiality, whereby bishops, together with the pope, share in exercising supreme power over the entire church (*Lumen Gentium*, nos. 21-22). From the very beginning of the council, the bishops assembled for Vatican II struggled to find a way to affirm the authority of bishops without separating it from the pope's authority.[15] Pope John

XXIII signaled his own collaborative style already in the preparations for the council's first session. Instead of having the bishops from around the world respond to an agenda established in Rome, he wanted his fellow bishops to be actively involved in setting the council's agenda.[16] When John died on June 3, 1963, it was left to his successor, Pope Paul VI, to oversee the continuing discussions concerning the nature of the church and the relationship between pope and bishops. Paul was keenly aware of the opposition to the notion of collegiality. He felt compelled to intervene in the revision of *Lumen Gentium* in order to insure the constitution's ratification at the council.

Brazilian Archbishop de Proença-Sigaud expressed the consequences that some bishops feared if Vatican II adopted the idea of collegiality. In addition to believing that collegiality has no basis in either scripture or tradition, de Proença-Sigaud claimed that, if it were nonetheless endorsed, collegiality "would give rise to a lack of discipline in the Church, whether with respect to the bishops and the pope, or priests and bishops . . . Bishops would be subjected to episcopal conferences, that is a collective authority, the worst kind there is . . ."[17] Ultimately, an explanatory note was added to Chapter 3 of the constitution, with the intention of defining the sense in which collegiality was to be understood.[18] The secretary general, Archbishop Felici, solemnly read the note in council on November 16, 1964, and he made it clear that the final, formal vote on *Lumen Gentium* a few days later was to be governed by this interpretation.

The note was presented as if it came from the Theological Commission, but its real author was Paul VI, who apparently intended it as his final attempt to win over those who had ceaselessly opposed the doctrine of collegiality ever since the second session (1963). In the speech (September 14, 1964) with which he had opened the third session of the council, Paul had identified the nature and function of the episcopate as "the weightiest and most delicate" of the important topics the council was to treat.[19] The explanatory note clarifies that "college" does not denote a group of equals who transfer their powers to their chairperson, but the body of bishops who are in communion with the pope and with each other. The bishops act as a college only when acting together with the pope and never independently. On the other hand, the pope's headship of the college does not preclude his acting on his own. This explanation was apparently sufficient to reassure the critics of collegiality that the doctrine would not contradict the church's tradition or undermine the pope's authority. The supporters of collegiality were content that, although the note distinguished the powers a bishop receives through sacramental consecration (i.e., teaching, sanctifying, governing) from the exercise of those powers that requires a juridical determination by hierarchical authority, the constitution clearly affirmed that in the college the bishops, "while faithfully upholding the primacy and pre-eminence of their head, exercise their own proper authority for the good of their faithful, indeed even for the good of the whole church, the organic structure and harmony of which are strengthened by the continued influence of the holy Spirit."[20]

Although no document of Vatican II experienced more thorough-going revision between its first draft and the final approved document, *Lumen Gentium* has been regarded as "the most momentous achievement of the Council, both because of its important contents and because of its central place among the Council documents."[21]

Ladislas Örsy, S.J.

Ladislas Örsy was born in Hungary on July 30, 1921. He entered the Society of Jesus in Budapest (Hungary) in 1943 and was ordained to the priesthood in 1951 at Louvain (Belgium).

Fr. Örsy earned a licentiate in philosophy at the Gregorian University in Rome in 1948, followed by a licentiate in theology at the Jesuit College at Louvain in 1952. Five years later he obtained his doctorate in canon law at the Gregorian University. In 1960 he earned an M.A. degree in civil law, which is equivalent to the J.D. degree in the United States, from the Honours School of Jurisprudence at Oxford University. Fr. Örsy taught at the Gregorian University from 1960 until 1966, when he came to the United States. In addition to being a visiting professor at the Graduate Theological Union (Berkeley, CA), the University of Fribourg (Switzerland), and the Pontifical Oriental Institute (Rome), Örsy taught at Fordham University (1967-1974) and at the Catholic University of America (1974-1991). Since 1991 he has been a professor of law at the Georgetown University Law Center, teaching philosophy of law, Roman law, and canon law.

Internationally respected as a leader in canon law, Fr. Örsy has writ-ten hundreds of articles in a variety of journals. His books include, Marriage in Canon Law *(1986),* The Church: Learning and Teaching *(1987), and* Theology and Canon Law: New Horizons for Legislation and Interpretation *(1992).*

During the Second Vatican Council he worked as a peritus for par-ticipating bishops.

A Lesson in Ecclesiology[22]

It was through the council that I got my most important lesson in ecclesiology, and in particular that I learned about the hierarchy of truth and the role of the magisterium.

I did my theological studies before the council at the Jesuit Theological School in Louvain from 1948 to 1952. It was the time of the "new theology": its newness consisted in fresh approaches to the old mysteries. It promised well: it brought forth insights in abundance. The leaders were Henri de Lubac, Teilhard de Chardin, Yves Congar, M. D. Chenu, Karl Rahner, Edward Schillebeeckx, John Courtney Murray, and many others. There were exciting exchanges. Disputations enlivened the investigations. We, mere students, watched and sensed that there was good wine in the making. At some point, however, the movement ground to a halt. A cold air of suspicion swept over the church, alarms were heard, censors and "visitators" were named and sent. They acted dutifully. They meant to pre-serve the tradition. In the name of the magisterium, and always for "prudence's sake," one outstanding theologian after another was removed from his chair or was ordered to keep silent on some issues, or quite simply in the name of obedi-ence, was given a new job. Then the encyclical *Humani Generis* was published. Its aim was to protect the Catholic community from error; it brought no inspiration for a new understanding of the old mysteries.

Once again, it seemed that there were no prophets in Israel; there was sadness in the land.

Then—who could have foreseen it?—an ecumenical council was called by the newly elected pope, John XXIII.

By those years, I was already teaching at the Gregorian University in Rome. We watched the preparations for the council. Over seventy documents were drafted covering the whole field of theology. Archbishop Felici (later cardinal), the secretary-elect of the council, foresaw one session, lasting at the most for two months, at which the episcopate of the world assembled in Rome would approve all that had been diligently prepared (mostly) under the direction of the Roman experts.

The council opened. And, lo and behold, theologians who a few years before were officially condemned, or effectively silenced, or discreetly transferred, were arriving in the Eternal City. They held seminars for bishops and gave lectures for all who cared about the great synod. That was just the beginning. As the council progressed, the very same theologians were helping the bishops to draft constitutions, decrees, and declarations. The once-exiled experts were offering new wine to the shepherds, and the shepherds liked it.

There I was, and I saw, and I watched: through the deliberations and decisions of the council, the magisterium was correcting the magisterium. That is, the extraordinary magisterium of the council was supporting much of the new theology. It kept completing, rectifying, even reversing what was presented earlier as the "official teaching of the church." The council proclaimed not only a new hierarchy of truth, but also showed in a practical way how the authority of day-to-day official teaching of the Holy See ought to be understood.

Thus, I received an existential training in the interpretation of "official teachings"—a training that has served me well to this day.

The Conversion of a Pope

Another event in my theological formation is difficult to classify. I had the grace to watch what might be termed the "conversion of a pope." Let me explain what I mean.

The council came to a critical point during the first session when the council fathers turned to the discussion of the sources of revelation. The draft was untouched by any new theology. In its paragraphs condemnations abounded. The discussion soon revealed that the majority of the bishops were against the draft. When the first "indicative" vote was taken, some 60% of the council fathers opposed its further discussion. By the rules of the council, however, two thirds were needed to take the document off the floor. As the results were announced, the absurdity of the situation became manifest. The council had to go on discussing a document that the majority wanted to reject.

On that day, I happened to have dinner at the English college. A bishop from Down Under was another guest. He just arrived from the session at St. Peter's. He was upset and told me (there are words once heard that you never forget): "I am going home. This is a farce, not a council."

He did not leave. What he saw as a farce was turned into a council by Pope John XXIII.

By the evening the Vatican Radio announced that the draft on the Sources of Revelation would be taken off the floor by the pope's order and sent back to a committee newly constituted. Moreover, so decided the pope, the council would have for all issues its own committees, each consisting of 24 members, eight appointed by the pope, 16 elected by the council fathers. These new drafting groups would have the authority to change prepared texts and the power to propose new ones.

We know what those committees ultimately did: they quietly rejected nearly all the material studiously prepared, and created the documents that brought the church into our modern world.

While the organization of the committees was under way, a story circulated in Rome. It was reported that a small deputation went to see the pope, a deputation consisting of persons of power and dignity from the Roman curia. They carried a warning to the Supreme Pontiff: "Holy Father, there is a danger. You must be careful. If you give that much freedom to the bishops, they will run away with the Council. You will not be able to bring them back." It was reported that Pope John replied: "They too have the Spirit."

There was a magisterial statement, if ever there was one! The successor of Peter perceived the presence of the Spirit in the successors of the apostles and was willing to trust them. Out of this trust, the real council was born and produced plentiful good wine.

Of course, there is no way to know if Pope John XXIII really made that utterance. *"Si non e vero, ben trovato"* ["If it isn't true, it's well put."]. Whether he said it or not, the events proved that he created a climate of trust. But why do I speak of the "conversion of the pope"? Because before the opening of the council, it was well known that John XXIII was fully satisfied with the preparatory documents. He approved each one of them. Indeed, he was delighted with them. After all, he named the commissions that drafted them; he presided in person over the whole process. In all probability, he too expected their swift approval by the bishops at the council. Yet when the signs of the times warned him that his expectations were misplaced, he responded with humility and was willing to enter into new horizons with all the risk that such a step entailed. Yes, John XXIII had the greatness to learn from his bishops—without ever losing his effective leadership and apostolic authority. The pope called the council, and the bishops created the vision of the council.

The lesson? It is in that simple sentence: "They too have the Spirit." Creativity flourishes in a climate of trust.

Martin E. Marty

Martin E. Marty was born February 5, 1928—three hours before his fellow-Chicagoan Father Andrew Greeley—in West Point, Nebraska. He attended Lutheran seminaries, was ordained in 1952, and served as a parish pastor for 11 years. Meanwhile he received the Ph.D. at The University of Chicago, where he taught ("The Fairfax M. Cone Distinguished Service Professor") from 1963-1998. He has been an editor at the Christian Century *since 1956 and was founding president of the Park Ridge Center for the Study of Health, Faith, and Ethics. Among his many boards has been that of the Regents at St. Olaf College, Northfield, Minnesota (1988-2001), where he was chair and where he served as interim president late in 2000. He holds 70 honorary degrees. Among his other honors are The National Humanities Medal, The National Book Award, and The Medal of the American Academy of Arts and Sciences. He has been president of the American Catholic Historical Association, the American Society of Church History, and the American Academy of Religion. The Martin Marty Center at the University of Chicago, the Martin Marty Prize of the American Academy of Religion—both devoted to a concept that has concerned him for decades, "Public Religion"—and the Martin Marty Chair at St. Olaf College honor his themes.*

At the time of the council he had just moved from parish ministry to his teaching role at the University of Chicago. He has written more than fifty books, including the three-volume Modern American Religion *(1997). He edited* Second Opinion *and continues to edit the newsletter* Context. *Marty now shares a "studio/study" with his photographer son Micah, with whom he has collaborated on five books. He enjoys and shares the interests of his musician-wife Harriet and the company of their extended family, is working on four books, and does regular lecturing and consulting.*

Certainty and Condemnations

My journalistic assignment was to cover the latter part of the third session of the council in autumn, 1964; a different *Christian Century* editor reported on each session. Members of the press ordinarily did not have a seat in the *aula*. But it happened that Bishop Peter Bartholomew of St. Cloud, Minnesota, inspired by the fact that the first bishop of his diocese had been named Martin Marty, generously provided a courtesy pass. So for six weeks this unofficial observer enjoyed the rights, privileges, and perspectives of both press and observers.

That first October day was one of the two most memorable and decisive council moments for determining an aspect of my vocation. (The other was the day when Pope Paul VI frustrated the efforts of those who were writing and promoting the "Declaration on Religious Freedom," and when Chicago's Albert Cardinal Meyer and theologian John Courtney Murray rallied forces to project that debate into the fourth session).

I arrived on October 29, 1964, the day four cardinals made tentative moves toward proposing a reexamination of the question of birth control as presently treated by the church. The story of how their move was also frustrated is not important for the lesson I drew from the occasion. And what I drew is based not on anything that appears in the council minutes or proceedings, but on an anecdote passed on by the arch-anecdotalist among the observers, the late Professor Albert Outler.

As he heard and told it, there was much stir among the council fathers the evening of October 29 after the four speakers had shaken the serenity of many. The climactic encounter in Outler's hearing and telling occurred between an arch-conservative hierarch, who vehemently opposed the very idea of raising the question of reappraisal, and a more moderate one who thought it worth examining. If we change church teaching on contraception, argued the former, won't people expect other teachings to be changed? And what would now be the status of souls who we said had committed mortal sin by violating the church's norms concerning contraception?

This quandary was expressed again in dramatic form almost two years later. At the final meeting of the Papal Birth Control Commission on June 20-21, 1966, Bishop Carlo Colombo spoke vehemently against backtracking on contraception. Father Marcelino Zalba, a Spanish Jesuit, chimed in his support: If we change the church's teaching on contraception, what about "the millions we have sent to hell if these norms are not valid?" Patty Crowley, a married Catholic from Chicago, shot back: "Father Zalba, do you really believe God has carried out all your orders?"[23] Long after I lost the pounds I had gained while being entertained by various religious orders—Rome was a great place for Protestants to enjoy hospitality that year—and after the vivid recall of sights, sounds, smells, and textures of that halcyon autumn began to wane and fade, I have lived off the meanings of that kind of question. And I have carried it over into subsequent ecumenical and inter-faith encounters or Christian-secular debates, where the temptation to be too sure about whom we save and whom we damn is strong.

I took from that little exchange not the notion that "we," in church and world, do not get to or do not have to make decisions. The council fathers and their *periti* had to deliberate and the bishops had to vote on important issues with which we, non-Catholics and Catholics alike, still live. But how they deliberated and what they have done since the council voting does matter.

Much of my work in recent years has had to do with militant fundamentalists, ethno-nationalists, uncivil citizens, and those who by actions and talk born of their cocksureness militated against ecumenical, reconciling, and civil speech and action. Often in their presence I have wanted to invoke the spirit of Oliver Cromwell, who wanted some opponents "by the bowels of Christ" to consider that they might be mistaken.

The need to ask whether God ratifies all our decisions is most appropriate when the deepest questions, the eternal puzzles, get deliberated. In the case of those two council participants the issue was eternity and destiny itself. Those in authority and those who gravitate to the viewpoints of the over-sure church authorities are quite confident that they and God know and decide the same things, thanks to their interpretation of scriptures or of magisterial churchly teaching. So they can consign those with whom they disagree to hell, hereafter or now. Should the condemner be so sure about divine ratifications?

Martin Luther has sent shivers into the minds of some theologians who have read in the reformer's debates the shocking notion that *Deus absonditus* [the hidden God] is hidden not only in revelation (e.g., in bread and wine and water and grammar) but also behind revelation. "Now we know in part . . . ." The best book title this Lutheran has read on Luther's thought is *Let God Be God*, something that Luther, a regular consigner-to-hell of his foes, intended to do but often did not. Patty Crowley, who questioned Fr. Zalba in 1966, and the cardinal, who challenged the conservative hierarch in 1964, were both letting God be God.

From Protestant theologian Reinhold Niebuhr I have learned and adopted an ironic perspective. It is a biblically grounded awareness that inside our knowledge there is enough ignorance; inside our innocence there is enough guilt, along with our virtue there comes enough vice, that no matter what our actions, they will not always turn out to be as positive as we had designed and thought and hoped them to be. As one adopts this perspective there is a danger that we might retreat into cynicism and lapse into the expression of an "after all, everything has been tried, so why should we act," or a "what fools these mortals be" dismissive spirit.

Niebuhr went on to say that, in the spirit of Psalm 2:4, the same God who sits in the heavens and laughs at and holds in derision the prideful and cocksure, also holds us responsible and does not dishonor human aspiration. So I took from the best of the council fathers and the most promising of their actions a sense that they must make decisions, but leave some of the consequences and judgment about their validity to the God in whose name the council was convoked.

I hope my own life, work, and ministry were altered by a second-hand report of a second-level conversation at the council. I certainly intended it to, and have made decisions in the light of a calling reinforced in Rome. Whether or not God ratifies all those decisions . . . ? Read Psalm 2:4.

Charles E. Curran

Charles Curran was born on March 30, 1934, the third of four children, to Gertrude Beisner Curran and John F. Curran. He went to the seminary in Rochester, New York, graduating with a B.A. from St. Bernard's College and Seminary in 1955 before going to study in Rome. After receiving a doctorate in sacred theology from the Gregorian University in 1961 and a doctorate in sacred theology with a specialization in moral theology from the Accademia Alfonsiana, Curran returned to teach moral theology at St. Bernard's Seminary in Rochester, New York, from 1961-1965. His teaching career at the Catholic University of America from 1965-1988 was marked by three significant events—in 1967 the faculty and students went on strike and successfully overturned the original decision of the Board of Trustees not to renew Curran's contract; in 1968 he was the spokesperson for a group of over 600 Catholic scholars who issued a statement of dissent from the major conclusions of the encyclical Humanae Vitae; *in 1986 after an eight-year investigation, the Congregation for the Doctrine of the Faith concluded that Curran was neither "suitable nor eligible to exercise the function of a Professor of Catholic Theology." After losing a lawsuit to retain his right to teach Catholic theology at Catholic University of America, Curran ultimately accepted the Elizabeth Scurlock University Professorship of Human Values at Southern Methodist University in 1991.*

Fr. Curran has served as president of three national academic societies—the Catholic Theological Society of America, the Society of Christian Ethics, and the American Theological Society. The Catholic Theological Society of America in 1972 named him the first recipient of the John Courtney Murray Award for distinguished achievement in theology. The Catholic Press Association of the United States in May 2000 awarded The Catholic Moral Tradition Today: A Synthesis *(1999), the latest of his thirty theological books, the prize as the best book from a small publisher.*

The Church as the Pilgrim People of God

The Diocese of Rochester, New York, sent me to live at the North American College and to study theology at the Gregorian University in Rome in September 1955 to prepare for ordination to priestly ministry. The vast majority of the Jesuit professors of theology at the Greg had been teaching there for twenty years or more. The professor's book in ecclesiology insisted from the very first thesis that the Roman Catholic Church was the kingdom of God on earth, founded by Jesus with a hierarchical structure emphasizing the role of the papacy. Such was my understanding of the church.

In 1958 my bishop informed me (that was the way things went before Vatican II!) that beginning in the fall of 1959 I should work toward a doctorate at the Gregorian in moral theology in order to teach moral theology at the diocesan seminary of St. Bernard's. In addition to going to the Greg, I also attended lectures and eventually obtained a second doctorate from the Accademia Alfonsiana that specialized in moral theology. At the Alfonsiana I encountered a new approach to moral theology that emphasized the universal call of all Christians to holiness with a strong biblical and liturgical basis. Bernard Häring was the primary but not the only professor working in this direction. I invited many of my fellow graduate student priests to go over and listen to Häring's lectures.

From Häring I also learned a different understanding of the church. In a course on conversion, he insisted that the church too was in need of conversion. We are a pilgrim people. Likewise the church is the people of God with all, not just hierarchy, religious, and priests, called by God to holiness.

I left Rome in June 1961 to begin teaching moral theology and canon law at St. Bernard's Seminary. (Some of my students had already studied more canon law there than I had studied in Rome!) I left Rome with a different understanding of the church from what I had first learned there. But I also left Rome with the feeling that neither Pope John XXIII nor the future Vatican Council were going to bring about much change. Such a feeling needs to be explained.

I was in St. Peter's Square the early evening of October 28, 1958, when John XXIII was elected and came to the balcony to give his first blessing. In fact, on the basis of a tip I found in either *Time Magazine* or the *New York Times*, I won five dollars by betting on Roncalli.

My first impression of the new pope was not positive. Pius XII was an aristocratic figure with a lean posture, who raised his eyes to God and blessed the crowd with three very precise signs of the cross. John was a rotund man who, before finishing the triple blessing, started waving to the crowd. This very young, impressionistic, newly ordained priest was somewhat taken aback.

However, John XXIII's unpretentiousness, gentleness, and pastoral concern scored high points. Some excitement accompanied his announcement on January 25, 1959, that he planned three works for the renewal of the church—a synod for Rome, the updating of canon law, and an ecumenical council.

I was doing graduate work during the Synod of Rome in the last week of January 1960. In my estimation it was a disaster. The 755 statutes were prepackaged and dealt primarily with insignificant things such as clerical dress and attendance at the opera and movies. The format was even worse than the content. The participants simply sat, listened to what was read out, and then all voted yes. There was no discussion of any kind. This was the old ecclesiology at work with no participation of those who were voting members of the synod. Such an approach did not augur well for the future ecumenical council.

In June 1960 the pope appointed the preparatory commissions to draft the documents for the council. The cardinals of the Roman curia chaired these commissions, and most of the members came from the Roman approach to theology. No one expected these curia officials to bring about much change.

I left Rome in late June of 1961. Just before leaving, Father F. X. Murphy, who had been a professor of mine at the Alfonsiana, invited me to a long lunch. F. X. regaled me with stories of the shenanigans and intransigent approach of the Roman curia, especially with regard to the upcoming ecumenical council. As a result of this conversation and my awareness that his mother's maiden name was Rynne, I knew who was the author of the famous "Letter from Vatican City" that appeared in the *New Yorker* at the very beginning of the first session of the council.

My first year teaching in the seminary (1961-62) was very busy but most gratifying. The news I heard from Rome, however, was quite negative. Josef Fuchs, my moral theology professor at the Greg, was forbidden to teach undergraduate seminarians. Similar restrictions had earlier been placed on two professors at the Biblical Institute.

When Vatican II opened in October 1962, I was not expecting much. But things changed in a hurry. The opening address of John XXIII clearly indicated he saw the need for reform. He emphasized *aggiornamento* [updating], castigated the prophets of doom who saw nothing but prevarication and ruin in the modern world, insisted on the need for mercy and a positive presentation of church teaching rather than severity and condemnations, and distinguished between the substance of the deposit of faith and the way in which it is expressed and presented.

The first session proved that the curial agenda was not going to prevail. The more progressive draft on the liturgy, which providentially was the first one discussed, showed that the vast majority of the participants favored significant change in the church's liturgy, which had repercussions for a changed understanding of the church. The council participants rejected the prepared documents on divine revelation and the church that came from the curia-dominated preparatory commissions. The newer draft on the church prepared for the second session of the council emphasized the church as the people of God, a pilgrim church with a hierarchical structure. The subsequent sessions had their tense moments, but it seems after the first session that the general direction of the council and its understanding of church were now clear.

My assessment of John XXIII differs from that of others. I do not think he had a clear idea at all of what he wanted the council to do when he first called it. The greatness of John XXIII was that he was open to the call of the Spirit—both in the tradition of the church and in the signs of the times.

Over the years I have had my own tensions with the church, but the understanding of the church as the pilgrim people of God has always sustained me.

Richard Rohr, O.F.M.

Father Richard Rohr is a Franciscan of the New Mexico Province. He was born in 1943 in Kansas. He entered the Franciscans in 1961 and was ordained to the priesthood in 1970. He received his master's degree in theology from the University of Dayton, and did further studies in scripture at the University of Notre Dame and the University of San Francisco.

Rohr was the founder of the New Jerusalem Community in Cincinnati, Ohio, in 1971, and the Center for Action and

Contemplation in Albuquerque, New Mexico, in 1986. After the initial founding periods, he handed both groups over to lay leadership and direction. New Jerusalem is still an alive community today in Cincinnati, and Rohr presently works with the Center in Albuquerque.

Rohr is probably best known for his numerous audio and videotapes. Articles by Fr. Richard have appeared in numerous publications, many of his tapes have come out in 14 different books, and many of these have been translated into other languages. His best known books include The Great Themes of Scripture: Old Testament *(1987),* The Great Themes of Scripture: New Testament *(1988),* Job and the Mystery of Suffering *(1996),* Everything Belongs *(1999), and* Hope Against Darkness *(2001).*

Fr. Rohr now lives in a hermitage behind his Franciscan community in Albuquerque and divides his time between local work, the county jail, and preaching and teaching on all continents. He considers the proclamation of the gospel to be his primary call and uses many different platforms to communicate that message. Scripture, the integration of action and contemplation, community building, peace and justice issues, male spirituality, the enneagram, and eco-spirituality are all themes that he makes use of for the sake of the gospel.

Honesty and Creativity in the Church

I was fortunate to be studying philosophy at Duns Scotus College in Detroit during the years of the Second Vatican Council. Because we had some very well-trained Franciscans at that time, they taught us how to think—how we know what we know instead of just what we should know, which seems to be more common today. Through phenomenology and what we called "philosophical psychology," we learned to assess and make use of our own "audio-visual aids," which developed a wonderful capacity for self-critical thinking and historical critical thinking too. In short we were taught an awful lot about our humanity before we piled too much divinity onto it.

By the time I moved to theology at St. Leonard's in Dayton in 1966, I was given a further gift. Our province had been wise enough to send a group of talented young friars to study theology in Rome during the very years of the council. They returned just in time to teach us! Again, we were not given simple doctrinal conclusions as much as the process of getting to those conclusions. We were not propagandized as much as educated. We were not formed into "system men" (a reasonable position for a Franciscan), although we were given a deep respect for how the system got to where it is, both its strengths and its weaknesses. As you would expect, it led us to know how to work within the historical situation with honesty and even courage because we knew we had been given the tools to do so with integrity. We had not been lied to. We had not been kept inside a closed system. The veil of the Wizard of Oz had been parted for us. We had nothing to hide from or to hide from others.

As wise people will know, this only gave us more self-confidence and more courage. We had faced our questions and doubts in a faith-filled context, and with wise and educated men who could lead us through our doubts and criticisms. We did not have to spend the rest of our lives resolving or reacting or repressing. Only thirty years later do I know how unique and how blessed was that period. Most of my brother priests before my time were not given such an opportunity for honesty; many of my brother priests formed in the last fifteen years do not even want such honesty, or, worse yet, seminaries are afraid to give it to them. Yet, we are the very people who quote Jesus as saying that "the truth will set us free." I wonder if we believe it.

"Afraid" is the key word. Truth and gospel can only flourish in a situation where fear is not in control, or at least where our fears are faced honestly. Today we do not have such a safe harbor. It feels like everybody is afraid of everybody: seminarians of faculty and faculty of seminarians, priests of bishops and bishops of priests, Rome of bishops and bishops of Rome, laity of clergy and clergy of laity. Who would have believed that things could change so much in one lifetime?

We know from history that greatness does not emerge in times of mere survivalism. Greatness emerges when people are forced to think honestly and creatively. I thank God profoundly for the time in which I was educated and formed. I thank God for such wise and holy teachers as that period produced. I know now that I enjoyed both a safe harbor and a wonderful window of opportunity that few people have enjoyed in history. So sad that the window closed so quickly. So sad that the church cannot create harbor in an unsafe world. It is the next generations of the church that will suffer. It is the gospel itself that is taking a back seat to fear, protectionism, and power.

We never seem ready for Jesus' great and self-effacing adventure.

Daniel E. Pilarczyk

Daniel E. Pilarczyk was born in Dayton, Ohio, in 1934. He attended Catholic elementary schools and entered St. Gregory's Seminary in 1948. After high school and two years of college there, he studied philosophy and theology at the Pontifical Urban University in Rome. He was ordained a priest in 1959 and earned a doctorate in theology in 1961.

Upon his return to the archdiocese of Cincinnati, he became assistant chancellor and began studies in classical civilization. He earned an M.A. from Xavier University and a Ph.D. from the University of Cincinnati. In 1963 he was assigned to full-time teaching at St. Gregory's Seminary, where he became rector in 1968.

In 1974 he was appointed auxiliary bishop to Joseph Bernardin, then Archbishop of Cincinnati. Pilarczyk was vicar for education in addition to being vicar general. He became archbishop of Cincinnati in 1982.

During his years as archbishop he served as representative of the United States hierarchy to the International Commission on English in the Liturgy and chaired its episcopal board from 1991 to 1997. He served as vice-president (1986-89) and president (1989-1992) of the National Conference of Catholic Bishops. He also chaired several committees of the conference, including education, liturgy, and doctrine.

Archbishop Pilarczyk has received seven honorary degrees and published about twenty books, including Twelve Tough Issues: What the Church Teaches and Why *(1988; rev. ed., 2002), and* Live Letters (2002), *a series of commentaries on the second readings for Sunday liturgies.*

Bringing Old and New Together

Nineteen sixty-nine was a terrible time to be a seminary rector. Everything in the country seemed to be up for grabs, and much of what was in the church as well. Seminarians were demonstrating all over the country for greater freedom and greater say in their preparation for the priesthood. Nobody knew exactly what lay ahead, most certainly not the rector of St. Gregory's Seminary in Cincinnati.

I had been appointed rector the year before at age 33 in what was, as I learned later, a desperation move by our eighty-three-year-old Archbishop Alter. During my first year in office, I made some rather minor changes in the seminary program. These were greeted with enthusiasm by both students and faculty, and I thought that I had solved the seminary's problems for the foreseeable future. Toward the end of that first year, however, some faculty members came to me to say that, while things were pretty quiet for the present, there would almost certainly be big trouble unless further, more sweeping changes were made. In a state of chronic panic, I established a committee of faculty and students whose purpose was to build up anew from top to bottom the whole seminary program.

One aspect of the changes was the academic program. It had been clear to me for some time that the college "theology" program was inadequate. I put together another committee to deal with this particular question. I don't remember now what we did about most of the program, but I do recall that one of the committee's members, who had been a *peritus* at Vatican II, urged us to set up a course in the council's "Pastoral Constitution on the Church in the Modern World." He said it was the obvious way to introduce college freshmen to contemporary ecclesial realities.

I volunteered to teach this course. Although I had a degree in theology, I had never done any regular teaching of it before. I had to do lots of reading, since the kind of theology that I had studied in Rome before 1961 was not exactly the kind of theology that lay beneath the council's teaching. I also had to do lots of thinking, since the council's whole mindset was different from the mindset I had absorbed. In addition to that, I had to learn how to teach through lectures rather than through the analysis of texts that I had become proficient in as a teacher of Latin and Greek.

During the summer of 1969, I spent hours each day reading about the history of the council and about Christian secularity. Here in *Gaudium et Spes* I was faced with a theological world that was concrete rather than abstract, practical rather than theoretical, oriented toward the world rather than heaven, toward the future rather than the past, toward the community rather than the individual. I remember walking around the seminary campus trying to figure out how all this new stuff fit in with what I had been taught. It was hard work, and sometimes frightening.

That autumn I taught the course for the first time to our college freshmen. Once they got the hang of my teaching methods and of what I expected of them, they loved it. *Gaudium et Spes* spoke loud and clear to them. By popular demand, I offered the course again during the second semester of that year and four more times during the years I remained as seminary rector.

Meanwhile there were suggestions from the students that other courses in the Vatican II documents be made available. Since I had come up with a method of study and presentation with *Gaudium et Spes*, I was not unwilling to go a little farther afield. I taught courses in *Lumen Gentium, Sacrosanctum Concilium, Dei Verbum,* and several other council documents. These were electives and had to be taught in the evening so that students from several classes could participate. Eventually I set up a plan for studying and teaching all the council documents. This project had to be scrapped, however, when I was appointed auxiliary bishop and left seminary work.

In the process of responding to what my faculty colleague and I had perceived to be the theological needs of the students, I had backed into a whole new theological specialty. It was hard work, not only because of the quantity of reading and study that it required, but also because of the effort to understand how these new approaches and new insights could be in harmony with what I had learned before. But it was a wonderful way to prepare to be a bishop. My work in the teachings of Vatican II reshaped my view of church and ministry and revelation and world and gave me excellent spiritual and intellectual equipment for the exercise of church leadership. Nobody planned it that way. Things more or less just happened. But that's the way God's providence often works.

As I go about my work in the Archdiocese of Cincinnati, I often encounter priests who were my students in their seminary days. It's not unusual for us to trade memories about our time together with *Gaudium et Spes* and *Lumen Gentium.* I am grateful to them for their kind reminiscences, and grateful to the Lord for the way in which he has provided for all of us and for his church.

Francis Sullivan, S.J.

Francis Sullivan was born on May 21, 1922, in Boston. After graduating from Boston College High School, he entered the novitiate of the New England Province of the Society of Jesus and was ordained to the priesthood in 1951. During his course of studies, he obtained the M.A. in philosophy at Boston College in 1945, the M.A. in classics at Fordham University in 1948, and the S.T.L. at Weston College in 1952. After ordination he was sent to Rome for further study of theology at the Pontifical Gregorian University, where he obtained the S.T.D. in 1956. Although he had expected to return to his province to teach at Weston College, he was then assigned to teach ecclesiology at the Gregorian University. He continued to do this for the next 36 years, serving also as dean of the faculty of theology from 1964 to 1970. After being declared emeritus in 1992, Sullivan returned to New England, where he, as of 2002, was an adjunct professor of theology at Boston College.

He has published seven books and numerous articles. His more recent important works include Magisterium: Teaching Authority in the Catholic Church *(1983),* Salvation Outside the Church? *(1992), and* Creative Fidelity: Weighing and Interpreting Documents of the Magisterium *(1996), and* From Apostles to Bishops *(2001).*

For his outstanding contributions to theology, Sullivan was awarded the John Courtney Murray Award of the Catholic Theological Society of America in 1994.

Vatican II on the Charisms of the Faithful

During the month of October 1963, the bishops at Vatican II were discussing the draft of the "Dogmatic Constitution on the Church." This draft included a paragraph on "the charisms of the faithful." From time to time the bishops from the United States would meet at the North American College to discuss issues that were coming up at the council, and they would usually invite a theologian to give them his ideas on the issue and respond to their questions about it. It happened that I was the theologian who was asked to give a presentation on the question of the charisms of the faithful.

At that time I had been teaching ecclesiology at the Gregorian University for about six years, and I have to confess that this was the first time I had ever prepared a lecture on the charisms of the faithful. My study of the question led me to realize that there are two quite different notions of "charism" current in Catholic theology. According to the article in the *Dictionnaire de Spiritualité*, charisms are extraordinary gifts of grace, such as one finds in the lives of saints and mystics. However, A. Lemonnyer, author of the article on charisms in the *Dictionnaire de la Bible, Supplement*, drew quite a different notion of charism from an analysis of the teaching of St. Paul. According to this view, charisms are gifts of grace that equip people for the roles and ministries that they are to have in the body of Christ. Some of these gifts are extraordinary, but many are not, and they are distributed widely among the faithful, in view of the contribution that each is intended to make to the life of the whole body. I also found that it was this notion of the charisms that had been affirmed in works by Yves Congar and Karl Rahner. This, then, was the view that I presented in my talk to the American bishops. I later learned that this was also the view that Cardinal Suenens defended in a speech that he gave at the council in response to Cardinal Ruffini, who had insisted that charisms were extraordinary gifts that one could not expect to find among the ordinary faithful.

After I had given my talk at the North American College, the thought came to me that the paragraph in the draft text that treated the charisms of the faithful could be improved, especially by making more ample use of the teaching and language of St. Paul. So I composed a paragraph that I thought was better than the one in the draft. But I was not a *peritus* of the council and did not have a way to submit an emendation on my own. However, a Jesuit from the New England Province, who had been my rector in the novitiate and subsequently my provincial superior, was now the Bishop of Kingston (Jamaica) and hence a member of the council. I had spoken with him a number of times during his stay in Rome, and now I recalled that he had once invited me to give him any thoughts that he might be able to use for an intervention at the council. So I told him about the paragraph that I had composed about the charisms of the faithful. The bishops were invited to submit in writing any emendations that they wished to propose for the improvement of the draft texts. Bishop McEleney graciously accepted my text and promised to submit it in his own name. When the constitution *Lumen Gentium* was promulgated,

I had the pleasure of seeing that the paragraph on the charisms of the faithful now corresponded substantially with what I had written. And when the *Acta Synodalia* were eventually published, I was able to verify the fact that in reworking that paragraph, the Theological Commission had accepted an emendation that had been proposed by Bishop John McEleney of Kingston, Jamaica.[24]

Impact on My Life and Ministry

The immediate impact that Vatican II had on me was on my ministry as a teacher of ecclesiology. Before the council began, I had been teaching the course on the church at the Gregorian for six years, and obviously I had been teaching pre-Vatican II ecclesiology. The conciliar decrees, especially the "Dogmatic Constitution on the Church" (*Lumen Gentium*) and the "Decree on Ecumenism" (*Unitatis Redintegratio*), had a significant impact on the course of ecclesiology that I offered to my students in the aftermath of the council.

About two years after the close of Vatican II, a development took place that in some respects was influenced by the council, and which eventually had a profound effect on my life and ministry as a priest. This was the entry of the Charismatic Renewal into the Catholic Church. I am convinced that Vatican II's positive teaching concerning the charisms of the faithful had a great deal to do with the acceptance of the Charismatic Renewal in the Catholic Church. I can hardly imagine that it would have met such acceptance if the council had adopted the view of Cardinal Ruffini that charisms are not to be found among the ordinary faithful. In any case, I think it unlikely that if the council had accepted Ruffini's view, I myself would have had an open mind about the claims that people were making about the charisms they had received through their participation in this movement.

I was not at all inclined to take part in it myself, but it excited my interest, and I took the time to become more informed about it. It was at least partly due to the positive teaching of Vatican II on the charisms of the faithful that I was able to come to the conclusion that many people could be experiencing genuine charisms as the fruit of being "baptized in the Spirit." That remained a theoretical judgment, with no basis in personal experience, until about five years after the council, when Fr. Carlo Martini, S.J., who at that time was a professor at the Biblical Institute, invited me to a meeting of a prayer group that had formed in Rome. Although my progress toward full involvement was hesitant and gradual, I continued to meet regularly with that prayer group until I left Rome 20 years later. Membership in "Lumen Christi" proved to be a great grace for my spiritual life, and also gave me new opportunities for ministry. Through the mysterious working of Divine Providence, the Second Vatican Council, and especially its teaching on the charisms of the faithful, has had a significant impact on my life and ministry.

Lawrence S. Cunningham

Lawrence S. Cunningham was born in 1935 and raised in Florida. He was educated both in Rome at the Gregorian University, where he received the S.T.L. degree, and in the United States at Florida State University, where he earned an M.A. in English and a Ph.D. in humanities. After teaching at Florida State and the University of Scranton, he joined the faculty of the University of Notre Dame in 1988. Cunningham served as chair of the Theology Department there for six years. Currently he is the John A. O'Brien Professor of Theology at Notre Dame.

Cunningham is the author or editor of 17 books. He lectures frequently here and aboard. His most recent book is Thomas Merton and the Monastic Vision *(1999), which is the fruit of his long engagement with the writings of Thomas Merton, the third volume of whose journals (1952-1960) he edited under the title* The Search for Solitude.

During his four years in Rome, Cunningham witnessed the death of Pope Pius XII, the election of Pope John XXIII, and, purely by chance, was present at the Basilica of Saint Paul-Outside-the-Walls when Pope John announced his decision to call an ecumenical council.

Tensions in Vatican II
and How to Proceed Today

I remember quite clearly running to a news kiosk near Saint Peter's Square to get a newspaper to read the biography of Angelo Roncalli, who had just been proclaimed pope from the loggia of the basilica by Alfredo Cardinal Ottaviani. Unknown to me at that moment, the new pope would quickly gain our attention both by his pastoral concerns and by his almost casual announcement at the Basilica of Saint Paul-Outside-the-Walls, shortly after he attained the papacy, that he intended to (1) convoke a Roman synod (the first in centuries); (2) begin the revision of the Code of Canon Law; and (3) convoke an ecumenical council.

As a theological student at the Jesuit-run Gregorian University, I was well aware that many things were stirring in the Catholic world. The Assisi Conference had gingerly raised the issue of a vernacular liturgy. We were reading the hitherto suppressed works of Teilhard de Chardin (mailed from outside of Italy because his works were not easily found in the Roman bookstores). Josef Fuchs, who was newly appointed to the chair of moral theology at the Gregorian, was a fresh voice in the casuistic field of ethics, and Bernard Lonergan was opening for us new ways to think theologically. We also knew that in France, despite the heavy hand of the Holy Office, important reform movements were afoot. The first tentative steps toward ecumenical exchange were in process. I also began to read books that opened up a whole new way of thinking about theology. I still have on my shelf Bernard Häring's *The Law of Christ,* in French, and Edward Schillebeeckx's *Christ the Sacrament of the Encounter with God* —two books that gave me an entirely new way of thinking theologically.

When I look back to my hopes and dreams for that coming council, a few things stand out. In comparison to what the council actually did, our expectations were rather modest. Despite listening to lectures in Latin, reading texts in that language, as well as taking Latin oral examinations, hopes were raised that more vernacular would be permitted as a pastoral improvement. Would we at least get permission to celebrate the sacraments in the vernacular and, further, was it beyond possibility that some of the Mass would be in the vernacular? We thought that the proclamation of the scripture readings would make a good start.

While we were beginning to see the writings of theologians who provided a more holistic view of theology, as opposed to the desiccated neo-scholasticism still lingering at the Gregorian, it was clear that the gap between what the scripture scholars and the theologians were offering was wide. I still recall my uneasiness with the rococo mariology handed to us, because it seemed that as a discipline mariology was constructed independently of solid biblical or patristic foundations. But I still regard the decision to place the conciliar reflections on Mary within *Lumen Gentium* as one of the best moves of the council. It had the twin benefit of articulating the Catholic sense of Mary's role in salvation, but it did so in a fashion that would not prove a stumbling block to either the churches of the Reformation or the Orthodox tradition.

By the time the council was actually convened, I was back in the United States. How the council proceeded was a source of joy and gave me a sense, perhaps only half understood, that the conciliar fathers were putting into their decrees the thinking of our theological heroes: Yves Congar (who was, in my judgment, *the* theologian of the council), Henri De Lubac, Jean Danielou, Bernard Häring, Edward Schillebeeckx, Karl Rahner, and those many others who were in the forefront of the liturgical movement (like the late Cipriano Vagaggini, O.S.B., and my own professor, Hermann Schmidt, S.J.) and the early pioneers of ecumenism.

The achievements of Vatican II cannot be considered an unqualified success, even though they did constitute a sea shift in church life and practice. Persons of a certain age speak of their experiences in terms of the pre- and post-conciliar days. Such comparisons are a sure sign of impending old age, since descriptions of the "old" Catholic Church are meaningless to the students I teach today. The various documents coming out of the council ranged from the banal (the "Decree on Communications") to those that seem today somewhat safe and half-hearted. Even the crucial "Dogmatic Constitution on the Church" (*Lumen Gentium*) shows an interior tension between an ecclesiology whose roots are in the older tradition of scholasticism, and the newer thinking, whose roots are in Newman, Möhler, and whose fruition comes from Yves Congar. Even *Gaudium et Spes* (the "Pastoral Constitution on the Church in the Modern World") presents a problem in that parts of it ring with the somewhat sunny optimism of the 1960s while not directly touching on issues that have come to the forefront of present-day discussions.

Whatever the tensions one sees in the conciliar discussions (and documents) of Vatican II, one does see a foundation on which we might advance. What needs to be advanced? Only the most naive think that we have fully worked out the relationship between the local and the universal church. That relationship requires a balance between the bishop as pastor of the Catholic Church fully realized in its local instantiation and the claims of the papacy as the focal point of the unity of the church. The centralizing tendency of Rome is not only the result of the style of the current pontiff (although that is part of it, to be sure), but also the result of a deeper problem because the role of the local church has yet to be fully articulated, despite the efforts of some fine theological work like that produced by the late lamented Jean Marie Tillard in his brilliant book, *L'Eglise Local*.

A more "sociological" problem to be faced is the necessity of developing a concept of the church for that huge number of Catholics who have no experience of the church before Vatican II. What are we to make of those tendencies that, on the right, seek a kind of restoration, and, on the left, veer toward something like liberal Protestantism? How do we articulate and sustain that retrieval of the *fontes* [sources or founts] in a sane and nourishing fashion? That issue goes on apace while demographics herald what all of us know viscerally: the near collapse of traditional religious life (especially so among women), the rapid aging of the clergy, the rising number of Hispanic Catholics in this country, the polarization of Catholic intellectuals and those who would like to be so named.

These "crises," of course, are not unfamiliar to readers of church history, even though knowledge of the past is no excuse for complacency. If there was one creative tension found in the deliberations of Vatican II it was in the desire to affirm the transcendent force of Christian belief with a concomitant conviction that the deepest reality of the Incarnation is to be found in serving others and not being served. The sign value of the church is best illustrated in the (hundreds of) thousands of experiments in community outreach to the poor, in the witness of our contemporary martyrs, in the willingness to be counter-cultural witnesses to the worst excesses of the age. In a famous observation, written two generations ago, Karl Rahner said that the Christian of the future would either be a mystic or would not be a Christian at all. By "mystic" Rahner meant those who experienced something beyond the epiphenomena of church observance. That "something beyond," of course, is the reality of God in Jesus Christ. As long as there are Christians drawing on the ancient wisdom of the gospel, the passing of forms and the changing of ministries will be incidental to the authentic witness of the gospel.

What sustains me today? As a Catholic theologian with thirty years of teaching behind me, it is the edifying (I use the term technically!) image of the many students, past and present, who have left our university to do volunteer service here and abroad or those who have entered into forms of ministry or gone on to do advanced work in theology to teach or work for the church. I have devoted my life to form them, and they, in turn, have formed me in the adamantine conviction that this is gospel work.

Richard P. McBrien

Born on August 19, 1936, in Hartford, Connecticut, Richard McBrien was educated in public and parochial schools and at St. Thomas Seminary, Bloomfield, Connecticut. He did his major seminary studies at St. John Seminary, Brighton, Massachusetts, earning an M.A. in Theology (1962). Ordained on February 2, 1962, for the Archdiocese of Hartford, he served as a parish assistant and college chaplain (1962-63), and then did doctoral studies in theology at the Gregorian University in Rome (1963-65) during the Second Vatican Council, receiving an S.T.D. in 1967. McBrien served on the faculty and as Dean of Studies at Pope John XXIII National Seminary, Weston, Massachusetts (1965-70), and then at Boston College (1970-80), where he was also director of the Institute of Religious Education and Pastoral Ministry (1975-80). He became the Crowley-O'Brien-Walter Professor of Theology at the University of Notre Dame in 1980 (changed to Crowley-O'Brien Professor in 2001), serving as chair of the department from then until 1991.

McBrien was president of the Catholic Theological Society of America in 1974-75 and received its John Courtney Murray Award in 1976. His major publications include Catholicism *(1980; new ed., 1994) and* The HarperCollins Encyclopedia of Catholicism *(1995), for which he served as general editor. His most recent books are* Lives of the Popes *(1997) and* Lives of the Saints *(2001).*

Renewed Commitment to Vatican II as Best Preparation for the New Millennium

I had the great advantage of doing my doctoral studies in Rome during Vatican II's second and third sessions (1963-64). I had been released from my pastoral obligations in the Archdiocese of Hartford at the request of Cardinal Richard Cushing, Archbishop of Boston, to serve on the faculty of the yet-to-be-constructed seminary for so-called delayed vocations in Weston, Massachusetts. The original plan was to name the seminary after Pope Pius X, but Cushing later decided—to my great relief and satisfaction—to change the seminary's patron to John XXIII, in honor of the pope who had named him a cardinal. Cushing sent me to Rome to study for a doctorate in theology at the Pontifical Gregorian University.

Within a week of my arrival in the city, I was included in a private audience with the recently elected pope, Paul VI, in the company of Cardinal Cushing and several Boston priests and seminarians. (One of those Boston priests, Msgr. Daniel Cronin, was serving at the time in the Vatican's Secretariat of State. He would later become my archbishop in Hartford.) Soon thereafter, I managed to obtain the necessary credentials to attend at least one of the conciliar sessions in St. Peter's Basilica, and I also attended several press conferences that were held each day for the English-speaking media in one of the press offices along the Via Conciliazione. The panels included a few bishops and several *periti*. Their task was to describe and interpret the day's debates and votes (if any). These press conferences proved far more interesting and educationally fruitful than the Latin lectures to which we were exposed in the Roman universities.

I also served on the speakers committee at the North American College's graduate house, the Casa Santa Maria dell' Umiltà, where I resided during my two years in Rome. The Casa was situated between the Gregorian University and the Pontifical Biblical Institute (which was just out the back door), and the Trevi Fountain, a popular tourist attraction. Through my involvement in the lecture series, I had the opportunity to meet distinguished theologians and bishops, such as John Courtney Murray, who sat next to me at fellow Jesuit Gustave Weigel's lecture on ecclesiology, and Bishop (later Archbishop) Mark McGrath, C.S.C., of Panama, one of the chief architects of the "Pastoral Constitution on the Church in the Modern World" (*Gaudium et Spes*), then known simply as "Schema 13." Because of our common association with the University of Notre Dame, where Mark served on the Board of Trustees, he and I would become good friends after 1980, the year I joined the Notre Dame faculty. I invited him to address my doctoral seminar on the council several years ago. The students were very much taken with him, in spite of his speech difficulties created by the onset of Parkinson's disease. I reminded them that they had the great privilege of hearing someone who not only attended the council, but also exercised a leadership role at it, particularly with regard to *Gaudium et Spes*. Archbishop McGrath's participation in my seminar was later written up in Charles Morris's widely read book, *American Catholic* (Times Book, 1997, pp. 334-35).

That the council made a profound and lasting impact on my work as a theologian, and as an ecclesiologist in particular, is self-evident to anyone who has read even a sampling of my monographs (especially *Do We Need the Church?* [1969], *Church: The Continuing Quest* [1969], *The Remaking of the Church* [1973], and *Catholicism* [orig. ed., 1980, 2 vols.]), and of the weekly columns I have written for the Catholic press since July 1966 (a selection of which were published as *Report on the Church: Catholicism After Vatican II* [1992]).

The general orientation of any Catholic theologian educated around the time of the council—either during it or just afterwards—was inevitably shaped and directed not only by the documents of the council, but also by the whole conciliar event. And those of us who had the opportunity of doing our graduate work in Rome at the very time that the council was in session were privileged in a way that cannot easily be exaggerated. Undoubtedly, it is because I am such a grateful product of Vatican II myself that I may occasionally become impatient with a few younger Catholics who speak and act as if the council is, at best, an important historical event that is over and done with and no longer of continuing relevance, or, at worst, a mistake that a naive Pope John XXIII perpetrated, with many harmful consequences to the life of the church—consequences that were made even worse during the allegedly indecisive pontificate of Paul VI. In the minds of such observers, it has been John Paul II's special mission to undo whatever damage the council did, without ever faulting the council directly, and then to tighten the reins of discipline and to re-energize the church's spirituality. Such critics pay no discernible heed to John Paul II's own testimony of gratitude to the council in his *Sources of Renewal: The Implementation of Vatican II* (1979; orig. Polish ed., 1972), or to his calling of an extraordinary synod in 1985 to give tribute to the council as a work of the Holy Spirit, or to his insistence in *Tertio Adveniente Millennio* (1994) that the "best preparation for the new millennium...can only be expressed in a renewed commitment to apply, as faithfully as possible, the teachings of Vatican II to the life of every individual and of the whole Church" (n. 20).

Some three and a half decades after the council, I continue to think, and to teach, and to write under its positive influence. My large undergraduate Catholicism course, which I teach every fall semester at Notre Dame, has a significant component on the council, made all the more necessary in light of the fact that none of these students was even alive when the council adjourned in December 1965. A much greater portion of my M.A./M.Div. course on the church, which I teach every spring, is devoted to the council, and my doctoral seminar, taught every other fall, is devoted almost entirely to the ecclesiology of Vatican II. Finally, it is a relatively rare weekly column of mine that does not touch directly, or at least indirectly, on the abiding impact of Vatican II on the life, mission, and ministries of the church in our day.

While still archbishop of Krakow, Karol Wojtyla wrote his *Sources of Renewal* as an act of gratitude to the council, "to acquit himself of a debt" to it and to the Holy Spirit (pp. 9, 10). I, too, remain in their debt, and my whole life and work as a Catholic theologian can be seen as a way of rendering that debt, gladly and ever gratefully.

Part Four

REVELATION, SCRIPTURE, AND TRADITION

Introduction to Revelation

William Madges

I remember the neighbor with whom my family shared a backyard fence in Detroit as I was growing up. He was a Lutheran. I cannot recall exactly the circumstances, but I think the occasion for my speaking to him was that my grade school was selling candy as part of a fundraiser. He noted that he saw us go to church every Sunday, but he saw us also sometimes going to church in the evening during the week. He wanted to know if those weekday visits were for Bible study, as was the case in his church. I told him, "No, we go for a novena." He asked me to explain what a novena was. I tried to explain as best as I could as a fifth-grader what this devotion to Mary, specifically Mary of Perpetual Help, meant. Our neighbor looked at me puzzled. He asked in response, "Where in the Bible do you Catholics find this notion that you should worship Mary?" At the time, I was not able to make the classic Catholic distinction between veneration of Jesus' mother and the saints, on the one hand, and worship of God, on the other. From my upbringing, however, I was convinced that our devotion to the saints and Mary was permissible because our parish priest promoted it. As I got older, I learned that these devotions were justified in terms of an appeal to the tradition of the church. That meant, even if the Bible didn't endorse some of our religious devotions—as our neighbor alleged—they were still okay because God had revealed their goodness through the tradition promoted by priests and bishops, and taught to us children in Catholic parochial school.

This was the understanding of the authority of scripture and tradition that Catholics, young and old alike, had prior to the Second Vatican Council. Whereas Protestants believed that there was only one medium through which God communicated divine revelation, Catholics believed that there were two media, scripture and tradition. From the Catholic perspective, the scriptures were the written "source" for Christian knowledge about God, morality, etc., whereas tradition was the unwritten source, passed on orally from Christ to the apostles, and then from the apostles to their successors, the bishops. So Catholics were not dismayed if they could not produce conclusive evidence on the basis of scripture alone to establish the legitimacy of certain Catholic practices or beliefs (e.g., purgatory). This issue, the authority of the Bible and the relationship between scripture and tradition, had separated Protestants from Catholics since the sixteenth-century Reformation. It was taken up at Vatican II. The fruit of the lengthy debate concerning this topic and related issues was given expression in *Dei Verbum*, the "Dogmatic Constitution on Divine Revelation."

Dei Verbum is one of the most important documents to be produced during the Second Vatican Council. At the time of the council, scholars such as R. A. F. MacKenzie and Francis X. Murphy hailed the document as equal in importance with the "Dogmatic Constitution on the Church" (*Lumen Gentium*).[1] Looking retrospectively at the document from the distance of three decades, Giuseppe Ruggieri largely concurs with MacKenzie's and Murphy's judgment. He writes:

> The common judgment is no exaggeration: the period from November 14 to December 8 [1962], and especially the week of November 14-21, which was devoted to discussion of the schema on the sources of revelation, represented a turning point that was decisive for the future of the Council and therefore for the future of the Catholic Church itself: the turn from the Church of Pius XII, which was still essentially hostile to modernity and in this respect the heir to the nineteenth-century restoration, to a Church that is a friend to all human beings, even children of modern society, its culture, and its history.[2]

The discussion of the first draft of the document on revelation, entitled *De Fontibus Revelationis* ("On the Sources of Revelation"), was heated and long. The draft or schema, which was prepared by the Preparatory Theological Commission under Cardinal Ottaviani, consisted of five chapters. The principal topics of these chapters were the "two sources" of revelation; the inspiration, inerrancy, and literary genres of scripture; the Old Testament; the New Testament; and holy scripture in the church.[3] From the very beginning debate centered upon the notion of two sources of revelation. The Council of Trent (1545-63) had applied the term "source" to the gospel. But in this text the term was applied to scripture and tradition, which were regarded as the two "fountains" of revelation. This way of thinking about "two sources" had emerged in the context of Catholic apologetics vis-à-vis Protestantism. By regarding scripture and tradition as two separate, virtually independent sources of divine revelation, Catholic apologists could justify as authentically Christian those Catholic beliefs and practices that Protestants claimed had little or no basis in scripture. The wave of renewal that was coursing through some channels of theology in the first half of the twentieth century, however, challenged this idea of two sources. Instead of regarding scripture and tradition as two independent sources, this new theological movement spoke of them as a cohesive whole that transmits God's word to successive generations in different ways. Scripture communicates in written form; tradition, in unwritten form. But neither is independent of or contrary to the other. Speaking from this perspective, Yves Congar declared: "There is not a single dogma which the Church holds by Scripture *alone*, not a single dogma which it holds by tradition *alone*."[4] Whereas the former, apologetic perspective presented a Catholic position clearly differentiated from, if not also antithetical to, the Protestant position, the latter perspective offered a Catholic position that displayed considerable common ground with the Protestant insistence upon the authority and sufficiency of scripture. These two perspectives clashed at Vatican II.

As in the case of debates about other topics at the council, the *periti* or theological experts—such as Martelet (France), Schillebeeckx (Netherlands), and Rahner (Germany)—provided the council fathers with perspectives and conclusions drawn from recent scholarship that they could use to evaluate the cogency and appropriateness of the draft document they were now considering. Schillebeeckx's and Rahner's written critiques of the draft on revelation were particularly influential.[5] Although it is difficult to know which of their critiques had a greater impact, it is important to note that "nearly all of the arguments found in their texts would be used during the discussion in the hall."[6]

The debate concerning the original draft began on November 14, 1962, during the first session of the council. Cardinal Ottaviani spoke first. Anticipating criticism of the draft as neither pastoral in tone nor up-to-date in theological content, he declared that authentic doctrine was the firm foundation of pastoral theology and that the traditional content of the draft had been prepared by men who, although not sympathetic to the "new theology," were nonetheless scholars themselves. Monsignor Salvatore Garofalo, the official reporter for the draft, spoke next. He claimed that the primary goal of the council was to defend and promote Catholic doctrine in its most precise form. The draft on the sources of revelation, therefore, was clear in its condemnation of erroneous positions concerning the sufficiency of scripture and equally clear in its promulgation of the proper understanding of the relationship of scripture and tradition as two sources of revelation.[7]

Cardinal Liénart from Lille, France, rose at once to lead the opposition. He insisted that the draft needed to be completely re-written because it did not deal accurately and well with the relationship of scripture and tradition. "There are not and never have been two *sources* of revelation," he claimed. There is only one source of revelation: the Word of God, announced by the prophets and revealed by Christ.[8] Cardinal Frings from Cologne, Germany, who followed Liénart to the podium, criticized the document both for its content and its tone. Contrary to Ottaviani's assertion, the document's content is not "traditional," but rather reflects the mentality of the anti-Protestant Catholic controversialists of the seventeenth to the nineteenth centuries. Their teaching corresponds neither to the understanding of revelation that patristic and medieval theologians espoused nor to the language of the Council of Trent. The tone of the draft, Frings declared, is not pastoral, but rather is offensive to Protestants.

This initial exchange of diverse judgments concerning the suitability of the draft continued as additional defenders and critics took the floor. Some bishops defended both the content and tone of the draft as necessary to prevent "modernist" biblical scholarship from infecting Catholic faith. Other bishops argued against the draft and in support of Catholic biblical scholars who were opening up new paths of investigation. Cardinal Bea, one of the strongest advocates for renewal at the council and head of the Secretariat for Christian Unity, noted, for example, that of all the references in the draft to the work of biblical scholars, only one was a favorable mention. Bea stated that the schema must be made shorter, clearer, more pastoral, and more ecumenical. Bea's intervention gave clear expression to the orientation that Pope John XXIII wanted the council to have.[9] While some bishops called for amending the draft, others—such as Cardinal Ritter of St. Louis—called for its total rejection. Cardinal Ottaviani, however, challenged the notion that a draft document could be rejected outright. He and other defenders of the draft intimated that the document could not be rejected because it had been "approved" by the pope. In point of fact, the pope's consent had not been given to the content of this schema or the others, but simply to their being sent out for discussion in the hall. Nonetheless, it became necessary to consult formally the regulations pertaining to conciliar procedures. Art. 33.1 of the Rules of Procedure made it clear that schemata or drafts could be discussed, amended, or rejected.[10]

The see-saw debate continued over the next couple of days. Some wanted the council to avoid condemning the more recent methods of biblical scholarship, and to adopt a more pastoral tone and a stance more open to diverse interpretations of scripture.[11] Others, however, wanted to defend a single, clearly articulated position that sharply distinguished Catholic teaching from Protestant.

By November 19, 1962, it was clear that an impasse had been reached. Although the majority of the bishops were not in favor of the draft, they were not convinced of the wisdom of rejecting it outright. And yet they also could not hope for significant changes if the document were simply sent back to the Commission that had originally prepared it because that Commission was headed by Cardinal Ottaviani and staffed by many people who supported the original draft. Bishop De Smedt of Bruges, Belgium, who was a member of the Secretariat for Promoting Christian Unity, insisted that the draft would have to be re-written in a more ecumenical vein if the council did not want to destroy the great hope of Pope John XXIII and others, who were waiting for a significant step toward greater unity with non-Catholic Christians. De Smedt further noted that although the Secretariat for Promoting Christian Unity had offered to collaborate with the Theological Commission in preparing the first draft on revelation, the Theological Commission had declined the offer. As a way out of this impasse, Archbishop Garrone of Toulouse, France, formally proposed that a mixed commission be established to write a new draft. The idea of a mixed commission had been discussed and endorsed earlier by the Secretariat for Christian Unity in its private deliberations. This mixed group would consist of members of the Theological Commission (which had prepared the original), the Secretariat for Christian Unity, and theological *periti*.[12]

On the next day, November 20, the secretary general of the council, Pericle Felici, told the council fathers that they were to vote on whether to table further discussion of the original draft. The question was formulated, however, in such a way that many bishops did not understand the meaning of the vote. Several clarifications were made. The result of the vote showed that 1,368 of the 2,209 bishops present were in favor of halting discussion of the present draft and in favor of preparing a new schema. Although a large number disapproved of the document, they were still 105 votes short of the necessary two-thirds majority. Thus discussion of Chapter One of the draft continued.[13]

On the following day, there was a dramatic announcement. Archbishop Felici announced that Pope John had decided that the schema should be withdrawn, even though the two-thirds majority required by the procedural rules had not been reached. This declaration took almost everyone by surprise. The pope's intervention made it clear that the Counter-Reformation attitude that had dominated the Catholic Church for centuries needed to be abandoned. Pope John gave the task of creating a shorter, more ecumenical and pastoral draft to a mixed commission, consisting of "liberals" (Cardinals Frings, Liénart, and Meyer), "traditionalists" (Cardinals Browne and Ruffini), and a centrist (Cardinal Lefebvre), with Cardinals Ottaviani and Bea serving as joint presidents.

As Francis X. Murphy (the pseudonymous Xavier Rynne) observed at the time, the most important single disclosure of this first session of the council was the great strength shown by the advocates of renewal and reform.[14] Previously it had not been known just how influential this tendency in the church really was. Among the members of the curia, the chief spokesperson for the new approach was Cardinal Bea. Under his leadership, the Secretariat for Promoting Christian Unity was able to evade domination by the Holy Office. The fact that Bea had been directed by papal decree to collaborate with Ottaviani in drafting a new schema on the sources of revelation meant that he now had the right to be heard on strictly theological matters, which, up to that point, Ottaviani had successfully retained within the exclusive control of the Holy Office.

Although a revised version of the schema on divine revelation was ready for the second session of the council in the fall of 1963, this text was not presented to the council fathers for discussion until the following year. Between 1963 and 1964, the schema underwent further revision. When formal discussion of the text began during the council's third session, Pope Paul VI had been pope for about a year, having succeeded John XXIII, who had died on June 3, 1963. The revised text reflected a moderate position on many points, which was more satisfactory to modern biblical scholars. Instead of identifying one fixed and absolute interpretative approach to the Bible, the revised document acknowledged that the church, under the inspiration of the Holy Spirit and conversant with the development of human knowledge, could grow in its understanding of revelation communicated through the Bible. Whereas the original draft had concentrated attention upon the "sources" or "founts" of revelation and the relationship between scripture and tradition, the revised draft focused upon the sacred scriptures themselves and their message. This new emphasis allowed for the validity of several modern theories concerning the biblical texts. It was precisely this moderate acceptance of pluralism that Cardinal Ruffini of Palermo, Sicily, opposed. During the debate on October 2, 1964, he repeated a point he had made previously: to encourage—as the present version of the text did—consideration of literary genres in determining the meaning of biblical texts was tantamount to admitting that the church had not properly understood the scriptures until quite recently. Pope Pius XII's 1943 encyclical *Divino Afflante Spiritu*, however, had given cautious endorsement to the consideration of genre and context in the determination of the meaning of biblical texts.

In the final speech of the day, Cardinal König of Vienna, Austria, addressed the sensitive issue of the historical and scientific accuracy of the Bible. König argued:

> Lest the authority of Scripture suffer, we must say sincerely and without fear that the sacred writer's knowledge of historical matters was limited according to the conditions of his time, and that God moved him to write in keeping with his background and education. In this way we see the complete condescension of the Divine Word, making Himself conform in all things to human conditions, including the limitations of human speech.[15]

This admission horrified those bishops who were convinced that every word of the Bible was true and that this truth was guaranteed infallibly. When discussion resumed at the beginning of the next week, the issue of inspiration and inerrancy was revisited. Although some bishops argued for an understanding of inspiration broader than regarding it as the divine means of guaranteeing the truthful communication of a series of propositions, others argued just as vigorously for a concept of inspiration sufficient to preserve the historical veracity of the scriptures in their entirety. Bishop Philbin of Down and Connor, Ireland, for example, rejected the use of literary genres in exegesis because he feared it would undermine the historicity of the gospels. And Bishop Carli of Segni, Italy, insisted that modern biblical methods, such as form criticism, threatened to undermine the faith of the church. Abbot Butler of Downside, England, tried to allay the fears of Philbin, Carli, and others by assuring them that the modern biblical movement did not intend to jeopardize the historical nature of God's revelation. Rather, it hoped to provide a wider and deeper appreciation of the biblical witness to God's word.[16]

In light of the many suggestions for revision made by the council fathers, it was not possible to offer the entire text for a final vote before the close of the third session of the council. Therefore, final consideration of the text was carried over to the fourth and last session in 1965. Although the overwhelming majority of bishops were generally satisfied with the document as a whole, there was still some discontent about the document's treatment of the three issues that had provoked earlier debate. Those issues were the relation of scripture and tradition, the inerrancy of the Bible, and the historical nature of the gospels. A significant number of revisions were proposed for each of the chapters when the document was considered in September 1965. These revisions were evaluated by the sub-commission charged with preparing the final version of the text (headed by Cardinal Florit) and by the Theological Commission. Some council fathers, however, complained to Pope Paul VI that their recommendations were not receiving proper attention in the Subcommission and Theological Commission. The pope, therefore, directed Cardinal Cicognani, the secretary of state, to send a letter to the Commission requesting that the text be reconsidered with an eye to reaching a better consensus, especially with regard to the three disputed points. Paul VI also expressed his wish that Cardinal Bea participate in those discussions.

Those discussions yielded revisions of Chapters 2, 3, and 5 of the document, which the council fathers had approved in September 1965.[17] Some wanted the text to state clearly that the Bible was not sufficient to convey all necessary Christian knowledge (as Protestants claimed) and, consequently, that not every Catholic doctrine can be directly proved on the basis of scripture alone. In response, the following sentence was added in section 9 of Chapter 2: "Thus it is that the church does not draw its certainty about all revealed truths from the holy scriptures alone." The section concluded with the same sentence as had been previously approved by the council fathers: "Hence, both scripture and tradition must be accepted and honored with equal devotion and reverence."[18] It is important to note the careful wording of this addition. It does not claim that the Bible is materially insufficient in conveying Christian knowledge, but leaves open the possibility that the whole deposit of Christian faith is contained in the Bible. It *does* insist that the church's certainty about the faith rests upon both scripture and tradition, and for this reason both scripture and tradition must be revered.[19]

Concerning biblical inspiration, many bishops wanted to make clearer that the scriptural inerrancy that derived from the divine inspiration of the biblical authors was not restricted simply to matters of faith and morals. They wanted, therefore, to change the sentence in section 11 of Chapter 3 that stated that "the books of scripture completely and in all their parts must be acknowledged as teaching solidly and faithfully, fully and without error the truth of salvation." Many bishops simply wanted to drop the words "of salvation"; others wanted to substitute different wording so that there would be no doubt that the "truth" that scripture teaches would be understood to mean the *facts* mentioned in scripture that were connected with the history of salvation. After considerable deliberation, the text was changed to read: "Since, therefore, all that the inspired authors, or sacred writers, affirm should be regarded as affirmed by the holy Spirit, we must acknowledge that the books of scripture, firmly, faithfully and without error, teach that truth which God, for the sake of our salvation, wished to see confided to the sacred scriptures."[20] In order to understand scripture properly, this document asserts that we must determine carefully what truth God intended to communicate through the Bible. This way of understanding scriptural inerrancy has permitted Catholics, for example, to read the creation accounts in the book of Genesis as expressing that all things come from God and that everything God has created is good, without requiring the additional belief in the creation of the universe in seven days and the denial of evolution.

The final major area in which change was sought and approved was the historical character of the gospels. Some bishops did not think it was sufficient for the text to state that the gospel authors told the "honest truth about Jesus." They wanted the document also to affirm that the gospels told the *historical* facts of Jesus' life and teaching. In response to these concerns, a phrase was added to underline the church's confidence in the *general* historical character of the gospels, without insisting that every last detail of the gospel narratives is factually true. The final revision of section 19 of Chapter 5 was made to read: "Holy mother church has firmly and with absolute constancy maintained and continues to maintain, that these four Gospels, whose historicity it unhesitatingly affirms [this was the phrase that was added], faithfully hand on what Jesus, the Son of God, while he lived among men and women, really did and taught for their eternal salvation, until the day when he was taken up (See Acts 1:1–2)."

The Theological Commission's handling of the desired revisions was overwhelmingly approved by the council on October 29, 1965. Out of 2,115 bishops voting, 2,081 approved the emended text as a whole. The formal promulgation of the "Constitution on Divine Revelation" took place on November 18.

Avery Cardinal Dulles, S.J.

Avery Dulles, S.J., an internationally known author and lecturer, was born in Auburn, New York, on August 24, 1918. He received his primary school education in New York City and attended secondary schools in Switzerland and New England. After graduating from Harvard College in 1940, he spent a year and a half in Harvard Law School before serving in the United States Navy, emerging with the rank of lieutenant.

Upon his discharge from the Navy in 1946, Dulles entered the Jesuit Order and was ordained to the priesthood in 1956. He received the Ph.L. degree in 1951 and the S.T.L. in 1957, both from Woodstock College in Maryland, and was awarded the doctorate in sacred theology in 1960 from the Gregorian University in Rome.

During the time of Vatican Council II Fr. Dulles was teaching at Woodstock College, a position he held from 1960 to 1974. He was a professor at The Catholic University of America from 1974 to 1988. Since 1988 he has been the Laurence J. McGinley Professor of Religion and Theology at Fordham University. He has also been a visiting professor at universities and seminaries both in the United States and abroad. The author of over 700 articles on theological topics, Dulles has published 21 books including The Catholicity of the Church *(1985),* Models of the Church *(1987),* Models of Revelation *(1992),* The Assurance of Things Hoped For: A Theology of Christian Faith *(1994), and his latest book,* The New World of Faith *(2000).*

Past president of both the Catholic Theological Society of America and the American Theological Society, Dulles has served on the International Theological Commission and as a member of the United States Lutheran/Roman Catholic Dialogue. He serves as a consultor to the Committee on Doctrine of the National Conference of Catholic Bishops and an associate fellow of the Woodstock Theological Center in Washington, D.C. His awards include Phi Beta Kappa, the Croix de Guerre, the Cardinal Spellman Award for distinguished achievement in theology, the Boston College Presidential Bicentennial Award, the

Religious Education Forum Award from the National Catholic Educational Association, America *Magazine's Campion Award, the F. Sadlier Dinger Award for contributions to the catechetical ministry of the church, and 28 honorary doctorates. In February 2001 Pope John Paul II elevated him to the status of cardinal in the Catholic Church.*

Vatican II and Myself

I was not at the Second Vatican Council, but I feel almost as though I had been. In January 1959, when Pope John XXIII announced that he was convening an ecumenical council, I was in Rome, doing my doctoral studies in theology at the Gregorian University. Like everyone else, I was caught by surprise. I had come to think that there would not be any more ecumenical councils, since Vatican I's definition of papal infallibility gave the pope authority to do by himself all that an ecumenical council could do.

There was much confusion in most people's minds about the purposes of the coming council. Many, including highly placed curial officers, seem to have thought that it would simply give conciliar authority to the principal teachings of Pius XII and condemn positions that seemed to be opposed to them. But John XXIII's statements about updating the Catholic Church, avoiding condemnations, and promoting Christian unity seemed to presage a more open type of council. Hans Küng in his immensely popular *The Council, Reform, and Reunion* clearly favored the latter alternative.

By the time Vatican II first assembled, I was back teaching at the Jesuit theologate in Woodstock, Maryland. Two professors from our faculty—Gustave Weigel and John Courtney Murray—were heavily involved with the council: Father Weigel with the "Decree on Ecumenism" and the "Declaration on the Jews"; Father Murray (from the second session on), with the "Declaration on Religious Freedom." The two of them shared drafts of various council documents with the Woodstock faculty, sought out our reactions, and briefed both faculty and students on the inner politics of the council. All of us were also avidly reading the spicy reports by "Xavier Rynne" in the *New Yorker.*

Neither Father Murray nor Father Weigel was in good health. Father Weigel came back gloomy and depressed from meetings of the Secretariat for Promoting Christian Unity and from the first two sessions of the council. With his habitual pessimism, he was convinced that curial opposition would defeat all healthy initiatives from open and reform-minded bishops. He died of a heart attack shortly after the close of the second session, at the age of 57. Father Murray was ill at the fourth session and had to spend some time in a hospital in Rome. That may have been providential, because it gave European thinkers a better opportunity to offset what otherwise might have an excessively "American" tone in the document on religious freedom. Father Murray survived a year and a half beyond the council, and died of a heart attack in 1967 at the age of 62.

Having written my dissertation on "Protestant Churches and the Prophetic Office," I was keenly interested in the documents on ecumenism and on the church. In effect, the council made my dissertation moot because the "Decree on Ecumenism" simply proclaimed what I had laboriously striven to prove about the Christian value of non-Roman Catholic bodies.

I did not carefully study the "Dogmatic Constitution on the Church" until just after the council, when Father Walter Abbott asked me to write the introduction and footnotes to *Lumen Gentium* for his edition of *The Documents of Vatican II*. In studying that document, I was surprised by the ease with which it settled the long-standing disputes about the sacramentality of episcopal ordination and incorporated the relatively new theme of episcopal collegiality. In many respects *Lumen Gentium* endorsed the results of the best theology of the past fifty years, with which I was somewhat familiar from my recent studies.

As a teacher of the seminary course on revelation, I was especially concerned with *Dei Verbum*. It confirmed what I had already been teaching at Woodstock with the help of authors such as Romano Guardini, Karl Adam, Henri de Lubac, Yves Congar, and René Latourelle. I appreciated the council's understanding of Jesus Christ as "the mediator and fullness of all revelation." I was pleased that it treated scripture and tradition not as two separate sources, but as two resources that must be used in combination to get at the word of God given to humankind in Jesus Christ. I liked the idea of treating tradition, as *Dei Verbum* did, before scripture, and of seeing tradition primarily in active terms, as the process of transmitting the word of God to new generations. To my satisfaction, also, the council looked upon tradition as capable of progressively clearer articulation in the course of time.

The statements in *Dei Verbum* on the inspiration and inerrancy of scripture harmonized excellently with what I was already teaching. I resonated with the council's nuanced view of the historicity of the gospels and its reserve in identifying the human authors. I particularly relished the section on the interpretation of scripture, which distinguished between different levels of exegesis, from the historical-critical to the more ecclesial and theological.

In short, I found no difficulty but only support from the various council documents. My only worry was that in trying to speak to so many questions the council might trespass too much on theological territory, thus obscuring the necessary distinction between the roles of the magisterium and the theologians.

Almost immediately after Vatican II, and to some extent even before it ended, I became involved in trying to explain its achievements to various Catholic and ecumenical audiences in the United States—bishops, priests, religious, and laity. Father Murray, before he died, exhorted me to pursue this educational apostolate because he felt that the council could not achieve its proper effect unless its documents were rightly explained.

Most of us, in the first years, tended to place too heavy an accent on what was new in the teaching of Vatican II, thus casting the continuities in the shade. Without going to extremes, I sometimes overemphasized the novelties. With the election of John Paul II and the Extraordinary Synod of 1985, a more balanced interpretation has come to prevail, and I welcome this turn of events. We Catholics really need the magisterium.

John Dominic Crossan

John Dominic Crossan was born in Nenagh, Co. Tipperary, Ireland, on February 17, 1934, and received his primary education at the Christian Brothers School in Naas, Co. Kildare, followed by secondary education at St. Eunan's College in Letterkenny, Co. Donegal. Crossan received a doctorate of divinity from Maynooth College, Ireland, in 1959, and did postdoctoral research at the Pontifical Biblical Institute in Rome from 1959 to 1961 and at the Ecole Biblique in Jerusalem from 1965 to 1967. He was a member of the Servites (a religious order founded in the thirteenth cen-

tury) from 1950 to 1969, and was ordained a priest in 1957. Crossan taught for six years at his order's major seminary as it relocated from Stonebridge Priory, where he was a professor during the Second Vatican Council, to Mundelein Seminary and eventually to the Catholic Theological Union near the University of Chicago. In 1969 he was dispensed from his vows as monk and priest, married Margaret Dagenais, a professor at Loyola University, and taught at DePaul University in Chicago until his retirement as professor emeritus in its Department of Religious Studies (1969-95). He was co-chair of the Jesus Seminar from 1985 to 1996 as it met in twice-annual meetings to debate the historicity of the life of Jesus in the gospels. He was chair of the Parables Seminar in 1972-76, editor of Semeia: An Experimental Journal for Biblical Criticism *from 1980-86, and chair of the Historical Jesus Section in 1993-1998, within the Society of Biblical Literature, an international scholarly association for biblical study based in the United States.*

Crossan has received awards for scholarly excellence from both the American Academy of Religion in 1989 and DePaul University in 1991 and 1995. In the last thirty years he has written 20 books on the historical Jesus and earliest Christianity. Four of his most recent books, The Historical Jesus: The Life of a Mediterranean Jewish Peasant *(1991),* Jesus: A Revolutionary Biography *(1994),* Who Killed Jesus: Exposing the Roots of Anti-Semitism in the Gospel Story of the Death of Jesus *(1995), and* The Birth of Christianity *(1998) have been national religious bestsellers for a combined total of 22 months. His work has also been translated into ten foreign languages, including Korean, Chinese, and Japanese. He has lectured to lay and scholarly audiences across the United States as well as in Ireland and England, Australia and New Zealand, Scandinavia and Finland. He has been interviewed on over 160 radio programs and on television programs in Great Britain (Weekend TV's "Two Thousand Years of Christianity," Channel 4's "The Real Jesus Christ," and BBC's "Lives of Jesus") and in the United States (many of A&E's "Mysteries of the Bible" segments, PBS's "From Jesus to Christ: The First Christians," and ABC's "Peter Jennings Reporting: The Search for Jesus" as well as ABC's 20/20 segment on "Mary").*

After Margaret's death in 1983, he married Sarah Sexton in 1986, and they now live in Central Florida.

Bliss at Dawn, Darkness at Noon

> There is a Third Vatican Council. The Pope convenes all the bishops
> of the entire world. Then, in a solemn public ceremony in St. Peter's
> Basilica, they all implore God to take back the gift of infallibility and
> grant them instead the gift of accuracy. (From Crossan's *A Long Way
> from Tipperary*, page 98.)

I was ordained within the thirteenth-century Servite Order in 1957 and sent
immediately for a doctorate in divinity at Ireland's Maynooth College and then
for a post-doctoral licentiate at Rome's Biblical Institute. I returned to teach
scripture from 1961 through 1965 at the Servite major seminary outside Chicago
and after that went for a two-year sabbatical to Jerusalem's Ecole Biblique. Those
dates meant that I had finished my post-graduate education just before the start
of the Second Vatican Council and that my first four years of seminary teaching
coincided with its proceedings from 1962 through 1965.

The amount of the Bible that I had covered in either undergraduate or post-
graduate studies was unbelievably minuscule, and even if done well in depth,
was certainly not covered at all in breadth. I never had a wide-sweeping survey
course. And I had absolutely nothing on theory or method. At the Biblical
Institute, for example, I had a course not on the New Testament, not on Paul,
not on Romans, but on Romans 5:12b (actually, just on three Greek letters in
that half-a-verse). There was also one about the Sermon on the Mount that
never mentioned Q, and one about the Song of Songs that never mentioned sex.
But, back in that Servite seminary, I was the entire Biblical Studies Department,
and so, over a four-year curriculum, I had to teach the entire Bible, from Genesis
to Apocalypse, slowly, steadily, unhurriedly, comprehensively. I had eight successive semesters for Pentateuch, Prophecy, History, Wisdom, Gospels, Acts,
Epistles, and Apocalypse. It was a fantastic remedial education for whose necessity I am still most grateful. I had only two classes a week and usually distributed about ten footnoted pages every preceding weekend (remember mimeo-
graph machines?). There were three results from that relentless concentration of
time and focus.

One result was that my Father Prior became a little nervous about those hand-
outs, as I was not using any tried-and-true textbooks filled with *sana doctrina*
[safe doctrine], preferably in Latin. (Having defended my doctorate in Latin and

taken classes in Latin at the Biblicum, I can witness that it totally concentrates the mind on what you can say rather than on what you might think.)

Another result was that, in those years of the Second Vatican Council, I was rather more involved in my biblical classes and ministerial students than on the council's ongoing deliberations and eventual documents. None of that meant indifference. Quite the opposite: it was bliss in that dawn to be alive. But blisser still to be actually doing what it was announcing.

I was using critical history to understand the Bible, and the council was using critical history to understand the church. It intended "aggiornamento" [updating] of ecclesiastical community, and I was totally involved in "aggiornamento" of biblical tradition. I scarcely had time to read the council's proclamations (although I always had time for "Xavier Rynne") as I was so completely involved in typing and copying the next week's notes. But what was common between Bible and council was historicity, the presumption that nothing on earth escapes the historical conditioning of its time and its place. As I saw it then and now, the theological name for that was incarnation and the ecclesiastical result of that was sacrament. I found all of that to be, if I may borrow the phrase, a seamless garment. I emphasize one point. None of that made me presume any ascendancy of Bible over tradition or either over community. What I was finding in the Bible was exactly what was happening in the council. Tradition was the living, ongoing, changing life of a community, and just as once it had created the Bible as its constitutive past, so now it had convoked the council as its determinative present. And, as far as I could discern, the Spirit of God had not changed procedures at any point along the way.

For me, however, the Second Vatican Council was finished up by Paul VI on December 8, 1965, and finished off by Paul VI on July 25, 1968. After *Humanae Vitae* I asked and received dispensation from my vows as a monastic priest in order to get married, but in the sure conviction that I would still have left even if a married priesthood had been an option. I could no longer be both an obedient priest and an honest scholar. I was in research and development rather than either marketing and sales or publicity and public relations. All of those functions are necessary in any public institution, but it is equally necessary to know which is which, which you are, and never to confuse or collate one with the other.

Maybe this is a better or more biblical way to put it. In Israel's long march across the desert it needed a single leader, but also a band of scouts. The scouts went way up ahead of the march and found themselves in a very strange position, hidden under flax stalks on an alien rooftop, saved by a woman's courage. But, no matter what happened then or thereafter, they had been inside the promised land and had felt it beneath their feet. They had made it there even if only for an initial visit. The leader, however, never got there. He climbed only to the peak of Pisgah and was buried in the midst of Moab.

I epigraphed this reminiscence with lines from my fuller memoir. I conclude with another unsolicited suggestion, not this time for the next Vatican Council but for the next Holy Father. Listen to your scouts but, still, buy binoculars.

One final biographical note: During the years of the Second Vatican Council, I was a newly ordained priest and newly degreed professor teaching biblical studies at the Servite major seminary outside Chicago, in Lake Bluff, Illinois. I am no longer a priest, it is no longer a seminary, but biblical studies and the Servite Order are still doing well.

Joseph A. Komonchak

Joseph Komonchak was born in Nyack, New York, on March 13, 1939, the son of Joseph Bernard and Hazel Meehan Komonchak. He attended Cathedral College and St. Joseph's Seminary at Dunwoodie, receiving the B.A. from the latter in 1960. For the next four years he studied theology at the Pontifical Gregorian University, from which he received an S.T.L. degree. Ordained to the priesthood on December 18, 1963, Komonchak returned to the Archdiocese of New York and served as a curate at St. Bartholomew's Church, Yonkers. In 1967 he was assigned to teach dogmatic theology at St. Joseph's Seminary. He received a Ph.D. from Union Theological Seminary in 1976.

Since 1977 Komonchak has taught theology in the Department of Religion and Religious Education at The Catholic University of America, Washington, D.C. His areas of specialty are ecclesiology, modern Catholic theology, the thought of John Courtney Murray, and the

history and theology of Vatican II. Komonchak was the chief editor of
The New Dictionary of Theology *(1987), co-edited with Mary Collins*
and Dermot A. Lane, and is the editor of the English edition of the
History of Vatican II *now in the course of publication. He was the recip-*
ient of a Woodrow Wilson fellowship at the Smithsonian Institute. He
now holds the John C. and Gertrude P. Hubbard Chair in Religious
Studies at The Catholic University of America.

He was a seminarian in Rome during the Second Vatican Council.

Dei Verbum and Cardinal Bea

When I was in the seminary, it was the custom that before our common meals a brief passage be read from the scriptures, the *Imitation of Christ,* or some other work of edification. This practice was also followed at the North American College, where I resided from 1960 to 1964. An exception was made, however, when the Second Vatican Council was in session: for those few months a summary of the day's discussions in the council hall was read out to us before evening meals. The summary was drawn from the official releases of the conciliar press office. Particularly during the first session of the council, these releases were not terribly informative. Apparently feeling constrained by the promise of conciliar secrecy and perhaps out of fear of giving scandal if they were to report more fully the conciliar debates, the authors of the communications were sparse with details. The communiqué about the events of the day concerning the debate on the draft-text on the liturgy read: "Of the fathers who asked to speak, twenty intervened this morning, some to defend the schema, others to attack it." Nevertheless, those who had some interest in and knowledge of the issues at stake in the conciliar debates were often able to read between the lines and discern the drama of the unfolding discussions.

I just used the term "drama," and it is important to emphasize this character of the conciliar event, especially now that there are already generations of Catholics for whom the council is accessible only through the published final documents and through contemporary journalistic accounts or more critical histories. It is not rare that some who read the texts for the first time wonder what all the fuss is about. But for Catholics of the time, especially those resident in Rome, the council as it unfolded, particularly during its first session in 1962, was experienced as a tense drama. It was a drama we were living, with daily ups and downs depending on one's judgments of the issues at stake, and it was a drama whose outcome was by no means certain. We weren't watching a play whose plot we already knew; this was a story that we were involved in, had a stake in, and whose plot, course, and dénouement were quite undetermined.

I remember quite clearly the debate and the vote on the schema on the sources of revelation during the first session. The text would have settled prematurely the ecumenically delicate question of the relation between scripture and tradition, and it would have impeded the work of Catholic biblical scholars. Vigorous critiques of the draft were offered by many conciliar fathers, but they seemed to be counterbalanced by strong defenders of it. It was decided to ask the bishops if they wanted to table this text. A two-thirds vote was required, but only about 61% of the bishops voted to end the debate. The results of the vote were read out to us in the refectory that evening, and a good number of us were very disappointed that the debate on what we thought a very imperfect text would begin.

The next evening, however, we learned from the press release that Pope John had intervened. Judging that too large a percentage of the fathers were opposed to the prepared text, he ordered it withdrawn and assigned for revision to a mixed commission. Many of us regarded that moment as defining the conciliar identity. A good majority of the bishops had indicated what kind of documents they wished to produce (or at least what kind they did not want to issue), and the pope had backed them. There was a feeling among us of liberation. One fellow-student, not usually inclined to hyperbole, said that it did indeed feel like the "new Pentecost" that Pope John had asked the church to pray for.

Only later would I learn two anecdotes that expressed the contrasting moods of participants and observers of this dramatic moment in the council. People asked who had persuaded the pope to intervene. Rightly or wrongly (and the matter is still not clear), responsibility was assigned to Cardinal Augustin Bea, head of the Secretariat for Christian Unity. Those happy with what Bea was thought to have done, were exultantly quoting a large billboard in Rome urging people to make use of British European Airlines. "*Volate BEA*," it said. "Fly BEA!" Those displeased at Bea's alleged part, went around muttering: "*Bea culpa; Bea culpa; Bea maxima culpa!*" [Bea's fault; Bea's fault; Bea is most to blame.]

Donald Senior, C.P.

Donald Senior, C.P., is president of Catholic Theological Union in Chicago, the largest Roman Catholic graduate school of ministry in the United States, where he is also a member of the faculty as professor of New Testament. Born in Philadelphia in 1940, he is a member of the Passionist Congregation and was ordained a priest in 1967. He received his doctorate in New Testament studies from the University of Louvain in Belgium in 1972. He is a frequent lecturer and speaker throughout the United States and abroad.

Fr. Senior has published extensively on biblical topics, with numerous books and articles for both scholarly and popular audiences. He is the general editor of the acclaimed Catholic Study Bible *(1990) and editor in chief of* The Bible Today. *Among his most recent works is a four-volume series of studies of the passion narratives, a new and expanded edition of his widely read,* Jesus A Gospel Portrait *(1994),* What Are They Saying About Matthew? *(1996),* The Gospel of Matthew *(1997) in Abingdon Press's new Interpreting Biblical Text series, and most recently, a full length commentary on the Gospel of Matthew in Abingdon's New Testament Commentary series (1998).*

Senior was the recipient of the National Catholic Library Association's 1994 Jerome Award for Outstanding Scholarship and was given the 1996 National Catholic Education Association's Bishop Loras Lane Award for outstanding service to Catholic education. He is past president of the Catholic Biblical Association of America (1997-1998) and is currently a member of the Executive Committee of the Association of Theological Schools of the United States and Canada. In fall of 2001 he was appointed a member of the Pontifical Biblical Commission, which advises the pope on issues of biblical translation and interpretation.

Vatican II and Biblical Renewal

Gauging the impact of Vatican II on the field of biblical scholarship is something like calculating the impact on space travel of Neil Armstrong's first footstep on the moon. Nothing will ever be the same!

When Vatican II got underway, I had just completed three years of philosophy in Chicago as a Passionist seminarian and was preparing to go to our school of theology in Louisville, Kentucky. The election of John XXIII was a time of wonder for those of us who had grown up thinking that the lean and elegant Pius XII defined what a pope was supposed to look like. This new pope, rotund, lumpy and smiling, was something entirely different. Little did I guess then what an impact he and his council would have on my life as priest.

I began to feel the impact of the council during my theology studies. I had the feeling of someone racing across an old bridge with the spans falling all around me. Old theology textbooks were shelved; English began working its way into the liturgy; for the first time we had Protestant theologians come and speak to us; our religious community began to discuss radical changes in our traditional way of life (including no longer rising to chant Matins at 2:00 A.M., a change not too many would lament). We Passionists had already been blessed with superb professors in scripture—Barnabas Ahern and Carroll Stuhlmueller—two giants who were in the forefront of the biblical renewal even before the council began, so the new emphasis on scripture that would emerge from the council was a seamless transition for most of us.

The council events reached right into our community when in 1964 Barnabas Ahern was selected by Cardinal Albert Meyer of Chicago to be his *peritus* at the beginning of the second session of the council. As things went in those days, my superiors "invited" me to begin preparation for a teaching assignment in scripture to eventually succeed Barnabas on our theology faculty. I loved my courses in scripture but had been looking forward to work as a Passionist missionary, the central focus of our corporate ministry. But I happily accepted this new assignment and during the summers began remote language preparation for my post-ordination graduate studies. I spent a memorable summer at Hebrew Union College in Cincinnati on a grueling crash course in Hebrew, one of three Gentiles in a large class of incoming rabbinical students. And I will never forget an intensive course at Harvard learning Arabic. Not only was the mystery of these Semitic languages a new discovery, but equally mysterious and wonderful for a young

Catholic seminarian in those days was the exposure to the worlds of Reform Judaism and Harvard Square.

After ordination in 1967 I went to Louvain University in Belgium for my doctoral studies in New Testament. Several of the faculty were by then veterans of the council, great theologians who with many other European colleagues had helped shape the extraordinary theological perspectives reflected in the council declarations: Gustav Thils, Albert Descamps, Gerard Philips, Philippe Delhaye, Frans Neirynck. It was during my years at Louvain—glorious years, by the way—that I felt I truly awakened to the diversity and reality of the church. There one could see very different expressions of church, in the Netherlands (which was at the height of its turbulent experimental phase), in Germany and France, and in what one of my history professors referred to as the "sub-Alpine" church of Italy. Mirroring the growing agitation against the Vietnam War in America, this was also the time of the student revolts in Paris, and the rumblings were felt even in more staid Belgium. There were student strikes in Louvain and on more than one occasion the invasion of our medieval university town by riot police and water cannon. These were exciting and somewhat ominous revolutionary times hard to imagine now.

My doctoral work was on the Gospel of Matthew under the direction of Frans Neirynck, a brilliant and demanding mentor. I was able to pursue my work on this with complete freedom, and I realized more than ever that this supportive atmosphere had been purchased at a great price. It was clear that the council had affirmed a whole generation of patient and courageous Catholic scholars, mainly in Europe, who had pursued biblical studies for more than half a century, often under suspicion and sometimes with intense suffering. Loyal Catholics such as Marie-Joseph Lagrange, O.P., of the Ecole Biblique in Jerusalem, Stanislaus Lyonnet, S.J., and Maximillian Zerwick, S.J., of the Biblical Institute in Rome remain heroes for me. They suffered greatly but never gave up, and their integrity won the day, for all of us.

When I completed my doctoral work and returned in 1972 to teach New Testament at the recently formed Catholic Theological Union in Chicago, the implementation of the council had already entered a turbulent phase. In my own community, as in most others, a whole generation of religious and priests had decided to resign. Controversies were raging over difficult moral issues such as contraception and nuclear warfare. Some early advocates of the conciliar reforms began to have second thoughts about some of the directions and the pace that the liturgical and structural changes were taking. But strangely—and wonderfully—

there seemed to be relatively little ambivalence about the now accelerated biblical renewal. No doubt some scholars and preachers played havoc by displaying seemingly cavalier attitudes to the historical roots of the biblical materials. But for most Catholics, the new biblical flavor of church teaching, preaching, and catechetics was a breath of fresh and livening air. It is something I would experience in every course and lecture and workshop that I would give over the next 30 years of ministry.

I think this biblical renewal is still going strong, even though there are countercurrents. Now and then I reread *Dei Verbum*, the Vatican II dogmatic constitution that confirmed the biblical renewal and gave it its new charter. Its final chapter, entitled "Sacred Scripture in the Life of the Church," recommended a series of initiatives for implementing the council's reforms: "wide open access" to the scriptures for all the faithful; new translations based on the original languages, including joint efforts with "separated brethren"; encouragement of more scholars to take up biblical studies; encouragement of theologians and catechists to use scripture in their materials; encouragement of priests, deacons, and catechists "to immerse themselves in the Scriptures by constant sacred reading and diligent study"; encouragement of bishops to provide the faithful with editions of the Bible that include explanatory notes. Coupled with these recommendations was the introduction of the three-year lectionary as part of the liturgical renewal that for the first time ever gave Catholic congregations the opportunity to hear wide expanses of the Old and New Testaments on a regular basis at their Sunday (and daily) Eucharist.

The list is breathtaking. Even more breathtaking is how many of these recommendations have been put into play and are still active in the church today. In 1943 Pius XII issued his groundbreaking encyclical on scripture, *Divino Afflante Spiritu*, which signaled a tidal change in the church's attitude to modern biblical scholarship. Fifty years later, with the council reforms concerning the use of scripture well on their way to implementation, the Pontifical Biblical Commission (over the signature of Cardinal Joseph Ratzinger) published a remarkable document entitled, "The Interpretation of the Bible in the Church." This official text is a stunning endorsement of the biblical movement, with its various methodologies and pastoral initiatives. It leads me to believe that, in fact, no decree of the council has been more faithfully implemented than the recommendations found in *Dei Verbum*.

Where will the story of Vatican II ultimately lead? None of us now can see that future with any surety. In my most hopeful moments, I think the biblical renewal is ultimately the most potent change that Vatican II has unleashed on the church. We should never forget the power of the biblical word. Over time, routine exposure to the Bible's passionate language, its compelling stories, its epic vision of God's relationship to humanity, and its strong portrayal of Jesus and his teaching could profoundly change the church's consciousness.

Barbara Reid, O.P.

Barbara E. Reid was born on May 26, 1953, in Detroit, Michigan. During the time of the Second Vatican Council she was a grade school student at St. Kevin School in Inkster, Michigan.

Reid studied at Aquinas College in Grand Rapids, Michigan, where she received a B.A. (Spanish) in 1975 and an M.A. (Religious Studies) in 1981. In 1974 she joined the Grand Rapids Dominicans and made final profession in 1980. Her Ph.D. was awarded in 1988 from The Catholic University of America in biblical studies, with a specialization in New Testament.

Sr. Reid has taught at the secondary and graduate levels of education. From 1976 to 1982, she taught and chaired the Spanish and Religion Departments at St. Mary Cathedral High School in Saginaw, Michigan. Since 1988 Sr. Reid has taught at the Catholic Theological Union in Chicago, where she is professor of New Testament Studies.

Sr. Reid is an active member of many professional societies, including the Society of Biblical Literature; the Catholic Biblical Association, where she serves as New Testament book review editor for the Catholic Biblical Quarterly, *and the Chicago Society of Biblical Research, which she served as president (2000-01). In 2001 she was awarded the annual Sophia Award for theological excellence in service to ministry from Washington Theological Union.*

Sr. Reid has published more than 100 articles, commentaries, and book reviews. They have appeared in journals such as The Bible Today, Biblical Research, New Theology Review, Chicago Studies, Currents in Theology and Mission, St. Anthony Messenger, *and* U.S. Catholic. *Her most recent books are the* Parables for Preachers *series (1999)*, A Retreat with St. Luke, *and* Choosing the Better Part? Women in the Gospel of Luke *(1996)*. In 1996 The Collegeville Pastoral Dictionary of the Bible, *of which she was a co-editor, was awarded first place in the category of theology by the Catholic Press Association. Sr. Reid's current scholarly work is in the areas of feminist hermeneutics, parables, and nonviolence in the gospels.*

Vatican II Opened a Window for Biblical Scholars

I was nine years old when the council opened in 1962. My third grade teacher, a Dominican sister, a great history buff, was very excited about it and tried to instill in us a sense of the momentous changes that were about to occur. In our little corner of the world, in Inkster, Michigan, a suburb of Detroit, I was far too young to understand all that was about to change in our church and how that would impact my life choices and profession. Although I had attended Catholic school all my life, I had never been exposed to scripture study. As youngsters we memorized the Baltimore Catechism. We knew Bible stories, and we had a big leatherbound family Bible on the coffee table at home, but the only time we opened it was to record family events, never to read it. Like most Catholic families, our preferred prayer form outside of Mass was the rosary. My first course in the Old Testament, taken as an elective in my sophomore year of college, sparked in me a thirst for scripture study that would remain insatiable.

For six years (1976-1982) I taught Spanish and religion at St. Mary Cathedral High School in Saginaw, Michigan. During those summers I completed a master of arts in religious studies at Aquinas College, always drawn most to the scripture courses. I was also experiencing how, since Vatican II, scripture was becoming more central to our faith life, both in my religious community and in my place of ministry. Liturgical preaching was now based on the scripture readings. The pastoral team at the cathedral was intent on forming a parish community firmly founded on the vision of Vatican II. I saw a growing hunger among people in the parish for praying with scripture, and reading and studying the Bible. I could also see that the thirst for scripture, but lack of formal study of it, was leading some to a fundamentalistic approach, or sometimes to a dangerous game of "Bible roulette," in which someone seeking for a word from God would randomly open the Bible, and whatever passage fell open was supposedly a direct message from God for what they were to do. I could see the need at every level for good biblical scholarship in the church. And I kept wanting to study more, knowing that there was so much about the Bible I did not know or understand. My notion that it was a "Protestant thing" to study the Bible was dissolving. In the fall of 1982 I began six years of study at The Catholic University of America, where I completed a Ph.D. in biblical studies with a concentration in New Testament.

One of the highlights of that time was a semester of study in the Holy Lands, ten weeks of which was led by Leslie Hoppe, O.F.M., from Catholic Theological Union in Chicago, and the remainder of which was spent working on my dissertation with tutelage from Jerome Murphy O'Connor and the Dominicans at the École Biblique et Archaéologique Française in Jerusalem. Another whole aspect of scripture study was opened up to me in this experience, as these leading scholars introduced me to the world of archaeology and love of the land and its culture and peoples. I never dreamed at that time that I would be leading groups there myself almost every year.

After completing my dissertation under the direction of John Meier at Catholic University of America, I began in the fall of 1988 to teach New Testament at Catholic Theological Union in Chicago (CTU), where I am now a tenured full professor. This graduate school of theology and ministry is a direct outgrowth of the vision of Vatican II. In 1967, on the heels of a visit of Cardinal Suenens to Chicago, three communities of men religious united to form CTU. Very shortly they would open their doors to women and lay students as well. Today the latter is the fastest growing population of the thriving student body of over 500 students. One of the most significant impacts of Vatican II is that the very notion of who ministers in the church and how that ministry is done has shifted dramatically. I don't know if I would have considered pursuing a doctorate in scripture in a pre-Vatican II church. And the possibility of my teaching scripture at the graduate level may have been slimmer yet.

The rise of feminist consciousness in the post-Vatican II church has resulted in a dramatic increase in the number of Catholic women biblical scholars. An increasing number of women have served in leadership, including president, of the Catholic Biblical Association. In addition, the ranks of Catholic biblical scholars now include a greater number of lay people, and people not from the dominant culture. There has been an increased consciousness that the social location of the interpreter is a determinative factor in the way in which biblical studies are done. There is an explosion of new methods since the time of the council, including not only further developments in historical-critical methods, but also a rise in various kinds of literary criticism, social science methods, liberation approaches, and post-modern hermeneutical perspectives. The open window of Vatican II has enabled Catholic biblical scholars to be fully immersed in these scholarly developments.

Another effect of Vatican II on scripture study is the encouragement of ecumenical exchange. The "Constitution on Revelation" reaffirmed for Catholic biblical scholars what had first been articulated in *Divino Afflante Spiritu* in 1943: we were encouraged to use all the critical tools of study already being developed by our Protestant colleagues. Shortly after the council, new translations of the Bible were done by ecumenical teams of scholars, based not on the Latin Vulgate, but on the original Greek and Hebrew texts. In Chicago ecumenical collaboration is a given. Catholic Theological Union chose to locate in the midst of the city, in a cluster of twelve theological schools of differing Christian denominations. Not only do students cross-register, but frequently the scripture faculty of the various schools appear as guest lecturers in one another's classes. The New Testament professors from the Association of Chicago Theological Schools meet four times a year to share a meal and a paper by one of its members. In addition, the Chicago Society of Biblical Research, of which I have been president, is one of the oldest ecumenical associations of biblical scholars in the country. The Catholic Biblical Association, for which I am New Testament book review editor, likewise is intent on fostering ecumenism. I am also part of the bilateral dialogue between United Methodists and Roman Catholics. This group also sees the need to ground the work toward unity in our common understanding of the scriptures.

Of the many ways in which Vatican II placed scripture at the heart of the life of the church was the emphasis on preaching from the scriptures. As a member of the Order of Preachers, I have been especially interested in how biblical scholarship is placed at the service of preachers. There is still a great need to form a biblically literate Catholic faithful. Seminaries and schools of theology face an especially great challenge of forming students to place the scriptures at the center of their prayer life, study, and ministry. A particular need is to teach them how to move from biblical exegesis to interpretation of the scriptures for liturgical proclamation.[21] My most recent series of books, one for each liturgical cycle, *Parables for Preachers* (1999, 2000, 2001), has attempted to put recent biblical scholarship into easily accessible format for preachers, teachers, and catechists. Likewise, my book *Choosing the Better Part? Women in the Gospel of Luke* (1996), has aimed to bring feminist perspectives to bear on interpretation of the Third Gospel for all interested students of scripture.

The horizons opened by Vatican II for Catholic biblical scholarship are vast and exciting. My life's journey has been directly shaped by its vision and energy, and will, I hope, continue to bring new life to the church and the world.

Joseph A. Fitzmyer, S.J.

Joseph Fitzmyer was born on November 4, 1920, in Philadelphia. After completing his education, he assumed a variety of teaching posts. At the time of the Second Vatican Council, he was teaching New Testament and biblical languages at the Jesuit theologate of the Maryland and New York provinces, Woodstock College in Maryland. He left there in 1969 and taught subsequently at the University of Chicago (1969-71), Fordham University (1971-74), Weston Jesuit School of Theology (1974-76), and Catholic University of America (1976-86).

Fr. Fitzmyer has published widely in the area of scriptural studies. He was the co-editor of The Jerome Biblical Commentary *(1968) and also of* The New Jerome Biblical Commentary *(1990). Some of his other important publications include* The Gospel According to Luke *(1981, 1985),* Acts of the Apostles *(1998), and* The Dead Sea Scrolls and Christian Origins *(2000).*

During the year 2000, Fr. Fitzmyer was the Royden B. Davis Visiting Professor at Georgetown University. Since 1990 he holds the position of professor emeritus and professorial lecturer in the Department of Biblical Studies at Catholic University of America.

The Word of God, Magisterium, and the Historical Character of the Gospels

I now recall how happy I was when in November 1965 the dogmatic constitution *Dei Verbum* was approved by the council fathers. Two of its assertions were and still are very important in my estimation. The first is the assertion in section 10:

> The task of authentically interpreting the Word of God, whether written or handed on, has been entrusted solely to the living teaching office of the Church (*soli vivo Ecclesiae magisterio*), whose authority is exercised in the name of Jesus Christ. This teaching office is not above the Word of God, but serves it, teaching only what has been handed on, as it listens to it faithfully, guards it scrupulously, and explains it faithfully by divine commission and with the help of the Holy Spirit.[22]

For the first time one finds in an ecclesiastical document the admission that the magisterium is not above the word of God in scripture or tradition, but serves it. This admission thus undercuts the accusation sometimes heard that for Catholics the magisterium is the ultimate norm of faith (because of the encyclical *Humani generis*).[23] Rather one can admit with Lutherans that scripture is *norma normans non normata* [the rule that measures, but itself is not measured] and tradition is *norma normata* [the rule that is measured—that is, measured by scripture], as Karl Rahner rightly saw.[24]

The second assertion is found in *Dei Verbum*, section 19, where once the "historical character" (*historicitatem*) of the four gospels is affirmed, the text goes on to admit the stages of the gospel tradition, which was commonly asserted by New Testament interpreters of that time:

> After the ascension of the Lord, the Apostles handed on to their hearers what he had said and done. (This they did) with that clearer understanding that they enjoyed after they had been instructed by the events of Christ's risen life (*eventibus gloriosis Christi*) and taught by the light of the

Spirit of truth. The sacred authors composed the four Gospels, selecting some things from the many which had been handed on by word of mouth or in writing, reducing some of them to a synthesis, explicating (*explanantes*) some things in view of the situation in their churches, and preserving the form of proclamation, but always in such fashion that they told us the honest truth about Jesus (*vera et sincera de Iesu*).[25]

Lest anyone fail to realize whence the substance of this double assertion was coming, the council fathers introduced section 19 with *Sancta Mater Ecclesia* [Holy Mother Church], using the very opening words of the Biblical Commission's Instruction of 1964, *De historica evangeliorum veritate* [On the Historical Truth of the Gospels].[26] For the double assertion was, in fact, a résumé of three paragraphs of that Instruction. In other words, *Dei Verbum* distinguished in effect, as did the Biblical Commission before it, three stages of the gospel tradition: (1) What Jesus of Nazareth did and taught (A.D. 1-33); (2) what the apostles proclaimed with post-resurrection faith and clarity about what he did and taught (A.D. 33-65); and (3) what the evangelists selected, synthesized, and explicated from stages one and two in their literary productions that we call the gospels (A.D. 65-95).[27]

Thus the interpretation of the gospels was liberated from earlier Catholic fundamentalism, which tended to equate stage three with stage one. Moreover, *vera et sincera de Iesu* was a carefully phrased expression that scarcely meant the same as "historical truth." Section 19 was, in fact, the product of much conservative and enlightened debate as *Dei Verbum* took shape in the council, and the struggle between the two groups of council fathers can still be seen in the contrast between the "historical character" (*historicitatem*) of the gospels asserted (in the first sentence) and the later nuanced double assertion (in the second and third sentences) of what the apostles and sacred authors have passed on to us, as the Biblical Commission had clarified.

Part Five

Ecumenism and Interreligious Dialogue

The Turn to the Other

William Madges

I can remember being taught in my early years in elementary school that if people wanted to be saved, they were "obliged" to belong to the Catholic Church, for it alone is the one true church established by Christ. When asked how I knew that no other church but the Catholic Church is the true church of Christ, the answer I had memorized through frequent recitation was because no other church has the four marks of Christ's church, that is, being one, holy, catholic, and apostolic. Although my Baltimore Catechism conceded that those who remained outside the Catholic Church "through no grave fault of their own and do not know it is the true Church" can be saved, the general impression with which I was left was that it was quite obvious that the Catholic Church was the true church. One would have to be blind or thick-headed not to see that.

From this perspective—as the Catholic Good Friday liturgy prior to Vatican II made clear—Orthodox Christians were "schismatics," and Protestants were "heretics." The Orthodox were called schismatics, even though they shared many beliefs in common with Catholics, because they did not recognize the pope as the legitimate head of the entire church of Christ. The Protestants were even further removed from the true church. They not only refused to recognize the pope as the rightful head of the church; they also deviated from the central, authentic doctrines of Christ's church. It is not surprising in this climate that Catholics were forbidden to visit the churches of other Christian denominations or to become too familiar with Protestant or Orthodox neighbors.

That situation changed in a dramatic way with the papacy of John XXIII. Prior to the Second Vatican Council, he established the Secretariat for Christian Unity (1960) and named five official observers to attend the third assembly of the World Council of Churches in New Delhi, India (1961). In addition, John XXIII declared that one of the principal purposes of the council was to contribute to the unity of the separated Christian churches.

The Second Vatican Council eventually produced two different documents that describe relationships with those who are not Catholic: the "Decree on Ecumenism" (*Unitatis Redintegratio*) and the "Declaration on the Relationship of the Church to Non-Christian Religions" (*Nostra Aetate*). The former document lays out Catholic principles of ecumenism and discusses how concern for restoring unity among Christians is to be put into practice. The latter document, which was originally a chapter in the "Decree on Ecumenism," addresses relations with non-Christians, with special emphasis placed upon the relationship with Jews. Both documents owe much of their spirit and content to the special committees established to deal with other Christians and non-Christians: the Secretariat for Christian Unity, established by Pope John XXIII in 1960 and headed by Cardinal Augustin Bea, and the Secretariat for Non-Christian Religions, established by Pope Paul VI in 1964 and headed by Cardinal Paolo Marella.

Let us turn our attention first to the "Decree on Ecumenism."

The Decree on Ecumenism

From early in the twentieth century, Protestants had become increasingly involved in what came to be called "the ecumenical movement." This phenomenon exhibited growing joint cooperation among the Protestant churches, beginning with interdenominational cooperation in missionary work. The World Missionary Conference of 1910 in Edinburgh, Scotland, which was the eighth in a series of international meetings of Protestant Christians begun in 1854, gave decisive impetus to the desire for greater Christian unity. This conference differed from previous meetings in that most of those who attended came not only as deeply interested individuals, but also as official delegates of the various missionary societies. Out of collaboration fostered by this conference grew the International Missionary Council, in 1921. Other areas of increasing ecumenical activity included youth work, Christian education, and united service to society. In 1908 the Federal Council of the Churches of Christ in America was founded, which merged in 1950 with a number of interdenominational agencies to form the National Council of the Churches of Christ in the U.S.A.

The Protestant ecumenical movement eventually broached even the more difficult issue of doctrinal differences, beginning with the first World Conference on Faith and Order, in 1927. By 1938 a provisional structure for a world council of Christian churches had been worked out, but its implementation was interrupted by the Second World War. Finally in 1948, the World Council of Churches was established, initially including 145 churches from 44 countries.

The Roman Catholic Church officially remained aloof from these developments. Official Catholic sentiment in the early twentieth century continued to be guided by papal teaching of the previous century. Pope Pius IX, in his "Syllabus of Errors" (1864), had rejected the idea that it was no longer necessary that the Catholic Church be held as the only religion of the state and that there should be freedom of worship for all. In the twentieth century, Pope Pius XI, although supportive of greater understanding of the Eastern churches, maintained a negative attitude toward Protestants. In his encyclical *Mortalium Animos* (1928), he declared that the only way in which the unity of Christianity could be fostered would be "by furthering the return to the one true church of Christ of those who are separated from it." This would involve their believing in "the infallibility of the Roman Pontiff in the sense of the Ecumenical Vatican Council [i.e., Vatican I] with the same faith as they believe in the Incarnation of Our Lord."[1]

In the light of this mindset, it is not surprising that, when Pope John strongly encouraged ecumenism, some members of the curia and others thought that he did not fully understand the doctrinal issues involved in the restoration of Christian unity. Others feared that his ecumenical openness would encourage those Catholic theologians who had been flirting with heterodoxy to minimize Catholic truth even further.[2] But Pope John persisted in his strong support of ecumenism. On October 19, 1962, he elevated the Secretariat for Christian Unity to the same level as the Preparatory Commissions, which had been charged with preparing the documents to be considered at the Second Vatican Council. He also invited Protestant and Orthodox communions to send observers to Vatican II; their presence at the council was unprecedented in the history of Roman Catholicism.

During the council Pope John met personally with the non-Catholic observers. Departing from custom, he received the delegates in the Hall of the Consistory, and then sat down with them in a square, in much the same way as he was accustomed to sit with the cardinals in consistory. As Francis Murphy noted at the time, it was quite significant that the pope sat on the same kind of chair as the delegates, rather than on his throne. This symbolic gesture of equality made quite an impression on the non-Catholic observers, who were introduced as "our brethren in Christ." In his talk Pope John emphasized charity and mutual understanding as the keys to progress in ecumenism.[3]

Initially, three separate documents, each dealing with a different aspect of ecumenism, were prepared for the consideration of the council fathers. The Theological Commission had prepared a document dealing with the theme of unity, especially with Protestants. The Secretariat for Christian Unity wrote a draft on general ecumenical principles. And the Preparatory Commission for the Oriental Churches prepared a document entitled *Ut unum sint* ("That They May Be One"), which was the first of the documents to be considered by the council. This document concerned itself exclusively with the means of achieving reunion with the Eastern Orthodox.

One might wonder why it had not been decided to present a single schema to the council, or at least three coordinated drafts that could later be fused into one. One factor was apparently the reluctance of the Theological Commission to cooperate with other commissions or groups because of its conviction that doctrinal matters were within the exclusive competence of the Theological Commission.[4]

During the discussion of *Ut unum sint* (November 26-30, 1962), a number of sensitive issues were hotly debated. One such issue was whether both sides were equally to blame for the split between Roman Catholic and Eastern Orthodox. Another was whether the Orthodox bodies were true "churches" or only "assemblies." On the final day of discussion, Cardinal Bea pointed out that many of the topics dealt with in *Ut unum sint* were the domain of his Secretariat for Christian Unity. He proposed that this document be fused together with the other two that had been prepared. The council fathers overwhelmingly endorsed this idea.

The new document that was prepared over the course of the next year was presented for discussion during the final two weeks of November 1963. It was radically different from the 1962 schema *Ut unum sint*. This revised schema now consisted of five chapters. The first dealt with the principles of Catholic ecumenism; the second, the practical aspects of ecumenism; the third, Christians separated from the Catholic Church. The third chapter was subdivided into two parts, one dealing with the Eastern churches, the other with the Protestant churches. Chapter Four was devoted to the Jews, and Chapter Five to religious liberty.[5]

On the fourth day of discussion of the revised schema on ecumenism (November 21, 1963), the council moderators announced that the council would proceed to an immediate vote on the acceptance of Chapters 1-3 as a basis for discussion. Archbishop Felici, secretary general of the council, added that the voting on chapters 4 and 5 would take place in a few days. A strong majority, 1,966 bishops, voted in favor of accepting the text for discussion (with 86 opposed). Ultimately the decision was made to handle the subject matter of chapters 4 and 5 in separate documents. The material of Chapter 4 grew into the "Declaration on the Relationship of the Church to Non-Christian Religions," which was approved on October 28, 1965, one year after the promulgation of the now shortened "Decree on Ecumenism." The material of Chapter 5 was developed into the "Declaration on Religious Freedom," which was also approved during the final session of the council (December 7, 1965).

During the debates about ecumenism at the council, two quite different perspectives came to light. On the one side were those bishops who defended wholeheartedly the mentality of the Counter-Reformation, according to which Christian unity meant nothing more than the return of others to the Catholic Church.[6] On the other side were those who believed that the gospel and the contemporary situation both called for a common witness to the faith, which meant acknowledging that not all Catholic truths are on the same level.[7] The differences were quite sharp. A variety of proposals were made for revising the text. At the conclusion of the second session, Cardinal Bea said that these suggestions would all be carefully considered in working out a revised text of the "Decree on Ecumenism" to be voted on during the next session.

In the intervening months, the Secretariat for Christian Unity had to sort through over a thousand proposed changes to the text. A new, revised version of the "Decree on Ecumenism" was presented again for discussion during the third session of the council in 1964. On the day before the final vote (November 19, 1964), Archbishop Felici announced that the printing of the final text was not yet completed. This meant that the council fathers would not be able to examine it before casting their ballots on the next day. Felici explained that the reason for the delay was that some changes, made on the authority of Pope Paul VI, had been introduced into the text to make it "clearer." The secretary general then read the 19 last-minutes changes, which had been submitted to, and accepted by, Cardinal Bea and the Secretariat for Christian Unity.[8] It appears that a minority of prelates who were dissatisfied with the progressive ecumenical tone of the text had appealed directly to the pope to change portions of the text. Paul VI did not forward the most destructive emendations to the Secretariat. The emendations that he passed along and that were incorporated into the text changed the emphasis, without altering the fundamental sense of the decree. A number of bishops and non-Catholic observers were irritated that the pope had proposed changes after it was too late for the council fathers to discuss them. The

Protestant observers were particularly upset by the apparently arbitrary way in which the changes were imposed upon the council at the last minute.[9] The next day, November 20, the council voted on the whole text, including the papal changes. The vote was 2,054 for, 64 against.

The decree goes beyond the traditional assertion that the Catholic Church is the true church to assert that Christ's Spirit is at work in the churches and communities beyond the visible boundaries of the Catholic Church. It acknowledges, moreover, that baptism establishes a communion among believers insofar as "all who have been justified by faith in baptism are incorporated into Christ" and therefore "have the right to be called Christians, and with good reason are accepted as sisters and brothers in the Lord by the children of the Catholic Church." (*Unitatis Redintegratio*, no. 3)[10] Dr. Oscar Cullmann, a Protestant observer at the council, rightly commented at the time: "This is more than the opening of a door; new ground has been broken. No Catholic document has ever spoken of non-Catholic Christians in this way."[11]

Declaration on Non-Christian Religions
For centuries it had been commonplace for Catholics to believe and to declare that "there is no salvation outside the church." And "church" meant the Roman Catholic Church. The Fourth Lateran Council (1215) had declared that there is "one universal church of the faithful, outside of which nobody at all is saved." The Council of Florence (1442) was more explicit in condemning those who remained outside the Catholic Church. In its Bull of Union with the Copts, also known as the Decree for the Jacobites, it explicitly declared that "all those who are outside the catholic church, not only pagans but also Jews or heretics and schismatics, cannot share in eternal life and will go *into the everlasting fire which was prepared for the devil and his angels* [Mt 25:41], unless they are joined to the catholic church before the end of their lives."[12]

It is no wonder, then, that the Jesuit Leonard Feeney (1897-1978) thought that the archbishop of Boston, Richard Cushing, was teaching heresy when he admitted that it was possible that non-Catholics might be saved.[13] Feeney was so convinced that church teaching was on his side that he persisted in his views and refused to leave Boston, although threatened with dismissal from the Jesuit order for refusing to do so. When he died, Feeney's ardent followers had the words *Extra Ecclesiam Nulla Salus* ["Outside the church no salvation"] carved into the bottom of his gravestone.[14]

What Vatican II was prepared to say on this issue was clearly a matter of deep concern and divided opinion. As Robert Graham observed shortly after the conclusion of the council, the development of the "Declaration on the Relationship of the Church to Non-Christian Religions" (*Nostra Aetate*) was one of the most dramatic stories of Vatican II.[15] As was noted above, this declaration began as Chapter Four of the "Decree on Ecumenism" and was focused exclusively on the Jews. The concern was not initially focused upon making a statement about the possibility of salvation for those outside the Catholic Church, but rather upon addressing the anti-Semitism that was rampant and so graphically embodied in the destruction of Jews during World War II.

As the debate on the "Decree on Ecumenism" got underway during the second session of the council in 1963, a number of council fathers, such as Cardinal Tappouni, the Syrian Patriarch of Antioch, argued for removing chapters Four and Five from the document on ecumenism. Tappouni declared that ecumenism has to do with the unity of Christians and, therefore, the church's relation to non-Christians ought not to be included in a document on ecumenism. Others, such as Patriarch Maximos IV Saigh, the Melkite Patriarch of Antioch, insisted that if Jews were to be mentioned, then the church's relation to Muslims must also be included in the document. If only the Jews were named, the statement could be misunderstood as a political endorsement of the State of Israel or of Zionism. If so understood, the Christian minorities living in Arab countries might suffer reprisals.[16]

Cardinal Bea, head of the Secretariat for Promoting Christian Unity, had to address these concerns in his address to the council on November 19, 1963. He defended the existence of Chapter Four by explaining that Pope John XXIII had personally directed Bea to formulate a statement on the Jews. Five months before his death on June 3, 1963, John had approved Bea's outline of the statement. Although the pope's approval did not necessarily settle the issue or bind his successor, Paul VI, Bea nonetheless was convinced that John's wishes resonated with a large number of council fathers and clearly reflected the spirit of Christ.[17] In response to the fear that the statement would be understood politically, Bea emphasized that the chapter on the Jews dealt only with the *religious* relation between Catholics and Jews. Bea proceeded to emphasize some of the most important aspects of the declaration's statement concerning Jews and Judaism. He stressed that Jews and Christians share a common spiritual heritage, and he denied that the Jews, either today or at the time of Jesus, could be blamed indiscriminately for the suffering and death of Jesus. In attempting to account for the recent persecution of Jews, Bea did not identify Christian prejudice against them, rooted theologically in the charge of deicide ("killing of God," that is, Christ), as the cause of the Holocaust. Rather, he suggested that the Holocaust, and the anti-Semitism that made it possible, perhaps had had a negative influence on the attitude of contemporary Catholics toward Jews. Although the gospel portrayal of Jewish responsibility for Jesus' death played a role in Christian attitudes toward Jews, it was not the principal cause of anti-Semitism. To find the principal cause, one would have to attend to social, political, and economic factors.[18]

During this second session of the council the bishops in attendance decided to separate Chapter Four (dealing with the Jews) and Chapter Five (dealing with religious liberty) from the rest of the statement on ecumenism. Debate on the subject matter of those two chapters would be postponed. The official reason given for the postponement was a "lack of time." Many, however, suspected that this reason was merely a pretext. A variety of political and theological considerations were thought to be the real reasons for postponement.[19] Between the conclusion of the second session of the council (December 4, 1963) and February 1964, the Secretariat for Christian Unity had revised and strengthened the text on the Jews. Two months later, however, at a meeting of the Coordinating Commission, several changes were made in the revised text to make it more palatable to the theological minority who opposed an overly conciliatory statement, and to the Arab world. The text was broadened to include mention of Muslims, Hindus, and Buddhists. And the passage exonerating the Jewish people of deicide was watered down. When news of these changes was leaked in early May, Jewish communities, especially in the United States, became upset.

It was this text that the council fathers considered when they met during the third session to discuss the issue again (September 28-30, 1964). Although there was still some small opposition to the document, the majority supported it. A significant number—including Cardinal Liénart of Lille, France; Frings of Cologne, Germany; Lercaro of Bologna, Italy; Léger of Montreal, Canada; König of Vienna, Austria; and the American cardinals Cushing (Boston), Meyer (Chicago), and Ritter (St. Louis)—advocated the restoration of passages that had been removed, particularly the passage that absolved Jews of deicide. It was even proposed that a request for forgiveness for Christian persecution of Jews be added to the text. Cardinal Ruffini of Palermo, Sicily, however, demurred. He proposed a linked process of exchange: the deicide charge could be dropped if certain anti-Christian statements in the Talmud were deleted.

In the final text that was approved on October 28, 1965, mutual understanding and respect were advocated. Although a Christian request for forgiveness was not added to the document, the declaration was unambiguous in its condemnation of anti-Semitism.

> Indeed, the church reproves every form of persecution against whomso-ever it may be directed. Remembering, then, its common heritage with the Jews and moved not by any political consideration, but solely by the religious motivation of christian charity, it deplores all hatreds, persecutions, displays of anti-semitism levelled at any time or from any source against the Jews.[20]

The declaration, however, goes far beyond a statement concerning Catholic relations with Jews. It affirms the unity of the human community (no. 1). And it acknowledges that, although the fullness of religious life is to be found in Christ, there are elements of truth and goodness in other religions (no. 2). Although expected to continue to witness to their own faith, Christians are therefore exhorted to "acknowledge, preserve and encourage the spiritual and moral truths found among non-Christians, together with their social life and culture."[21] The statements dealing with Hinduism and Buddhism are very brief and descriptive, rather than evaluative. The statements dealing with Islam and Judaism are much fuller and appreciative. "High regard" for Muslims is expressed (no. 3), while gratitude for the "nourishment" Christianity draws from Judaism is acknowl-edged (no. 4).[22] The declaration concludes with an appeal to all Christians to be at peace with all people (no. 5).

When one reads section 2 of *Nostra Aetate* together with section 16 of *Lumen Gentium,* he or she might wonder whether Vatican II is proclaiming new doctrine about the possibility of salvation outside the Catholic Church. In the early centuries of Christianity, the slogan "no salvation outside the church" was first directed against those (former) Christians who were separated from the church through heresy or schism or those Christians who were in danger of being sepa-rated through excommunication. After Christianity became the official religion of the Roman Empire at the end of the fourth century, however, the slogan began to be directed against non-Christians. The assumption was that the gospel had been proclaimed everywhere and that everyone had had sufficient opportunity to accept it. Those who had not accepted it—pagans and Jews, for example—were believed to be guilty of refusing God's offer of salvation, for which refusal they would be justly condemned. Lateran Council IV and the Council of Florence reiterated this belief. After the division of the Western church into Catholic and Protestant communities, the statement "no salvation outside the church" was widely interpreted to mean "no salvation outside *my* church."

Although earlier theologians, such as Thomas Aquinas in the thirteenth century, had reflected upon possible exceptions to the principle that salvation could not be obtained outside the visible church, new impetus for thinking about this matter was given by the European voyages of discovery. Beginning with Columbus' "discovery" of the so-called New World in 1492 and continuing with the voyages of the Spanish and the Portuguese explorers in the sixteenth century, European Christians encountered peoples who had never heard the gospel before. Was it possible for people living after the time of Jesus, who had never heard the Christian good news, to be saved? Or phrased differently, how could Christians continue to judge all pagans guilty of sinful unbelief, when they now knew that countless people had been living without the knowledge of the gospel, through no fault of their own?[23] Explicit faith in God, which could be interpreted to imply faith in Christ, and implicit desire for baptism might be sufficient to obtain the salvation of those who did not belong to the visible church.

Spanish theologians such as Francisco de Vitoria (c. 1485-1546) broke new ground. Vitoria judged that Native Americans were not culpable for rejecting Christian faith, if the faith had not been presented to them in a convincing way. Vitoria was keenly aware of how the identification of the faith with the behavior of the conquistadors made it difficult for the natives to affirm and adopt Christianity.[24] Juan de Lugo (1583-1660) extended the thinking of Vitoria and other contemporaries. By paying careful attention to the ways in which people come to faith, Lugo concluded that even people who had been exposed to the Christian message over a long period of time might not be culpable for failing to embrace Christianity. From his perspective, pagans, Jews, or Muslims were obliged by the first preaching of the gospel to inquire further into its truth. If they make this inquiry, but are unable to find sufficient reasons to embrace the Christian faith, their ignorance of the truth of Christianity is invincible. Lugo's ideas were revolutionary in their historical context. He "dared to suggest that some who sincerely sought the truth might not recognize it in the Christian religion, and might still be saved by the faith in God which they found in their own religion."[25]

Ideas such as these were developed slowly over the course of several centuries until they were explicitly endorsed at Vatican II. Without repudiating the teaching of Lateran Council IV (that there "is one universal church of the faithful, outside of which no one is saved"), the bishops at Vatican II developed a broader understanding of the church. The "Dogmatic Constitution on the Church" (*Lumen Gentium*) declared that all people are called to be "church," understood fundamentally as the assembly or people of God. And to the church, understood in this sense, "belong, or are related in different ways: the catholic faithful, others who believe in Christ, and finally all of humankind, called by God's grace to salvation."[26] The constitution proceeded to declare explicitly that Jews and Muslims are "related to the people of God in various ways" and are included in the plan of salvation. The essence of the constitution's teaching on the possibility of salvation outside of Christianity is summed up in section 16:

> Nor is God remote from those who in shadows and images seek the unknown God, since he gives to everyone life and breath and all things (see Acts 17:25–28) and since the Savior wills everyone to be saved (see 1 Tim 2:4). Those who, through no fault of their own, do not know the Gospel of Christ or his church, but who nevertheless seek God with a sincere heart, and, moved by grace, try in their actions to do his will as they know it through the dictates of their conscience—these too may attain eternal salvation.[27]

Roger of Taizé

Born on May 12, 1915, Brother Roger is founder and prior of the Taizé Community in France. Founding that community in 1940, Brother Roger tried to open ways to heal the divisions between Christians and among human beings in general. The community is made up of Catholic brothers as well as brothers from different Protestant backgrounds; they come from over 25 different countries. The Taizé community works for reconciliation and peace.

> *The brothers of Taizé make a life-commitment to celibacy, life togeth-er, and a great simplicity of life. Some brothers live in small groups that share the life of the poor across the world. Week after week, thousands of young adults from every continent go to Taizé to pray and to prepare themselves to work for peace, reconciliation, and trust among human beings. At the end of each year, a meeting brings together 70,000 to 100,000 young adults in a large European city. Gatherings are also held on other continents.*

> *Brother Roger has written many books, including* Struggle and Contemplation *(1974),* The Sources of Taizé *(1991),* Peace of Heart in All Things *(1996), and, together with Mother Teresa:* Seeking the Heart of God: Reflections on Prayer (1993).

> *Among the many awards Brother Roger has received are the Templeton Prize, London 1974; the Peace Prize, Frankfurt 1974; the UNESCO Prize for Peace Education, Paris 1988; Karlspreis, Aachen 1989; the Robert Schuman Prize, Strasbourg 1992; the Award for International Humanitarian Service, Notre Dame University 1997.*

Christ Is United to Every Human Being Without Exception

In the middle of the twentieth century there appeared a man by the name of John, born in a humble peasant family in the north of Italy. The vast pastoral responsibility that was entrusted to him in his old age undoubtedly caused an exceptional intuition of reconciliation to come to fruition in him. That man, John XXIII, made that intuition part of the vocation of multitudes of Christians.

It was Cardinal Gerlier, of Lyon, who in 1958 took the initiative of introducing us to John XXIII shortly after his election as pope. Wishing to place in his heart the question of the reconciliation of Christians, the cardinal asked John XXIII to give his first audience to Taizé. Why so quickly? The pope was elderly, explained the cardinal, he would soon be hearing a great many words, and it was important that he remember well what we would say to him.

John XXIII agreed and received us just after his inauguration, the first morning on which private audiences were held. He showed himself to be very attentive to the question of reconciliation and ended the conversation by asking us to return.

That first meeting with the pope communicated to us an unexpected impetus.

At the beginning of 1959, John XXIII announced the council. Brother Max and I were filled with gratefulness when we realized that he wished us to be present at the council as observers. I remember well the day when the letter arrived: to be invited to take part in that search made our hearts overflow.

Naturally, I had the impression that I was not made to participate in such an assembly. In the course of the four years of the council, however, I only missed two sessions. During the early days of the council, I used to read texts by Saint Teresa of Avila during the night. She gave me the courage to continue.

We rented a four-room apartment in the center of Rome. Our windows opened onto an inner courtyard, with no sun. Brothers took turns coming from Taizé to help with hospitality. Already early in the morning, we would meet for prayer. Then we left for the council. For the entire four years, as we went to Saint Peter's morning after morning, approaching the basilica awakened the same happiness when, as we came close to the Tiber, the sky opened up, a soft sky, filled with light....

As soon as we reached the basilica, before entering the section for the observers, we spent a moment of silent prayer with many bishops before the reserved Eucharist in a side chapel, long before the time of the daily assembly.

During the assembly, our attention was particularly awakened when we heard, under the dome of Saint Peter's, a bishop affirm what would open new ways forward for the future and corresponded to our own basic concerns: the presence of Christians in the contemporary world.

How often did we call to mind a face from the history of Christians, in particular, as soon as he died, the face of the beloved Pope John XXIII. Still today, I cannot forget the moment in 1963 when I learned of his death. From the depths of my being this question rose up: what would become of Taizé without John XXIII?

At the end of the morning, leaving the basilica, we found the bishops with whom we had made an appointment, and we brought them to our apartment for the midday meal. We had set up a tiny chapel there and we began with a sung prayer. Around the circular table for the meal, the topics of conversation were quite varied, depending on whether we were hosting Asians, Americans, or Africans. It was good to hear their concerns, to discover how they lived in faraway lands. The fourth year, women sometimes came to eat with us, when they were invited to the council as auditors. Around this table we also got to know Karol Wojtyla, the future Pope John Paul II, who was a young bishop at the time.

The meals were simple, sometimes overflowing with joy. We had so few resources that the food was frugal. We found out that some people used to say, "It's better to have something to eat before going to dine with the Taizé brothers!" There was usually rice and tomato sauce, a little wine, and we always found flowers to put on the table.

During the afternoon, people of the most varied sort came to visit us, particularly young people. At the end of the afternoon, often we replied to an invitation from a seminary to go and meet young people. Then we returned quickly through the crowded streets to come home for evening prayer and to welcome other bishops for a meal.

When there were letters to write, texts to compose, notes to prepare in order to express our viewpoint if it was asked for, it was only possible to spend time doing this at the end of the evening or late at night.

During those four years, we discovered multiple facets of that unique communion that is the church. We would perhaps have been unaware of them had we not had the opportunity of taking part in that event. Sometimes we wondered: why this vote, or that expression? Then the discovery of the mystery of the church returned again. And our hearts rejoiced once more.

At the beginning of the council, the ecumenical dynamism was such that it seemed as if a reconciliation would come to pass. John XXIII had called people "not to try and find out who had been wrong and who had been right." In his turn, as universal pastor, Paul VI had asked non-Catholics for forgiveness "if a wrong could be attributed to the Catholic Church regarding the causes of separation."

But were the denominations capable of seizing that historical moment? The weight of the past created irrational refusals, and after the council some people wondered whether an hour of ecumenism had been missed.

Great intuitions remain from the council. They are gospel treasures to respond to urgent needs at the beginning of the third millennium. For forty years now we have been welcoming a great many young adults to Taizé week after week, and we feel an unexpected hope: it is possible to discover in the spirit of the council responses to the longings of the younger generations.

There is one luminous gospel insight that the council brought to light; it had previously remained for a long time under the dust of the years: "Christ is united to every human being without exception." Later on Pope John Paul II, in his first encyclical, quoted those words and added: "... even if they are unaware of it." Multitudes of human beings are unfamiliar even with the name of God. But God is in communion with each person. This striking intuition can open up a new understanding of faith on earth. Yes, for every human being, the invisible God is a kind of influx of light, peace, and love.

Jeffrey Gros, F.S.C.

Jeffrey Gros is the associate director of the Secretariat for Ecumenical and Interreligious Affairs for the United States Catholic Conference of Bishops (USCCB). He was born in Memphis, Tennessee, on January 7, 1938. He completed his undergraduate education in Winona, Minnesota. He earned a master's degree in theology from Marquette University (1965) and a doctorate in theology from Fordham University (1973).

Brother Gros has extensive experience in teaching and research at the undergraduate and seminary level, including at Christian Brothers University, St. Mary's University of Minnesota, St. Mary's College in Moraga, California, and Memphis Theological Seminary. In addition, he has served as Director of Faith and Order with the National Council of Churches. For the past decade, he has served in the Secretariat for Ecumenical and Interreligious Affairs with the USCCB. He has participated in numerous international meetings of the World Council of Churches. Gros's current responsibilities include dialogue staffing with the United Methodist, Southern Baptist, Lutheran, Pentecostal, and Evangelical churches, as well as the Faith and Order Committee of the National Council of Churches.

He has published widely in the area of ecumenism, with numerous articles in a wide range of journals and anthologies. Among the books he has written or edited are: Building Unity *(1989), co-edited with Joseph Burgess;* Growing Consensus *(1995), co-edited with Joseph Burgess;*

Introduction to Ecumenism (1998), with Ann Riggs and Eamon McManus; That All May Be One: Ecumenism *(2000); and* Growth in Agreement II *(2000), co-edited with William Rusch and Harding Meyer.*

Among the special honors he has received are the James Fitzgerald Award (1986) from the National Association of Diocesan Ecumenical Officers and an honorary doctorate from Manhattan College (1995).

A Marvelous Beginning of a Pilgrimage Toward Communion

As a De La Salle Christian Brother, member of a lay religious community founded in 1680, with no clergy or theologically educated members since its foundation, my own calling has been to the ministry of education in the church. I graduated from college in 1959, with Pius XII dying in the fall, and John XXIII calling the council during the Week of Prayer that January. Studying in Minnesota and beginning teaching in Chicago, we were imbued with the liturgical movement and its hopes for reform, and the racial and social justice commitments of the church. My own teaching was in the field of biology.

In science, we were launching the post-Sputnik curricular reforms, moving from pedagogy based in memorization to more experimental and experiential forms of learning. In religion teaching, we were just beginning to incorporate the Bible/liturgy-centered kerygmatic methods. Our brothers had moved from catechisms in high schools, to narrative texts in the 1940s.

I was teaching in St. Louis during the third session of the council, when *Time* magazine ran an article noting that the Catholic Church was moving ecumenical. I wandered across the street to Concordia Lutheran Seminary, into the offices of Arthur Carl Piepkorn—a providential happenstance. He was an author who knew the Council of Trent from its Latin text, as well as interpreting the Lutheran Confessions in their most catholic sense. Three years later he was in the "freshman class" of the new Lutheran-Catholic dialogue that has turned out to be so productive. Attending his Lutheran "Masses" on Wednesday evening, the prejudices I had learned about "Protestants not believing in the real presence" were dispelled, and subsequent reading of Luther and the Confessions showed me how misguided had been Catholic polemics before the council. Luther always affirmed the faith of the church that taught the change of the bread and wine into the true body and blood of Christ. The real presence of Christ in the Eucharist is what separated Calvinists and Lutherans in the sixteenth century, a division we have had the opportunity to see overcome in our own lifetime (1997).

However, in those days of 1963 and 1964, before the council was over and before the dialogues had begun, it was exciting to recite compline in the Lutheran dorm chapel with the seminarians. Gary Pence would take us to Luther Memorial for Wednesday night Eucharist and explain the Lutheran liturgical tradition over pizza afterwards. We would take a car full of seminarians to the Easter Vigil, still celebrated in Latin, at Msgr. Martin Hellriegel's Holy Cross Church during Holy Week. We not only enjoyed learning about one another, but we also gained insights into our own worship tradition through these interchanges, long before there were books and articles available to explain our common heritage.

There are still a few Catholics who see fellow Christians in "us and them" categories. However, the position of the church, reinforced by the teachings of this Holy Father, the leadership of the U. S. bishops and their colleagues around the world, and the tireless work of the Pontifical Council for Promoting Christian Unity, demonstrates that, for the faithful Catholic, we have come to recognize that we share more than separates us, and that zeal for the unity of the church is central to Catholic identity.

A Fascinating Journey

In 1963 a program of theology was opened for lay persons and religious at Marquette University. Before that there had been a few pioneers, like Brother Luke Salm, F.S.C., who got a pontifical degree in theology at Catholic University, but there were few lay theologians in the world, even in religious communities.

In that year I was asked to enter doctoral studies, shifting from biology to theology. I graduated with a master's degree in 1965. With the council ending, we were able to get the documents, especially *Lumen Gentium*, in time to incorporate them into our preparations for comprehensive exams.

Of course, day-by-day events brought the results of the council, and contemporary American Catholicism, into our lives: talks by Dorothy Day, Bernard Lonergan, Daniel Berrigan, Bernard Häring; a conference in Washington between the sessions, with John Courtney Murray and other *periti*; and the like. This experience, along with doctoral studies at Fordham while working in a Black and Hispanic parish in the South Bronx, and professors of the stature of Bernard

Cooke, Avery Dulles, Robert McNally, James Hennessey, Ewart Cousins, and Herbert Ryan, began for me a pilgrimage of theological exploration that continues to open out to the richness of the tradition and the horizon of the church's future.

My own life, subsequent to the council, has been caught up in three dimensions of the reforms initiated there: 1) Catholic schools, 2) religious life, and 3) the church. In this brief essay I have been asked to reflect on reform of the church, and specifically the conversion of Catholicism to its ecumenical vocation, as I have experienced it. However, I am looking forward to reading a history of U.S. Catholic schools and their contribution to the reforms of Vatican II, including commitment to the visible unity of the churches.

I can sort out my own pilgrimage into three segments: 1) teaching in college and seminary, forming a new diocese; 2) working for the churches' ecumenical commitments in the National Council of Churches; and 3) serving the U.S. bishops in its Secretariat for Ecumenical and Interreligious Affairs. In all of these I have had an educational calling, which has enriched my spiritual life, strengthened my vocation to "service of the poor through education" as our brotherhood is called to do, and hopefully had some service to offer to the church.

In 1970 the diocese of Memphis was erected, its first bishop taking as a pastoral theme: "The Good Samaritan on the Banks of the Mississippi." Carroll T. Dozier was most known for his pastoral letters on peace and justice, his commitment to the council and its renewal of the roles of the laity and sacramental participation, and his advocacy of the place of women.

Among all of the things the diocese did was to implement the ecumenical commitment of the council. Those of us who were trained early on after the council were on deck for all of the renewal dimensions of the council. As "theological volunteers," who served diocesan concerns in our spare time after all of the teaching responsibilities, ecumenism seemed a rather minor, if central, dimension of all of the multiple reforms.

We had dialogues with Episcopalians, Southern Baptists, Presbyterians, and Lutherans—as well as close relations with Methodists and Disciples through the local interfaith agency. Relations with the Black Churches were strong (two national headquarters are in Memphis) because the bishop of Nashville had identified with Martin Luther King in the 1968 sanitation strike, and the 1973 pastoral letter on justice hit the press the same month that the public schools were integrated. We presumed this sort of ecumenical program was the standard of all

Catholic dioceses responsive to the council, especially the larger ones with more theological, pastoral, and financial resources than were available in Memphis.

When agreements with the Anglicans came out in the 1970s, the dioceses of Memphis and Nashville and the Episcopal diocese of Tennessee would collaborate in providing study days for the priests on the Eucharist and on the ordained ministry. It was a great opportunity to meet old friends, now as colleagues building the unity of the church. My kindergarten teacher, Annabelle Payne Whitamore, from a prominent Episcopal family, was now on the committee with me to prepare for the priests' study day on the Eucharist. When we hosted the study day on ministry, led by Bishop Arthur Vogel and Father George Tavard, we had the opening service in Grace-St. Luke's Episcopal Church, in whose gym I had passed my years as a boy scout years before. (Actually, this was my first time in the church sanctuary, since in the 1940s as Catholics we were not allowed to attend Boy Scout Sunday in the church with the rest of our troop.) We began a journey to give theological grounding to human relationships and sharing of faith, which had been part of my experience since childhood.

Southern Baptists are generally not seen as very ecumenical. However, there are so many Baptists in Memphis that they say there are more churches than filling stations. Indeed, the phone book lists more than 20 "first Baptist Church" of some part of town or another. We grew up with Baptists, we argued with them about their differences from us, and we learned from them. My father, a successful businessman and frequent leader in fund drives for parishes and schools, always complained about the stinginess of Catholics as compared with Baptists, who were frequently expected to tithe for their churches. We had African American "help" in our home, and I always used to enjoy joining folks for their Sunday worship in their Baptist congregation. There seemed to be so much more vitality and faith there in these Black congregations than in our staid and Latin Mass.

Today we still walk together, in many ways, even though—sadly—the present Southern Baptist dialogue will end in 2002. Thanks to Glenmary Home Missioners and dozens of other ecumenically oriented Catholics in local situations, there is a vast network of Southern Baptist and Catholic parishes who have close collaboration and deep spiritual relationships. In my years of service in the National Council of Churches, I have had the good fortune to host two conferences, which published results, bringing together Black churches, including Catholics and Baptists, to deepen the communion we share in Christ.

From Volunteer to Ecclesial Ministry

In 1981, after ten years of teaching at Christian Brothers University and Memphis Theological Seminary (Presbyterian), I took a position in New York at the Faith and Order Commission of the National Council of Churches. This was a great time of reception of the results of the (then) fifteen years of theological dialogue in which Catholics had been involved. In 1982 the Anglican-Roman Catholic International Commission submitted its *Final Report* to these two churches, and the World Council of Churches finished its fifty-year project *Baptism, Eucharist and Ministry* convergence text for the churches' evaluation.

Among other things, I had a rich ten years of theological ministry and administration helping the churches with their study of these and other ecumenical texts, like those emerging from the most productive Lutheran-Catholic dialogue and the variety of concerns brought by Orthodox members.

My "southern exposure" was a great resource, since it was during this decade that the Pentecostal, Holiness, and some evangelical churches came into full participation in these dialogues and the international dialogues. It was also a decade of linking the African American church concerns and the emerging feminist theological developments into the sixty-year tradition of Faith and Order theological discussions.

In 1991 I was called to serve the U.S. bishops in their ecumenical office. During this time the Holy See has provided the 1993 ecumenical *Directory*, the 1995 encyclical *Ut Unum Sint, The Ecumenical Dimension in the Formation of Pastoral Workers* (1998), the rich celebration of the 2000 Jubilee, which the Holy Father attempted to move from a papalist triumphal celebration to a time of ecumenical, social, and spiritual renewal.

The Lord has blessed the churches with a vision of visible unity unimagined by those of us formed in the 1950s, and with a rich harvest of dialogue and relationships that are a stimulus to even greater zeal on this pilgrimage toward full communion.

George H. Tavard, A.A.

George H. Tavard, Augustinian of the Assumption, was born in France on February 6, 1922, and ordained in 1947. Two years later he received his S.T.D. degree from the Facultés Catholiques de Lyon. Fr. Tavard came to the United States in 1959. He was chairperson of the department of theology at Mount Mercy (today, Carlow) College in Pittsburgh, Pennsylvania, when Pope John called the council.

Fr. Tavard has been a prominent figure in ecumenical activities for more than forty years. Since his first books in 1952 and 1954, he has pursued a teaching and writing career. After the council he served in some of the official ecumenical dialogues (internationally: the Anglican-Roman Catholic dialogue, ARCIC-I, and with the World Methodist Council; in the U.S.A., with Lutherans and with the Episcopal Church). He also served on some of the task forces that prepared the Joint Statement on Justification, signed by the World Lutheran Federation and the Catholic Church.

After teaching in Pittsburgh, he taught at Pennsylvania State University and Methodist Theological School in Ohio. He has been Visiting Professor at Wesleyan University, Princeton Theological Seminary, St. Thomas Seminary in Denver, the Josephinum School of Theology, Hekima Theological College in Nairobi, the Catholic University of America, Regis College at the University of Toronto, and Distinguished Professor at Marquette University. He has published 54 books, including The Pilgrim Church *(1967) shortly after the conclusion of Vatican II. His more recent publications include* The Church, Community of Salvation: An Ecumenical Ecclesiology *(1992) and* The Starting-Point of Calvin's Theology *(2000). A Festschrift has been published in Fr. Tavard's honor: Kenneth Hagen, ed.,* The Quadrilog. Essays in Honor of George H. Tavard *(1994).*

The Secretariat for Christian Unity and Ecumenism

In September 1960, after John XXIII had created the Pontifical Secretariat for the Unity of the Christians, I was named among the consultants. In September 1962 I was included in the first list of conciliar theologians (*periti*). As a consultant I attended the meetings of the Secretariat during the preparatory phase of the council. As a *peritus* I was involved in the writing of the decrees on ecumenism, on Judaism and other religions, and on religious liberty. In this double function I took part in the work of the Secretariat before, during, and between the sessions. Several brothers in my religious congregation were in the preparatory commissions, but I was the only one among the theologians of the council. The council's participants being classified according to their place of work, I figured among the Americans. Joseph Fenton wrote in his diary: "Tavard is here as an American (God help us)." Made by virtue of the pope's immediate jurisdiction, these nominations bypassed the usual channels of authority. The Secretariat for Unity met about eight times before the opening of the council, in the vicinity of Rome (once also in a convent in Bühl, Germany), for periods of four to six days.

When the council opened in October 1962, there was no talk yet of a decree on ecumenism. The Secretariat had prepared a few statements (*vota*) relating to ecumenism and partial drafts on prayer for unity, the Word of God, and religious liberty. None of them referred to common prayer or *communicatio in sacris*. The concern of the Secretariat, at that moment, was more basic: it was to attempt to insert an ecumenical note into the work of the council. There was as yet no way of foreseeing how far the bishops would be willing to go along this line. The task done by the preliminary Theological Commission scarcely permitted any optimism in regard to the ecumenical dimension of the council. But the picture changed dramatically as soon as it became clear that there was widespread dissatisfaction with the work of the Theological Commission, especially with its schema "On the Church." On December 1, 1962, the council decided, by a vote of 2083 to 36, that the Secretariat for Unity should prepare a document that would incorporate elements from the schema on "the Unity of the Church" (*Ut Unum Sint*) prepared by the Commission for the Oriental Churches, elements from the last chapter, "On ecumenism," of the rejected schema on the church, and an expanded version of the *vota* already prepared by the Secretariat.

In keeping with this resolution, the Secretariat formed several subcommissions, made up of theological experts and bishops, to work along the proposed lines. During the four sessions of the council, the full Secretariat met about once a week, in different locations. The language was a mixture of French and English, with an occasional intervention in Latin, German, or Italian. Every Friday the Secretariat met with the Orthodox and Protestant observers. Outside of this I had no regular contact with the observers, though I got to know the delegates of the French Reformed Church and Oscar Cullmann, Paul VI's special invitee, the Taizé brothers, and some of the Americans, especially the Quaker Douglas Steere.

The first version of the "Decree on Ecumenism" was distributed to the council fathers in May 1963. When the bishops turned their attention to the second chapter of this first version (November 25-27, 1963), a number of them asked for a positive statement on the possibility of some shared liturgical participation among separated Christians, especially, but not exclusively, in relation to the Orthodox. In keeping with these debates and the recommendations made in writing to the Secretariat, Chapter Two was re-written. In February 1964, meeting at the residence of Bishop Willebrands on Monte Mario, five *periti* were given the task of re-writing section 7 (now become section 8). Besides Michalon as the original author of section 7, there were Gregory Baum, Jerome Hamer, Emmanuel Lanne, and myself. Hamer chaired the meeting. At some point in our discussion of the issue, prior to writing anything on *communicatio in sacris,* Hamer stated, approximately: "The idea is simple; the problem is how to express it properly. There are two principles involved. The liturgy is an expression of unity. But it is also a means of grace. As an expression of unity, it presupposes oneness. As a means of grace, it brings it about." Just then, word came that he had a telephone call. While he was gone, I wrote a couple of Latin sentences formulating what he had said in French, the most common language of this small group. When Hamer returned from the telephone, I read my sentences aloud. A few words were changed. And this became the statement of the "Decree on Ecumenism" concerning *communicatio in sacris.* This new version was approved by the entire Secretariat for Unity at its session from February 25-March 7, 1964.

When Bishop Helmsing of Kansas City was given by Cardinal Bea the task of formally presenting Chapter Two of the "Decree on Ecumenism" to the council on October 6, 1964, William Baum conveyed to me Helmsing's request that I compose a suitable text for this *relatio* [report]. I spent the following Saturday writing a draft. On Sunday afternoon I brought it to the hotel where Helmsing and Baum were staying. On Monday afternoon I read it to the whole Secretariat for Unity.

One word was changed, and Bishop Helmsing read it to the council a few days later.

In the daily sessions of the council, I took a seat in the tribune next to that of the Superiors General. Fred MacManus; Godfrey Diekmann; Joseph Baker, adviser to Cardinal Ritter; William Baum from Kansas City; William Keeler from Harrisburg (these last two, future cardinals) were usually in the same area. The view was good. Occasionally I looked for bishops I knew. Cardinal Cody of Chicago never stayed long at his place. As Charles Helmsing, Bishop of Kansas City-St. Joseph, once told me, most bishops found the sessions painful, for if they are used to sitting at their desk all morning long, in more comfortable chairs, they tend to deal with one question after another and they seldom stay on the same point for long. The council sessions, however, called for a different kind of attention, and the seats were far from comfortable! Looking over the assembly I once caught Fulton Sheen distributing chocolate to his neighbors. From time to time I left the tribune to walk in the side aisles, talk with a bishop or two, or get a cup of something in one of the bars.

Personal reminiscences are of small value when compared with the achievements of Vatican Council II. They can nevertheless illustrate little-known aspects of the work that was done, especially by the mostly unrecognized conciliar *periti*. They should encourage younger scholars to delve deeper into the history of the most important religious event of the twentieth century.

Robert Drinan, S.J.

Robert F. Drinan is Professor of Law at Georgetown University. After completing elementary education, he earned both the B.A. (1942) and the M.A. degree (1947) from Boston College. He entered the Society of Jesus in the same year that he completed his undergraduate education, and he was ordained a Jesuit priest in 1953.

Fr. Drinan has served as guest lecturer and visiting professor at numerous universities in the United States, England, and Africa, including Oxford University (1988), the University of Michigan (1984), and

Swarthmore College (1984). From 1956 to 1970, he served as dean and professor of law at the Boston College Law School, where he specialized in criminal law, constitutional law, and the philosophy of law and church-state relations. In 1971 he was elected to the U. S. House of Representatives, where he served for the next ten years. During his time in Congress, he was a member of several important committees, including the House Committee on the Judiciary (1971-1981). In addition, he was part of official congressional delegations to Vietnam, China, South Africa, Israel, and the Soviet Union. Since leaving Congress, Fr. Drinan has been a professor of law at Georgetown University, specializing in international human rights, constitutional law, civil liberties, and arms control. Because of his expertise and concern for human rights, he served on human rights missions to Chile, the Philippines, and El Salvador, among others.

Drinan has been a regular contributor to several journals and newspapers, including the Christian Century *and the London* Tablet. *He has published nine books. Among his more recent publications are* Cry of the Oppressed: The History and Hope of the Human Rights Revolution *(1987),* Stories from the American Soul *(1990), and* The Fractured Dream: America's Divisive Moral Choices *(1991).*

Fr. Drinan has served on the board of numerous legal and human rights organizations, including Common Cause (1981-87, 1996—), People for the American Way (1986—), and the Lawyers Committee for Human Rights (1981—). For his distinguished work on behalf of human rights and civil liberties, Fr. Drinan has been awarded 23 honorary degrees.

The Declaration on Religious Freedom (*Dignitatis Humanae*)

I recall vividly the day, December 7, 1965, when Vatican II finally published its decree on religious freedom. I and countless others had followed that topic for many years. During my studies in the seminary I read diligently the articles of Father John Courtney Murray, S.J., in *Theological Studies* and the response to them by Father Fenton, a professor at Catholic University, in *The Ecclesiastical Review*.

By instinct I agreed with Father Murray's plea for religious freedom, but I recognized that the traditional view that the Catholic Church should disadvantage non-Catholic groups was ancient and firmly held in some quarters.

I almost thought that Father Murray's views would never get a hearing when Rome told Father Murray not to publish anything on the question of the church's view of proper church-state relations.

The views opposed by Father Murray seem incredibly wrong now. Catholic theologians actually held that "error has no rights." And that in nations where Catholics constituted the majority, the church also had the right to penalize and even to suppress Protestant churches.

For eight years before Vatican II issued its final declaration vindicating religious freedom, I was dean of Boston College Law School and an active participant in ecumenical activities. Beginning in 1962 it appeared possible, but apparently unlikely, that Vatican II would change the church's narrow view on its attitude toward a pluralistic society.

Everyone followed the five versions of the text on religious freedom. Three public debates were held at the council with a total of 120 speeches. Accurate text and reliable predictions were hard to come by in the days before e-mail and fax.

But the people—at least in Boston—knew that Cardinal Richard Cushing was going to speak at the council on what we used to say was the "side of the angels." He did speak—in Latin—and echoed the opinions of Father Murray—by then a *peritus* at the council.

When the final text of the "Declaration on Religious Freedom" was issued, it was clear that something monumental had happened in the church. The change took away the embarrassment and the humiliation of having to live with a tradition that contradicted the principle of religious freedom, which had long been recognized in the constitutional law of the West. The declaration brought a credibility to the church, which I had never before experienced. It was a joy to go to interreligious events. I saw in the declaration the ideas and even the words that Father Murray used in his many explanations of why religious freedom, and not merely tolerance, should be given to non-Catholic denominations.

For many years I have gloried in the thrust of Vatican II's defense of religious freedom. When I re-read some of it, I discover new implications. Father Murray, in his comments on the declaration in *The Documents of Vatican II* (edited by Walter Abbott, S.J), asserts that the church was "late" in acknowledging the validity of the principles of religious freedom.[28] But the document has more depth and is more thoughtful than some of the legal and philosophical explications of the free exercise of religion.

There are many passages in the document on religious freedom that I quote regularly in my talks, writings, and my class on international human rights at Georgetown University Law Center.

When I criticize the religious right movement in America, I like to cite these words of Vatican II: "However, in spreading religious belief and in introducing religious practices everybody must, at all times, avoid any action which seems to suggest coercion or dishonest or unworthy persuasion . . ."[29]

I always love to quote the language that comes directly from the writings of Father Murray. They express sound jurisprudential principles: "For the rest, the principle of the integrity of freedom in society should continue to be upheld. According to this principle, people's freedom should be given the fullest possible recognition and should not be curtailed except when and in so far as is necessary."[30]

Walter J. Burghardt, S.J.

Walter J. Burghardt was born in New York City on July 10, 1914. He earned the M.A. (1937), Ph.L. (1938), and the S.T.L. (1942) degrees from Woodstock College in Maryland. In 1941 he was ordained a priest in the Society of Jesus. Fr. Burghardt received his doctorate in theology (S.T.D.) in 1957 from The Catholic University of America. He then embarked upon a distinguished career of teaching and writing. He taught historical theology for 32 years at Woodstock College and The Catholic University of America. He has also been visiting lecturer or professor at Princeton Theological Seminary and Union Theological Seminary. Editor-in-chief of the journal Theological Studies *for 23 years, Fr. Burghardt is also coeditor of the ecumenical publication* The Living Pulpit *and the Ancient Christian Writers series of translations.*

A senior fellow of the Woodstock Theological Center in the District of Columbia, Father Burghardt has published 21 books and about 300 articles in over 70 journals. Among his most recent titles are Christ in

Ten Thousand Places: Homilies Toward a New Millennium (1999) and Hear the Just Word and Live It *(2000). Burghardt has published his memoirs,* Long Have I Loved You: A Theologian Reflects on his Church *(2000), recently awarded a first prize by the Catholic Press Association. Twenty-one colleges and universities have awarded him honorary degrees. In addition, he has received the William Toohey, C.S.C., Award for Distinguished Catholic Preaching from the University of Notre Dame (1984), the Warren Distinguished Catholic Service Award from the University of Tulsa (1991), and the Jerome Award from the Catholic Library Association for Outstanding Contribution and Commitment to Excellence in Scholarship (1999), among others. In 1996 a two-year Baylor University survey included him as one of the 12 "most effective preachers" in the English-speaking world. Fr. Burghardt was recently presented with the Life Achievement Award, Alpha Sigma Nu, Jesuit Honor Society, for contributions to the church, to the Society of Jesus, and to preaching of the gospel.*

Vatican II and Religious Freedom: The Role of John Courtney Murray, S.J.

When Vatican II opened, J. C. Murray was not there. In his own ironic word, he had been "disinvited." A decade before, he had incurred Roman displeasure by his writings on church-state issues and religious freedom. He had been informed through his Jesuit superiors that anything he wrote henceforth in those areas would require a prior critique—in Rome. With his love for the church and the Society of Jesus, Murray felt he could not disobey. But with his love for truth and the human person, he did not see how he could operate honestly in such chains. So he cleared the bookshelves in his room at old Woodstock College of those books that dealt with religious freedom, with church and state, with Catholicism and the American proposition. He saw no further use for them. Unable to present his position to his peers for challenge and criticism, Murray decided to forgo publication on these subjects until a more favorable climate was created.

Before Vatican II opened, New York's Cardinal Francis Spellman requested of Rome that Murray be named a *peritus*. According to the cardinal's secretary at the time, Patrick V. Ahern, the request was politely but firmly turned down by Cardinal

Alfredo Ottaviani, who headed the screening committee involved. Spellman replied sharply: I would not certify Father Murray if I were not sure of his credentials and his orthodoxy. Ottaviani responded: Thank you very much; the matter has been brought again before the screening committee; unfortunately.

> Cardinal Spellman's response to this letter has vanished from the arch-diocesan files, as has the other correspondence in the matter—victims, Bishop Ahern believes, of the cardinal's determination to expunge the record of unpleasantness that might "give scandal." But the bishop has no difficulty recalling the nature of the letter. "It came down to something like, 'Father Murray is going as my personal *peritus*,' he said. And if he doesn't go, I don't go." Then, of course, the final reply came back to the effect that Father Murray would be most welcome. I don't think there's any doubt that Cardinal Spellman singlehandedly got Father Murray into the Council.[31]

Murray himself was convinced that he owed his participation to Spellman. "Between us," he wrote to Notre Dame's Leo Ward, "it was my Eminent friend of New York who pried me in. He said (and meant it, I think) that the Jesuits had got too slim a deal about *periti*, and that it was 'no more than right' that I in particular should be there. Which was nice of him."[32]

The full story of Murray's influence on *Dignitatis Humanae* has still to be written. Early on he addressed a significant commission, decisive for the fate of the religious-freedom issue. He was commissioned by the Secretariat for Promoting Christian Unity to analyze the comments sent in by the bishops on religious freedom. He fashioned preliminary drafts of the document, addressed American and other national groups of bishops, shaped interventions for many a U.S. bishop, and eloquently interpreted the issues for reporters at the daily press panels. The Casa Villanova, where Murray lodged, "became the Council's intellectual crossroads. Cardinal and bishop, priest and layman, European and American, liberal and conservative were all part of the cast which lived, worked, prayed, and talked there. 'To be anything in Rome was to be at the Villanova,' [John] Cogley wrote in *Commonweal*."[33]

Still, even during the council, Roman hostility threatened Murray's full participation. The courageous moral theologian Bernard Häring recently revealed a discussion within a subcommission of the council's Doctrinal Commission, on a draft of the projected "Declaration on Religious Freedom" prior to its submission for public discussion. He reports that the task of co-ordinating secretary fell to him and that "the subcommission did not water down the text, but rather strengthened it."

> In view of this situation, Cardinal Ottaviani, the President of the Doctrinal Commission, tried delaying tactics. Since the admonitions from our side accomplished nothing, we had to request a decisive action by Pope Paul VI that forced Cardinal Ottaviani to place the text on the table for discussion in the full Commission as soon as possible. For this the bishops brought Father Murray along. Nevertheless Ottaviani refused to let him speak, despite loud protests from bishops. Since I had been chosen as speaker for this draft, I could not be refused the opportunity to speak. Ottaviani responded angrily that one did not need this whole text since there was already too much freedom in the Church. Now my patience was tested to the limit. I said: The fact that the head of the Holy Office answers thus is sufficient proof of the pressing need of this declaration and the necessity to allow the theologian whom he had so long condemned to silence the opportunity finally to speak. Ottaviani grimly relented. It was a pleasure to experience how magnificently Murray presented his viewpoint in beautifully fluent Latin and with sovereign dignity. The subsequent vote resulted in the overwhelming majority approving the strengthened text and passing it on to the Council.[34]

Dignitatis Humanae has often been styled the council's "American document." Here I counsel caution. (1) The declaration, approved 2,308 to 70, was an act of the universal church. (2) It was not the product of U.S. participants alone. Such an interpretation would overlook the crucial contributions of men like Jan Willebrands and Charles Moeller, Carlo Colombo and Yves Congar, Jérôme Hamer and Pietro Pavan, Augustin Bea and Emile Joseph De Smedt. (3) The most significant drafts set before the council emerged officially from the Secretariat for Promoting Christian Unity—a group whose competence to present texts with a theological content was disputed until October 22, 1962, when Pope John XXIII put that Secretariat on the same level as the other commissions and authorized it to lay drafts and schemata before the council. Still, we must recognize the startling truth expressed by Pietro Pavan, one of the document's architects:

> I took part in the Second Vatican Council from beginning to end. At the preparatory stage I was a member of two pontifical commissions, the

Theological Commission and the Commission on the Lay Apostolate. In the four sessions...I was a *peritus*. I am therefore in a position to say with full assurance that the impact of the American episcopate—above all, all the bishops of the United States—was decisive (1) in bringing about the "Declaration on Religious Freedom" and (2) in assuring that its main line of argument should be the one which it now exhibits.[35]

An important observation indeed. Still, another observation by the same Pavan is perhaps equally important:

In the drafting [of the third schema—separate from the schema on ecumenism] as well as in subsequent redraftings down to the time when the declaration *Dignitatis Humanae* took its final shape, an outstanding part was played by John Courtney Murray, S.J. He was distinguished at all times for his unique grasp of the subject, for his wisdom, his nobility of mind, his loyalty to the Church, and his love of truth.[36]

What was so important about the declaration? In Murray's summation, three doctrinal tenets: (1) the ethical doctrine—religious freedom as a human right; (2) the political doctrine—the functions and limits of government in matters religious; (3) the theological doctrine—the freedom of the church as the fundamental principle in the relations between the church and the sociopolitical order.

Timothy Unsworth

Tim Unsworth has been a columnist for the National Catholic Reporter *since 1982. His essays and reportage have also appeared in* America, Commonweal, U.S. Catholic, Salt *and* Salt of the Earth, Catholic Digest, Christian Century, Chicago Tribune *and a number of other publications. He was editor of* U.S. Parish *and* U.S. Church, *two month-*

ly newsletters. His writings have won three awards from the Catholic Press Association. He is the author of five books, including award-winning Last Priests in America *and* I Am Your Brother Joseph, *a life of the late Cardinal Joseph Bernardin of Chicago.*

Unsworth spent over twenty years as a teacher and administrator in Catholic secondary education before going to Chicago's DePaul University as its alumni director. He also worked in development at the University of Chicago and as an alumni director and development director at Northwestern University's Dental School. In 1986, he withdrew from higher education in order to devote his time to freelance writing. In addition to his books, he has written over 500 articles and over 50 encyclopedia essays. He resides in Chicago with his wife, Jean, an author and former professor of Fine Arts at Loyola University of Chicago.

Msgr. John Quinn and the Declaration on Religious Freedom

Eagle-eyed Vatican II scholars such as the legendary "Xavier Rynne," a Redemptorist priest now equally recognized by his real name of Francis Xavier Murphy, C.Ss.R, would likely only smile at the notion. However, I maintain that the 103,014 Latin words in the sixteen documents of the council, which heralded a new era of Catholicism, traced at least part of their inspiration to the late Msgr. John Quinn's two ice machines.

It's well nigh impossible to prove this thesis. Most of those who sat by the ice machines, cooled their beverages while discussing the great documents of the council, and wrote interventions are largely in their graves. But the energy that surfaced during these moments clearly made its way to the floor of the council.

If an army marches on its stomach, then clearly the American *periti* and a few other experts, who assisted the 2,240 council fathers during the three sessions of this council were fueled by the comfort provided by the two ice machines supplied to John Quinn by a U.S. airline with the soul of a St. Nicholas.

John Quinn was a Chicago priest. Ordained in 1940, he was on the episcopal track. In the jargon of the all male and often cynical priesthood, Quinn was a comer—a man whose behind was dipped in butter since his days as a seminarian. Educated as a canonist in the shadow of the Vatican, he could have fallen victim to "scarlet fever." But his penchant for helping people kept getting in the way. Time and again, Quinn chose pastoral decisions over political ones. In time, his nickname "pol" (for "politician") was used as a compliment, not a judgment. He became one of the nearly ninety percent of Roman-educated priests who do not achieve the fullness of the priesthood.

Quinn was well liked. His practice of doing favors for people—including high ranking Vatican clerics—derived from a pastoral heart. One of his friends from his Roman days was Cardinal Alfredo Ottaviani, a Vatican careerist, who was the head of the Holy Office (now the Congregation for the Doctrine of the Faith). Ottaviani was an intransigent conservative, especially on issues touching on religious liberty and papal authority. Named a cardinal by Pius XII in 1953, he was also known as a zealous priest. The facts are somewhat fuzzy here, partly because it is a delicate issue. But John Quinn earned Ottaviani's undying gratitude when Quinn obtained scarce toilet tissue for the Vatican following World War II. Quinn's reward was the purple piping of a domestic prelate. What is clear is that Quinn's invitation to be a *peritus* at Vatican II came through Ottaviani's clout. He was one of the twelve American *periti* appointed by John XXIII.

For the first session, held between October 11 and December 8, 1962, the American *periti* were housed in an old convent, which was barely adequate but which underscored the low esteem in which the council's 200 experts were held. The death-grip attitude held even when the Americans moved to nicer quarters for the three subsequent sessions. The American community room gradually became the center of good conversation and good drink—with ice. Even tourists to Rome have experienced the lack of ice in an alcoholic drink. One cube is deemed sufficient. Electricity is expensive. So is alcohol. The preferred beverage is wine at room temperature. *Periti* from other nations, including the Dominican Yves Congar, regarded by many as the "Father of Vatican II," were remembered for having come by for a bit of conversation and a drop of the creature.

John Quinn even got the use of a car and used it to shop for beverages and other necessities He also set up an informal currency exchange to change American dollars into Italian lire. He bought towels, soap, tissue, shaving materials, and other necessities for the moderately isolated and sometimes not very practical scholars. He actually deprived himself of scholarly time in order to meet the needs of his colleagues.

The late Jesuit theologian John Courtney Murray, principal author of the sixteenth and final document, the "Declaration on Religious Freedom" (*Dignitatis Humanae*), arrived for the opening session and promptly got seriously ill. Murray was the most important contributor to Catholic reflection on church and state and the question of religious liberty in the twentieth century. When Msgr. Quinn learned of Murray's illness, he found a competent physician and chauffeured Murray on numerous office visits. He saw to it that Murray had adequate get-well food and proper hygiene. Murray, who loved a good drink, was soon gathered with the others around the ice machine.

Some years ago, looking back, during a Wiener schnitzel dinner in a German restaurant in Chicago, John Quinn recalled that the council chamber was flooded with interventions on the religious freedom document. The American *periti*—and some of the American delegate bishops—were hobbled by the absence of a central office from which to issue their responses. They spent many an evening poring over and discussing the interventions of the curial bureaucracy while they cooled their drinks at the ice machine. They felt angry but helpless.

Eventually, the resentment began to mount in council father Cardinal Albert Meyer of Chicago. Initially rather conservative, his innate honesty transformed him into a dissident. At one point, reviewing some of the interventions that had reached the floor, he uttered to some colleagues something to the effect that "This isn't right," or "This isn't fair. We've got to do something."

Again, the dissidents turned to John Quinn. Cardinal Meyer and others prepared a response and turned it over to the man who had created ice. Somehow, Quinn wormed his way into the secretary of the council and duplicated hundreds of copies of the U.S. intervention. By the next morning, virtually every one of the 102 cardinals, seven patriarchs, 26 bureaucrats from the General Secretariat, 2,440 council fathers, 200 *periti* and 130 observers had a copy. (They weren't all there, of course, but this was the number of ticket holders. Attendance varied from 2,000 to 2,500. Two hundred seventy-four council fathers from Communist countries could not attend.) For the curial bureaucrats it was simply too late to quash the unwelcome American intervention.

Following the session in which the "Declaration on Religious Freedom" was accepted (it was promulgated on December 7, 1965, the day before the council closed), Msgr. John Egan of Chicago was in the community room waiting for the experts to gather. John Courtney Murray, who had been studying and writing on this issue for decades, came into the room and said: "We won, Jack! We won!" The document, which would make for a far better church, now belonged to the world.

After the council, John Quinn returned to Chicago, and in 1966 was named pastor of St. Andrew's Parish on Chicago's northside. He served until his then mandatory retirement at age 70. Typically, this writer met him while en route to the Synod on the Laity, held at the 'Vatican. Quinn was bringing a large box of frozen steaks and lobsters to his fellow Chicago priest, Paul C. Marcinkus, now a retired archbishop, but then the man who ran the Vatican. At 70, Quinn became pastor emeritus of St. Andrew's and lived there until his death on New Year's Day, 1998. Cardinal Ottaviani lived until 1979, dying in his 89th year. His successor as head of the Holy Office was Cardinal Joseph Ratzinger. Cardinal Albert Meyer, a dutiful priest, ponderous in speech and cautious in action, emerged from the council as a progressive. He died of a brain tumor in 1965.

John Courtney Murray returned to the U.S., where he continued to support the concept of religious freedom internally within the church. He died in 1967 while riding in a New York City taxi en route to visit his sister on Long Island.

It's likely that the two ice machines made their way back to the airlines.

Francis Cardinal Arinze

Francis Arinze was born on November 1, 1932, at Eziowelle in Anambra State of Nigeria. After secondary school studies in All Hallows Seminary, Nnewi and Enugu, he studied philosophy in Bigard Memorial Seminary, Enugu, Nigeria (1953-1955), and theology in Urban University Rome (1955-1960). He received the bachelor in divinity degree in 1957 from the Urban University, and earned the master's (1959) and doctorate in divinity (1969) from the same institution.

After his ordination as a Catholic priest on November 23, 1958, he became a lecturer in liturgy and philosophy at the Bigard Memorial Seminary, Enugu, 1961-1962, and then became Catholic Education Secretary for the Enugu Diocese, 1962-1965. He was in Rome as a young priest when Pope John XXIII announced the Second Vatican Council in

January 1959. As Catholic Education Secretary, he followed the first three sessions of the council from afar. During this time, he engaged in further study (1963-64), earning a diploma in education from the University of London Institute of Education.

On August 29, 1965, Arinze was ordained auxiliary bishop of Onitsha, Nigeria. Two weeks later, he joined other council fathers in St. Peter's Basilica, Rome, in the entire fourth session of the Second Vatican Council, from September 11 to December 8, 1965. Bishop Arinze, 32 years old at that time, was the youngest bishop in the church and at the council.

Arinze was made archbishop of Onitsha in 1967 and held that post until 1984, when Pope John Paul II transferred him to Rome and made him president of the Secretariat for Non-Christians. In 1985 he was made a cardinal. In 2002 he was made prefect of the Congregation for Divine Worship.

In addition to many articles, Cardinal Arinze has published seven books, including Sacrifice in Ibo Religion *(1970),* Answering God's Call *(1982),* Alone with God *(1986),* Church in Dialogue *(1990),* Living Our Faith *(1990), and* Meeting Other Believers *(1997).*

Vatican II Encourages Interreligious Dialogue

The attitude of the Second Vatican Council toward the people of other religions and its directives on dialogue with them are best understood if they are seen in the context of the open-arms approach that Pope (now Blessed) John XXIII gave to the council. The council wanted the church to meet every human being, whether that person be a Christian in a church or community not in full union with the Roman See, or a follower of another religion, or indeed a person of no declared religious conviction.

The council declaration *Nostra Aetate,* approved on October 28, 1965, spells out the attitude of the Catholic Church toward people of other religions. It is the first ever major document of a general council on the subject. In its earlier draft, the declaration was only on relations with the Jews. But over the years 1964 to 1965 it was expanded to cover relations with all other religions, with express mention of Islam, Hinduism, and Buddhism.

The underlying doctrine is also available in other Vatican II documents, especially the "Dogmatic Constitution on the Church" (*Lumen Gentium,* nos. 13, 16, 17); "Decree on the Church's Missionary Activity" (*Ad Gentes,* nos. 7, 9); and the "Pastoral Constitution on the Church in the Modern World" (*Gaudium et Spes,* no. 92).

Nostra Aetate exhorts Catholics to meet the people of other religions and, through dialogue and collaboration with them and in witness to Christian faith and life, to "acknowledge, preserve, and encourage the spiritual and moral truths found among non-Christians, together with their social life and culture" (*Nostra Aetate,* no. 2).[37]

On Pentecost Day 1964, between the second and third sessions of Vatican II, Pope Paul VI had instituted the Secretariat for Non-Christians as an autonomous dicastery of the Roman curia, the central offices of the church, for the promotion of interreligious dialogue. In 1988 the name was changed to the more positive one of Pontifical Council for Interreligious Dialogue.

Not everyone in the church immediately absorbed the spirit of the council as articulated in *Nostra Aetate.* Some people feared that an attitude of dialogue and friendship with other religions would discourage missionaries from preaching Jesus Christ and proposing faith and baptism to people. It has to be admitted that this risk exists, but only when dialogue is not properly understood or where it is conducted on erroneous theology.

Some of the encouraging developments following on the attitude of the Second Vatican Council toward other religions are the following. In 1974 Pope Paul VI instituted a Commission for Religious Relations with the Jews and a parallel Commission for Religious Relations with the Muslims. In 1986, Pope John Paul II took the unprecedented step of inviting representatives of the major world religions to come to Assisi (Italy) to fast and pray for peace, each religion according to its own tradition. It was the International Year for Peace. The Assisi event improved the general world climate for interreligious dialogue tremendously. The following year, the religions of Japan—especially Buddhists, Shintoists, Catholics, and Protestants—invited the major religions of the world to come to Kyoto, Hiroshima, and Nagasaki to pray for peace.

A yearly commemoration has been done in Japan ever since. And the Community of Sant'Egidio, a Catholic lay association based in Rome, has, since 1987, held a yearly commemoration of the Assisi celebration, from one city to another. In October 1999, in preparation for the Jubilee Year 2000, 200 representatives of 20 world religions held a four-day meeting in Vatican City to reflect on their collaboration in the forthcoming Third Millennium.

A development of great importance in the church is in the area of a Christian theology of religions. In the face of a world increasingly more pluralistic from the religious point of view, theology cannot be done today without attention to the fact of the existence of other religions. What is their place in God's plan of salvation? What is the relationship between dialogue and proclamation? What does inculturation of the gospel gain from the religious and cultural backgrounds of the people who receive the gospel?

For me, who has been able to follow these developments for over 16 years, it has been enriching indeed. To observe and take part in joint reflections between the World Council of Churches and the Catholic Church on aspects of interreligious dialogue, to meet Catholic seminary and university faculties over the question, and to visit and discuss with Muslims, Hindus, Buddhists, and followers of traditional religions: all these have been great graces indeed.

Thanks to Vatican II, the Catholic Church is irrevocably committed to meeting other believers.

Eugene J. Fisher

Eugene Fisher was born on September 10, 1943, in Detroit, Michigan. He received his B.A. from Detroit's archdiocesan seminary, Sacred Heart, in 1965 just as the council was coming to a close. In 1968 he completed his M.A. in Catholic theology from what was then the University of Detroit (now Detroit-Mercy). He was awarded a Ph.D. from New York University in 1976, in the area of Hebrew culture and education.

Prior to 1977, Dr. Fisher was director of catechist formation for the Archdiocese of Detroit, as well as adjunct professor of sacred scripture at St. John's Seminary in Plymouth, Michigan, and for the Religious Studies Department of the University of Detroit. At present, Dr. Fisher is associate director of the Secretariat for Ecumenical and Interreligious Affairs of the United States Conference of Catholic Bishops, in charge of Catholic-Jewish relations. He succeeded Father Edward H. Flannery, who held the post since its establishment in 1967 following the Second Vatican Council. Dr. Fisher is the first layperson to hold the post.

Dr. Fisher is an active member of numerous learned and professional societies and associations, such as the Catholic Biblical Association, the National Association of Professors of Hebrew, and the Society of Biblical Literature (SBL). He has lectured widely throughout the United States, Canada, Europe, Latin America, and Australia. He has published twenty books and monographs, and over 250 articles in major religious journals, many of which have been translated into French, Spanish, Italian, Portuguese, Polish, and German for publication in Latin America and Europe.

Most recently his writings, all of which seek to foster religious dialogue and appreciation, include: Catholics Remember the Holocaust *(1988), and* A New Millennium: from Dialogue to Reconciliation: Christian and Jewish Reflections *(co-edited with Rabbi Leon Klenicki).*

In April of 1981, Dr. Fisher was appointed by Pope John Paul II to be consultor to the Vatican Commission for Religious Relations With the Jews. In 1985, he was named a member of the International Vatican-Jewish Liaison Committee, representing the Holy See. In 1999, he was appointed by the Holy See as Catholic coordinator of the International Catholic-Jewish Historical Team, and in 2000 as Catholic coordinator of the International Catholic-Jewish Liaison Committee for its meeting in New York in June of that year. He has represented the Holy See on several occasions, most recently at the International Conference on Holocaust Education (January, 2000) and as Vatican Observer at the meeting of the Lutheran World Federation (September, 2001).

The Council and the Invention of Catholic-Jewish Relations

The Second Vatican Council happened while I was in college. It could not have come at a better time for me. The council's documents, which we read and studied and debated as they came out in stately procession from Rome, blew away my childhood impression of what Catholicism was all about and replaced it with a more dynamic sense of a community chosen by God to change history itself and to improve the lot of all humankind (I would have said "mankind" then). Salvation was not just a spiritual, personal thing. It was a challenge to humanity to overcome its own evil. College is a crucial time in one's life. For during it, one chooses who one will be and the basic values one will uphold for the rest of one's life. The council thus permeated my being thoroughly and permanently. One could say that the way I experienced the council and its remarkable teaching was not simply existential but ontological as well. The council's statements on ecumenism and interreligious understanding (*Nostra Aetate*) became, along with the rest, part of the fiber of my being.

After college, I attended St. John's Seminary for two years. There, I took some optional scripture and biblical Hebrew courses from John J. Castelot, S.S., who had written a popular series of introductions to the Bible. There were only two or three of us in these classes, which he held informally in his room in the evening. His evident love of scripture and his joy at probing its depth infused me. But what astonished me was the fact that the Hebrew Bible, read in its original, had a whole lot more in it than any translation can really convey. Genesis, for example, even its elegant and poetic creation accounts, is filled with puns and delightful and provocative word plays that satirize elements of the common world-view of the ancient Near East and give the reader a sense of the ironies of life. In scripture, tragedy and comedy constantly intertwine. The Bible is a far more sophisticated (and funny) set of books than our rather straight-laced approach to it as Christians allows us to see. It's no wonder that Jews are over-represented in American comedy. They've got a three-millennia long tradition going for them!

Then I wanted to go on for a doctorate in theology. I had sent in to, and been accepted by, both the Chicago and Princeton divinity schools, but would have had to take out major loans to pay for them. Dr. Marinoff suggested I write to his good friend David Rudavsky, at New York University's Institute for Hebrew Studies. I found the idea of studying the Hebrew Bible with the people who wrote them quite appealing, so I dashed off a résumé. He responded with a generous scholarship covering not only tuition, but modest living expenses as well. On a warm day in early September 1968, I walked out of New York's Grand Central Station with the address of the school in my pocket and two large suitcases. I did not know where I would spend the night, but I did know that my relatively sheltered midwestern life was about to change. I set the bags down for a moment to take it all in. A young man promptly picked one up and began to walk off with it, mumbling something about carrying my luggage for me. I chased after him, carrying the other bag and would have lost the race if a policeman had not intervened. Welcome to New York!

I didn't know it then, but I had stepped into a career in a field that did not even exist before the Second Vatican Council, Catholic-Jewish relations. The changes and challenges in life-style, intellectual environment, and religious perspective I experienced in New York were dramatic. This was the period of massive antiwar demonstrations, in which I took part with enthusiasm, thanks to the great vision of peace of John XXIII (*Pacem in Terris*), the council itself (*Gaudium et Spes*), and Paul VI at the U. N. "War no more! War never again!" as I recall the phrase from my seminary days.

I had been in the seminary just at the right moment to go through the council as it was happening, and been fortunate to be quite actively involved in the Civil Rights movement in Detroit during the same period. The winds of change promised a new and more equal American society, as the open windows of theological *aggiornamento* [updating] promised a reformed and more open Roman Catholic Church. For us, change represented hope, not something to be feared. One could acknowledge freely the shortcomings of the past, whether in society or the church, because both were actively engaged in rectifying what had gone wrong. Admitting American racism and Christian anti-semitism, then, was not to risk becoming mired down in the guilt of the past (as it continued to be for some time in Europe). It was simply to open oneself to hope for a better future.

When I saw Pope John Paul II visit Yad Vashem in Jerusalem and place a prayer of repentance in the name of the church in the Kotel (Western Wall), I thanked God that I have lived in a time in which the future has become a reality. Along with hundreds, perhaps thousands of veterans of the Jewish-Christian dialogue on all levels from parishes to the Holy See itself, I cried tears of joy. *Gaudium et Spes*, indeed.

John T. Pawlikowski, O.S.M.

John T. Pawlikowski, a priest of the Servite Order, was born in Chicago, on November 2, 1940. Educated at Loyola University in Chicago (A.B., 1963) and the University of Chicago (Ph.D, 1970), he did specialized study at the University of Wisconsin and at Mansfield College, Oxford University.

Since 1968 he has been a member of the faculty at the Catholic Theological Union in Chicago (CTU), where he currently holds the position of professor of social ethics and director of Catholic-Jewish Studies in CTU's Cardinal Joseph Bernardin Center for Theology and Ministry. He has been active in Christian-Jewish Relations locally, nationally, and internationally for more than three decades. He has served on the Christian-Jewish Relations Committee of the National Council of Churches, and continues as a member of the National Advisory Committee of the U.S. Catholic Bishops' Office for Catholic-Jewish Relations.

In 1980 he was appointed to the United States Holocaust Memorial Council by President Jimmy Carter. He was subsequently reappointed to three additional terms by Presidents Bush and Clinton. He currently serves on the Council's Academic Committee, Committee on Conscience and Strategic Planning Committee, and chairs its Church Relations Committee. In 2000 he was elected a vice president of the International Council of Christians & Jews, and was elected president of that council in 2002. He has also served as co-chair of the National Polish American-Jewish American Council. He has written or edited some 20 volumes, including Christ in the Light of the Christian-Jewish Dialogue *(1982),* Jesus and the Theology of Israel *(1989), and* Reinterpreting Revelation and Tradition: Jews and Christians in Conversation *(2000).*

Christian-Jewish Relations and Vatican II

My own academic and ministerial development was very much part of the Vatican II scene. I was in the final years of my preparation for the Catholic priesthood during the time of the council, with my ordination taking place in 1967.

The "Vatican II" spirit was very much alive at the Servite theologate in Lake Bluff, Illinois. A number of the professors there, including John Dominic Crossan (then a Servite priest), became involved in an ecumenical association of theologians in the Chicago area as a result of Cardinal Suenens' visit to the University of Chicago campus during the council. The visit and subsequent association led to the development of the Catholic Theological Union, where I now teach, and the move of McCormick Theological Seminary (Presbyterian) and the Lutheran School to the University of Chicago area, where they joined Chicago Theological Seminary, Meadville-Lombard Theological School, and the Divinity School of the University of Chicago in the Hyde Park Cluster of Theological Schools.

In 1967, a year prior to the opening of Catholic Theological Union, I enrolled in a doctoral program at the University of Chicago, at a time when Catholic students were entering the university in droves in response to the ecumenical atmosphere created by the council. This was a significant reversal for Catholics. When I was a senior in a Catholic high school in the late fifties and considering a choice of college, I was warned not to consider the University of Chicago for fear that I would lose my faith there. While at the University of Chicago, I came under the influence of Dr. J. Coert Rylaarsdam, a pioneer scholar in the rethinking of Christian-Jewish relations, and Professor Martin Marty, who had considerable interest in the present-day relations between Christians and Jews.

My more than three decades of interest in the Christian-Jewish relationship were in many ways the result of the influences of professors Crossan, Rylaardsdam, and Marty. Without their encouragement and insights, I doubt that I would have walked the road of Christian-Jewish encounter for so long a time.

My initial interest in Christian-Jewish relations must be laid at the feet of John Dominic Crossan. In his courses at the Servite theologate, Crossan instilled in me a tremendous respect and an appreciation for sacred scripture and an interest in the long history of Christian anti-semitism, which he saw as rooted in New Testament interpretation. Crossan delivered one of the earliest lectures on anti-semitism and the New Testament in light of *Nostra Aetate* at a public series on the Second Vatican Council held at Chicago's Loyola University, a lecture eventually published in *Theological Studies* (June, 1965). I was in the audience that evening as a proud student. It was only later on that I would recognize that, despite his deep commitment to the elimination of anti-semitism, his approach to the interpretation of Jesus' parables, rooted in the views of Rudolf Bultmann and his disciples such as Norman Perrin, contained the seeds of theological anti-Judaism with an emphasis on the displacement of "those who first heard the word" from the sacred table. Scholars such as Clemens Thoma have shown how destructive such parabolic interpretation can be for our image of Jews and Judaism.

Reflecting later on this dual experience of Crossan as both profound critic of anti-semitism and at the same time purveyor of theological anti-Judaism, it became apparent to me how deep-seated and yet subtle anti-semitism remains in Christian self-understanding so that even those who staunchly oppose its outer manifestations sometimes remain unaware of its subtle dimensions. Despite this lapse, I shall always be grateful to him for instilling in me a profound concern for anti-semitism and a deep commitment to develop a new, constructive theology of the Jewish-Christian relationship. Without his encouragement in the midst of the new spirit of the Vatican Council, I doubt I would have ever made Christian-Jewish relations such a central part of my academic and ministerial career.

When I entered the University of Chicago in autumn 1967, I had no intention of pursuing Christian-Jewish relations as the focal point of my doctoral work. But under the influence of J. Coert Rylaarsdam, I began to see the importance of a new look at the Old Testament and to recognize how significantly Jesus and the early church were influenced by the progressive Jewish forces of their day. I began to see a rethinking of the Christian-Jewish relationship as critical to the overall reform of the Catholic Church that had been mandated by the council. I remain convinced that a renewed, constructive understanding of this relationship remains central to the full implementation of Vatican II's call for liturgical renewal, enhancement of the role of the laity, and an openness to all other religious traditions. My one, ongoing criticism is that Christian theology has not taken seriously enough the fundamental restatement of the church's self-identity that occurred in Section 4 of *Nostra Aetate*, where the council repudiated the centuries-old christology and ecclesiology rooted in the notion of Jewish covenantal displacement.

My encounter with Martin Marty at the University of Chicago introduced me to the debate about continuing anti-semitism in the churches. I became acquainted with the early pioneers in this area, such as Franklin Littell, Alice and Roy Eckardt, John Oesterreicher, and Edward Flannery. My world, incidentally, had now become ecumenically Christian, not just Catholic (although my "Catholic" identity was in fact strengthened in an institution where, as I said above, my high school teachers feared for my faith). This was the prevailing spirit at the University of Chicago Divinity School and was very much in keeping with the orientation of the council. This experience solidified my life-long interest in combating anti-semitism, starting with the decision to use the St. Louis University studies on prejudice in Catholic teaching materials (which had directly impacted support for the passage of *Nostra Aetate* at the council) as the basis of my doctoral dissertation.

The era of the council, which coincided with my ordination and pursuit of doctoral studies, has set the basic framework for my life. Vatican II taught how destructive it is to try to confine God's redemptive presence.

Part Six

World Issues and Social Justice

The Church and the World: Reading the Signs of the Times

Michael J. Daley

Though she always shakes her head whenever I say something like this, I could not resist telling my wife that the movie we were watching, *Chocolat*, would make a great introduction to an article I was writing.

The movie opens in a small French village gathered together for Mass on a windswept Sunday morning on the eve of Lent. The year is 1959. The opening lines and images convey to the viewer that this village is a place of tranquility, guided by tradition. Whether it be religious, political, economic, or social—things had remained pretty much the same since the late sixteenth century. It was then that the villagers threw the Huguenots, French Calvinists, from their homes and land. This world would soon be turned on its head, though, with the unplanned and unannounced arrival of three things: an unmarried woman, her daughter, and a chocolate shop.

Viewed from afar, the woman is immediately considered an occasion of sin. Her marriage status, good looks, and vocational choice were enough to make her almost demonic. Representing the town's conscience, the mayor, a Jansenist if there ever was one, is offended at what seemed to be her lack of discretion—opening up a confection store during Lent. Over the course of several weeks, any and all means are attempted to shut the store and see to it that this woman and her daughter leave town.

In a last ditch effort on the eve of Easter (no midnight vigils yet!), the mayor breaks into the store and begins destroying all of the shop's delicious offerings only to fall victim to its seductive smells. Unable to refrain any longer, in a fit of uncontrolled passion, he consumes as much chocolate as he possibly could fit into his stomach. At which point the mayor passes out in the store's front window. By chance, on his way to church Easter morning, the village's young curate comes upon the mayor and rescues him from imminent personal and professional embarrassment. Additionally, by the grace of a strong wind, the priest finally gets the chance to say his own sermon, which usually was prepared by the mayor but had blown away.

With great determination in his voice, the curate looks out over the congregation and, encapsulating the preceding days and events of the village, says: "Here's what I think. I think we can't go round measuring our goodness by what we don't do, by what we deny ourselves, what we resist, and who we exclude. I think we've got to measure goodness by what we embrace, what we create and who we include." Knowing that I still had an introduction to write, the words *gaudium et spes* ("joys and hopes") echoed in my ears.

And the Walls Came Tumbling Down

Rather than avoid the world as a den of iniquity, the Catholic Church at the Second Vatican Council embraced it as a graced community, placing itself at the service of all of humanity whom it sought to make more whole through Christ. This conciliar sentiment is found most expressly in "The Pastoral Constitution on the Church in the Modern World" (*Gaudium et Spes*), which was issued during the council's last session and approved on December 7, 1965. Its introduction, though written decades ago, still reads with the freshness of wet ink:

> The joys and the hopes, the griefs and the anguish of the people of our time, especially of those who are poor or afflicted, are the joys and hopes, the grief and anguish of the followers of Christ as well. Nothing that is genuinely human fails to find an echo in their hearts. For theirs is a community of people united in Christ and guided by the holy Spirit in their pilgrimage towards the Father's kingdom, bearers of a message of salvation for all of humanity. That is why they cherish a feeling of deep solidarity with the human race and its history.[1]

Considering the church's recent history up to that point, the content and tone of the document caught many Catholics off guard.

From the end of the eighteenth century up to the very eve of the council, says University of Notre Dame historian Jay P. Dolan, a general mood existed within the Catholic Church that cast "an attitude toward the world or secular society that was quite negative. Church leaders frequently spoke as if Armageddon was just around the corner. The power of darkness seemed to be in control, and religious error, like 'a sheep in wolf's clothing,' prowls about the earth seeking whom it may devour. Though European Catholics were more extreme in this regard, Americans also evidenced a hostile attitude toward the world."[2]

The culprits were easily seen. In France, with the Revolution (*ca.* 1789), the prerogatives of the church seemed at risk everywhere you turned. Religious life, for all practical purposes, was disbanded; thousands were forced to flee in exile. The grand cathedral of Notre Dame became a temple of reason. A non-religious calendar, with a new communion of saints (voices of reason rather than faith) was created. The Constantinian age of the church was falling and a new one characterized by separation of church and state was emerging. This was the case not only in France but throughout Europe and included what would be the countries of Italy, Austria, and Germany.

The person of Pope Pius IX (pope, 1846-78) and his *Syllabus of Errors* (appended to the encyclical *Quantra cura* December 8, 1864) perhaps best illustrates the church's siege or fortress mentality to the movements besetting it. In it Pius IX condemned 80 propositions including: pantheism, religious freedom, religious indifferentism, rationalism, socialism's position on the right to private property, denial of temporal power to the pope, freedom of the press, and separation of church and state. In the conclusion to the *Syllabus*, Pius refuted the notion that "the Roman Pontiff can and should be reconciled with, and agree to, progress, liberalism and modern civilization."[3] Long presumed, now declared, the church and the modern world were at odds with one another.

Yet alongside this "ghetto" attitude on the part of the church, exemplified by the pope becoming a "prisoner of the Vatican," was developing a world-engaging tradition of Catholic social teaching.[4] It has even been termed by some to be Catholicism's "best kept secret."[5] Most people see its beginning in Pope Leo XIII's encyclical *Rerum Novarum* (also referred to as "On the Condition of Labor"), in 1891. Responding to the excesses of the Industrial Revolution, Leo XIII stated that workers had rights—to work, to private property, to a just wage, and to form and join unions. This was followed by Pius XI's encyclical, *Quadragesimo Anno* ("The Reconstruction of the Social Order"), which commemorated *Rerum Novarum's* fortieth anniversary. This encyclical, written during the height of the Great Depression with its devastating economic and social effects and the emergence of European fascism, challenged both capitalism and socialism as economic systems.

It also introduced the concept of subsidiarity, which states that problems should be solved, as much as possible, at the local level.

In 1961, on the eve of Vatican II, following the example of his predecessors, Pope John XXIII issued *Mater et Magistra* ("Christianity and Social Progress"), which, in light of increasing internationalization and interdependence of economies, sought to bring attention to the gap between the rich (first-world) nations and poor (third-world) nations. During the council itself, just prior to his death, John issued another encyclical related to social justice, *Pacem in Terris* ("Peace on Earth"). Addressed to "all people of good will," in the aftermath of World War II and in the shadow of the Cold War, John called for an end to the arms race and stressed the common good of all humanity.

Thus, both on the eve of and during the council itself, it was hard to deny the presence and concerns of the wider world, whether they were economic, social, cultural, or political. Yet, as Fr. Donald Campion, S.J., relates, "despite the existence of such a body of authoritative pronouncements in the Church, the several commissions charged with drafting tentative texts for consideration by the council had not felt it necessary or desirable to prepare a document dealing with the theme of the Church in the modern world."[6]

The Origins of a New Church

Though *Gaudium et Spes* was the last document to be approved (December 7, 1965) by the council, its origin actually predates the council by almost six months. In March of 1962, Archbishop (soon to be cardinal) Leon Joseph Suenens of Malines (Belgium) had an audience with Pope John, in which they discussed the council's direction and overall plan. In the course of the conversation, Pope John asked him, "Who is attending to the making of an overall plan for the Council?"[7] At this seeming invitation from John XXIII to express his feelings on the state of the council's preparations, Suenens took "exception to the number of draft texts that had been prepared and were intended for discussion at the upcoming Council. There were...far too many, in my opinion. Their quality varied greatly, and in any case, their sheer bulk would have precluded *a priori* any possibility of useful and fruitful work within the Council."[8]

Taking advantage of Suenens' observations, Pope John asked him, "Would you then like to make a plan?"[9] After carefully studying the proposed schemata, Suenens states that he "drafted a preliminary note for Pope John. Its intent was to pare down the texts, and to give the Council a truly pastoral perspective. My note," he stressed, "was both negative and positive; the *idem nolle* [what I didn't want] was as essential as the *idem velle* [what I did want] and together they provided the groundwork for a more detailed plan."[10] This plan was finished by the end of April 1962 and met with the approval of Pope John and several other influential cardinals, with whom Suenens shared it including Montini, the cardinal archbishop of Milan and soon to be successor to Pope John XXIII.

Suenens' plan was basically divided into two parts: the church *ad intra* (inner life) and the church *ad extra* (outside world). Related to the church *ad extra*, Suenens wrote that "the Church must bring Christ to the world. The world has its own problems, and seeks with anguish for solutions; some of these problems are obstacles to the spread of truth and grace. Some of the major problems can be grouped as follows: What do men and women seek? They seek love in their homes; daily bread for themselves and their families; peace both within each nation and among nations. These are basic aspirations. Does the Church have anything to contribute at these levels?"[11]

On September 11, 1962, during a rather memorable radio address to announce and introduce the council, Pope John shared with others his vision. During his address it is clear that he had adopted Suenens' plan: "Considered in the relations of her vitality *ad extra*, that is, the Church facing the needs and demands of peoples—those human situations which turn them instead to appreciate and enjoy the things of earth—the Church considers it her duty to do justice to her responsibilities by her teaching...."[12]

Not to be forgotten in all of this development is a group whom some claim "gave the impulse which led to the decision to produce a schema on the Church in the world."[13] Led by Dom Helder Camara, who at the beginning of the council was an auxiliary bishop of Rio de Janiero but in 1964 was appointed archbishop of Olinda y Recife, they were known as "the Church of the Poor."[14] Canon Charles Moeller, a *peritus* at the council, relates that Camara "constantly discussed with visitors the problems of the Third World" and quotes Camara asking others: "What ought we to do now?... Are we to spend our whole time discussing internal Church problems while two-thirds of mankind is dying of hunger? What have we to say on the problem of underdevelopment? Will the Council express its concern about the great problems of mankind?"[15]

The first few weeks of the council were a whirlwind of activity and chaos. The assembled fathers were looking for direction in the midst of confusion. To make matters worse, Pope John's health was failing. In an attempt to give the council greater structure and order, Cardinal Montini wrote Pope John a letter, alluding at the end to Suenens' plan. Eventually, Suenens himself got into the act and was faced with the difficult decision: "Should I take the initiative and present my plan, or should I wait, since Pope John had wanted to be the one to choose the appropriate moment for making it public?"[16] On December 4, 1962, in the *aula* of St. Peter's, with the approval of Pope John, Suenens proposed his plan of the church *ad intra* and the church *ad extra* to the council fathers. "The unanimous endorsement of the Council," Suenens shared, "was further reinforced on the following day, when Cardinal Montini...spoke with enthusiasm in favour of my proposal, as also did Cardinal Lercaro."[17] For there to have been "The Pastoral Constitution on the Church in the Modern World" then, there first had to be the vision. By no means, however, did the existence of this vision make it any easier for the document to come to life.

Better Late than Never

As stated by numerous commentators on the council, no other document went through as laborious or precarious a process of birth as did "The Pastoral Constitution on the Church in the Modern World."[18] Jan Grootaers notes that this is indicated by the very name it was first given—Schema XVII. He goes on to say that "this odd bestowal of a purely numerical title is by itself enough to show the anonymity that marked a draft text that one group refused to study for a long time. It would be put on the agenda of the full assembly of Vatican II only in the fall of 1964 and then only after lengthy hesitation on the part of Paul VI."[19] The constitution would eventually take the "unlucky" working title of Schema XIII.

The two commissions given the task of developing the schema were the Doctrinal Commission and the Commission for the Lay Apostolate. Cardinal Suenens was named *relator* [reporter] of the schema by his fellow bishops. In the beginning this now mixed commission drew upon previously prepared material. Speaking of the constitution's first draft, Fr. Joseph Ratzinger, then professor of theology at Tübingen and conciliar *peritus* and now Cardinal Prefect of the Congregation for the Doctrine of the Faith, said:

> The prepared text did definitely broach topical contemporary questions. One of the texts treated Christian ethics in general; another dealt with marriage and family. But their solutions were too pat to be convincing. They were marked by an assurance which had no basis in revelation, and

by an authoritarian decisiveness which is simply no longer suited to the complexity of reality. They were put in categories that came more from classical antiquity than from Christianity. Marriage was discussed in terms of the basic category of "end"; its morality was deduced abstractly from the concept of nature. Here social utility was viewed as overriding the reality of the human person. The whole emphasis was on asserting and reiterating the rights of the Church. The Church's ministerial function was virtually forgotten.[20]

There was still much work to be done. The newly elected Pope Paul VI gave a needed boost to the schema's efforts when, in his address reconvening the council, he spoke of one of its aims being to dialogue with the modern world. Meeting in Rome, Malines, Zurich, and Ariccia, the work of the mixed commission would last three years and produce several texts for consideration and amendment. Not surprisingly, the schema "followed the course of development of all the conciliar texts, which moved from a more abstract, conceptual and timeless perspective towards a biblical, patristic, liturgical and conciliar outlook."[21] Furthermore, three papal actions would directly affect the document and would lead some to ask whether work on the schema was redundant—the publication of the encyclicals *Mater et Magistra* and *Pacem in Terris*, and the removal of any discussion of artificial birth control from the council with the establishment of a papal committee on birth regulation.[22] On December 7, 1965, before its public promulgation, the final vote was taken. Out of the 2391 votes cast, 2309 were in favor of the constitution.

The Document Itself

The longest of the council's sixteen documents, "The Pastoral Constitution on the Church in the Modern World" is divided into two main parts. The first part, "The Church and The Human Vocation" (nos. 11-45), articulates what can best be called a Christian anthropology or, in other words, what it means to be human in light of Christ. The second part, "Some More Urgent Problems" (nos. 46-90), speaks to issues related to marriage and family, culture, economics, politics, and war and peace.

Moving beyond the oft-quoted opening paragraph, the constitution seeks to enlarge the church's "audience" and "addresses not only the daughters and sons of the church and all who call upon the name of Christ, but the whole of humanity...." (no. 2). The means through which this will be done is conversation rather than diatribe (no. 3). This will enable the church not only to offer to the world the fruits of its "reading the signs of the times and of interpreting them in the light of the Gospel" (no. 4), but create the possibility and likelihood of the reception of these insights on the part of the world. As Bernard Häring, C.Ss.R., one of the twentieth century's greatest moral theologians and a council *peritus*, was quick to point out, "Christians never will mold the world if they do not pay attention to the signs of the times. Christian presence in the world is only possible if Christians are at the same time imbued with the spirit of the gospel and are men of their time."[23]

In looking at these "signs" the most easily recognized one is change. The council fathers recognized "the accelerated pace of history is such that one can scarcely keep abreast of it.... And so humankind substitutes a dynamic and more evolutionary concept of nature for a static one..." (no. 5). These areas of change included the social, psychological, moral, and religious. Usually, whether it's slow or fast, change brings imbalance and, "[i]n the midst of it all stands humanity, at once the author and the victim of mutual distrust, animosity, conflict and woe" (no. 8).

With this as the backdrop, the constitution spoke of the world in an almost paradoxical way, saying that "[i]n the light of the foregoing factors there appears the dichotomy of a world that is at once powerful and weak, capable of doing what is noble and what is base, disposed to freedom and slavery, progress and decline, amity and hatred. People are becoming conscious that the forces they have unleashed are in their own hands and that it is up to themselves to control them or be enslaved by them. Here lies the modern dilemma" (no. 9). The church's solution to the questions of the age is to be found in conveying to humanity that it is made in the image and likeness of God—as both persons (nos. 12-22) and community (nos. 23-32). Yet, the reality of sin blocks this recognition from taking place (nos. 13, 37).

Though tempted at times and having the opportunity to do so, "the Council refused to hurl anathemas."[24] Instead the church envisioned its role "to be a leaven and, as it were, the soul of human society in its renewal by Christ and transformation into the family of God.... In pursuing its own salvific purpose not only does the church communicate divine life to humanity but in a certain sense it casts the reflected light of that divine life over all the earth, notably in the way it heals and elevates the dignity of the human person, in the way it consolidates society, and endows people's daily activity with a deeper sense and meaning" (no. 40).

This leads the church to address what it considers "some more urgent problems." The second part begins by speaking to the challenges faced by those seeking to make and maintain marital commitments and support their families (nos. 47-52). One of the ways in which the council did this was by emphasizing conjugal love in marriage (no. 50). No longer was procreation said to be the sole objective of marriage. Unfortunately, though the need for "responsible parenthood" was admitted, the council was not allowed to discuss the issue of artificial birth control. Enda McDonagh makes the interesting observation that if the organizational and time pressures could have been overcome, and even if the council would have decided to maintain the traditional teaching, "it would probably have received much more widespread support than *Humanae Vitae* did subsequently."[25]

The next chapter looks at the church and culture (nos. 53-62). The council defines "culture" very broadly as "all those things which go to the refining and developing of humanity's diverse mental and physical endowments" (no. 53). It admits of new forms of culture and the anxiety that comes from that process of change or, for some, disruption. From this would come the challenge to be open to communicating the gospel in new ways. As Pope John often said, "The substance of the faith is one thing, the way in which it is presented is another."

With respect to economics (nos. 63-72), the constitution basically represents the themes of the emerging Catholic social tradition beginning with Leo XIII up to John XXIII. Echoing the first part, this chapter demands that "the dignity and vocation of the human person as well as the welfare of society as a whole have to be respected and fostered; for people are the source, the focus and the aim of all economic and social life" (no. 63). It highlights the growing international economic inequalities and advocates reform not just on the practical level, but in ideas and attitudes as well. This situation is well summarized in a quote used by the council fathers: "Feed the people dying of hunger, because if you do not feed them you are killing them" (no. 69).

Chapter Four concerns politics (nos. 73-76) and takes as its starting point the common good. With long entrenched political structures falling and new ones emerging throughout the world, the constitution urges that any political order must "provide all citizens with effective opportunities to play a free, active part in the establishment of the juridical foundations of the political community, in determining the aims and the terms of reference of public bodies, and in the election of political leaders" (no. 75). All the while the church remains ready "to preach the faith, to proclaim its teachings about society, to carry out its task among people without hindrance, and to pass moral judgments even in matters relating to politics, whenever the fundamental human rights or the salvation of souls requires it" (no. 76).

Finally, written during the heart of the Cold War, the last chapter deals with the promotion of peace as opposed to simply avoiding war and the building up of the international community (nos. 77-90). Here it calls special attention to the arms race, saying it "is one of the greatest curses on the human race and the harm it inflicts on the poor is more than can be endured" (no. 81). The second section of the chapter promotes greater cooperation between international institutions as a means to increase global progress and prevent war (no. 84). It states that "Christians should willingly and wholeheartedly support the establishment of an international order that includes a genuine respect for legitimate freedom and amity towards all" (no. 88).

The constitution ends with what could be termed a call to social action: "Christians can yearn for nothing more ardently than to serve the people of this age successfully with increasing generosity. Holding loyally to the gospel, enriched by its resources, and joining forces with all who love and practice justice, they have shouldered a weighty task here on earth and they must render an account of it to him who will judge all people on the last day" (no. 93).

Looking back now, some like to diminish the constitution's weight and vision by referring to it as a *pastoral* constitution rather than a *dogmatic* one like "The Dogmatic Constitution on the Church" (*Lumen Gentium*). Quoting the words of Archbishop Garrone, though, Bishop Mark G. McGrath, C.S.C., who was present at the council as a representative from Latin America (Panama), says that "The Pastoral Constitution on the Church in the Modern World" is "at the very heart of the Council. One could say that it is the only schema formally willed by John XXIII."[26] Seen in this light, as representative of the central purpose for the council, it could be argued that this document possesses the most authority.[27]

Mary Luke Tobin, S.L.

Ruth Tobin, daughter of William and Mary McGovern Tobin, was born May 16, 1908, in Denver, Colorado. She was educated in Denver public elementary and high schools. After two years at Loretto Heights College (Denver), Tobin entered the novitiate of the Sisters of Loretto, in Nerinx, Kentucky. At her reception into the congregation, she received the name Sister Mary Luke.

Sister Mary Luke received her B.A. degree at Loretto Heights College (1934) and her M.A. (1942) in history at Notre Dame University. After serving as principal in several Loretto high schools, Sister was elected in 1952 to the General Council of the Sisters of Loretto. In 1958 she was elected superior general, in which position she served two six-year terms.

From 1964 to 1967 Sister Mary Luke was president of the Conference of Major Superiors of Women. As leader of women religious in the United States at the time of Vatican II, Sister Mary Luke was invited to the last two sessions of the council. She was one of fifteen women auditors.

Since that time Sister has been active in issues of peace and justice, as well as in women's issues and ecumenism. After 1970 she served on the staff of Church Women United in New York. Later, drawing upon her early friendship with Thomas Merton during her years at the Motherhouse, she directed the Thomas Merton Center in Denver until 1995.

Sister Mary Luke is now in residence at the Loretto Motherhouse (Nerinx, Kentucky)—retired, but still championing issues of peace and justice, including the dismantling of racism, women's rights, and abolition of the death penalty.

Women Are Also "Church"

When the Second Vatican Council opened in 1962, I was Superior General of the Sisters of Loretto. Religious communities were aware that a new era was upon us and were studying proposed changes suggested by such authors as Archbishop Philippe, secretary of the Sacred Congregation of Religious, the Belgian Cardinal

Suenens, and many others. The liturgical movement in the United States, spear-headed by Godfrey Diekmann, O.S.B., was well under way.

In August 1964, I was elected president of the Conference of Major Superiors of Women in the U.S. This group had been working since 1950 to effect the renewal and adaptation called for by some far-sighted members of the Sacred Congregation. It was at their suggestion and encouragement, as well as that of my own congregation, that I proceeded to Rome during the third session of the council to learn from the periphery the developments occurring daily at the Vatican. On September 23, 1964, while watching the moon on the waters, I was summoned to the radio tower on the *S.S. Constitution* for three messages. The operator remarked that in his twenty years on this ship, this was the first time he had three messages for one person. The media had just been informed that fifteen women auditors had been invited to the council and that I was the one from the United States. The Associated Press was calling from New York wanting to be the first to offer congratulations. The other two were calls from Loretto superiors in Kentucky and St. Louis.

When interviewed, the layman in charge of the "auditors" indicated that women had been invited to participate in those sessions "which would be of interest to them." I made a mental note that I would never miss a session—a decision I later learned was shared by all the women. We were eight women religious and seven laywomen.

Early in the council, the bishops, in the "Dogmatic Constitution on the Church" (*Lumen Gentium*), insisted that the church should be titled "The People of God." The people *are* the church, with the result that as such the doors would be open for wider participation of all. From this understanding would flow the ideal of collegiality and the formation of parish councils.

The importance and dignity of the individual were becoming recognized, as well as the responsibilities of that person for participation and decision making within the total community. An outgrowth was the extension of the boundaries of the church to include all Christians and those of other world faiths. For the first time, Protestant Christian churches were acknowledged as churches.

The presence of women in and around the council hall called to consciousness the issues that women were facing. Although council documents spoke out clearly against discrimination, women were still looked upon (perhaps unconsciously) as second-class citizens. I recall an incident when Rosemary Goldie, an auditor who held a curial position in Rome, and I were attending a meeting in preparation for documents to be presented to the bishops. Father Yves Congar, after giving his position paper asked, "What do you think of my presentation?" Rosemary replied, "Père Congar, you can leave out all the pretty phrases about women and omit the flowers. Just make it clear that men *and women* constitute the church."

Related to the above incident, at the great outdoor Mass at the conclusion of the council, part of the program involved the presentation of certificates of honor to distinguished persons in various categories. Four philosophers, for example, were so honored; they walked across the platform and received from the hands of the pope some special insignia of recognition. Then four *literati*, four musicians, and so on, were singled out for praise. Finally, four women walked across the stage. And the announcer proclaimed that "women would be honored for their contribution to the church." I turned to Father Godfrey Diekmann and said: "But women are not a *category* in the church. They should not be honored as women more than men should be honored as men. Men *and* women are the church, aren't they?" Father Godfrey looked at me and said, "You're right, Sister; you women need to help us see this."

Two statements within the council documents speak out clearly against discrimination. In "The Pastoral Constitution on the Church in the Modern World" we see: "But any kind of social or cultural discrimination in basic personal rights on the grounds of sex . . . must be curbed and eradicated as incompatible with God's design."[28]

Also, in "The Dogmatic Constitution on the Church," we read that "the chosen people of God is, therefore, one: 'one Lord, one faith, one baptism' (Eph 4:5); there is a common dignity of members deriving from their rebirth in Christ.... In Christ and in the church there is, then, no inequality arising from race or nationality, social condition or sex, for 'there is neither Jew nor Greek; there is neither slave nor free man; there is neither male nor female. For you are all one in Christ Jesus'" (Gal 3:28 Greek; see Col 3:11).[29]

Unfortunately, an insensitive state of affairs regarding women in the church still remains. The open door that revealed to me the enormous discrepancy between Christian faith and practice, in the area of women in church and society, has only opened wider as I have become more conscious of the need to work ceaselessly for the goal of the equality of all persons.

However, the greater freedom, flexibility, experimentation, and new apostolic ventures were exciting to me. But I was perplexed and disappointed to discover later that the authorities at the Vatican were not equally enthusiastic about our plans for "the renewal and adaptation in the religious life" that had been called for.

In formal meetings of religious women as a follow-up to the council, these women were expressing their desire to have a part in the decision making that affected their lives, either by a deliberative vote or in a consultative manner.

In assessing the developments of the council, those which I consider healthy and hopeful include: 1) a more flexible liturgy; 2) wider participation of both men and women in pastoral ministry; 3) religious education, which has incorporated the teachings of Vatican II; 4) the establishment of parish councils (which now include women); 5) peace and justice commissions instituted at diocesan and local levels; 6) ecumenical involvement through participation in these commissions.

Although in many places it appears that the promises of Vatican II have not occurred, to me it seems that the event of Vatican II was a special epiphany of hope for the church in our time. The council was a door opened wide—too wide to be closed.

Elizabeth Johnson, C.S.J.

Born literally on the eve of Pearl Harbor, December 6, 1941, Elizabeth A. Johnson, C.S.J., is a teacher, writer, editor, and public lecturer in theology. Currently Distinguished Professor of Theology at Fordham University in New York City, where she teaches in both undergraduate and graduate programs, she began by teaching science and religion in Catholic elementary and high schools before moving on to teaching theology at the college (St. Joseph College, Brooklyn, NY) and university level (Catholic University of America, 1980-91). Her formal education includes a B.S. from Brentwood College (1964), an M.A. in theology from Manhattan College (1970), and a Ph.D. in theology from Catholic University of America (1981).

Former president of the Catholic Theological Society of America,

Elizabeth Johnson has written books that include Consider Jesus: Waves of Renewal in Christology *(1990);* She Who Is: The Mystery of God in Feminist Theological Discourse *(1992);* Women, Earth, and Creator Spirit *(1993); and* Friends of God and Prophets: A Feminist Theological Reading of the Communion of Saints *(1998). Her books, numerous scholarly essays, and popular articles have been translated into German, Portuguese, Italian, French, Korean, Dutch, Spanish, and Lithuanian. She serves on the editorial boards of the journals* Theological Studies, Horizons: Journal of the College Theology Society, *and* Theoforum.

Elizabeth Johnson loves to teach and was awarded Fordham University's Teacher of the Year Award in 1998. She has delivered numerous lectures and workshops to church and academic groups both at home and abroad.

Johnson's She Who Is *garnered major awards, including the University of Louisville Grawemeyer Award in Religion;* Friends of God and Prophets *received the annual Excellence in the Study of Religion Award from the American Academy of Religion. In addition, Johnson has received seven honorary doctorates, the University Medal from Siena Heights University (Adrian, MI), the Loyola Mellon Award in the Humanities from Loyola University (Chicago), the Elizabeth Seton Medal from Mount St. Joseph College (Cincinnati), the Sacred Universe Award from the ecological movement SpiritEarth, and the annual award from the journal* U.S. Catholic *for promoting the cause of women in the church.*

Deeply involved in the life of the church, she is a religious sister in the Congregation of St. Joseph, Brentwood, New York. Her public service in the church has included being a theologian on the national Lutheran-Catholic Dialogue, a consultant to the Catholic Bishops' Committee on Women in Church and Society, a theologian on the Vatican-sponsored dialogue between science and religion, and on the Vatican-sponsored study of Christ and world religions. She is now a member of the core committee of the Common Ground Initiative, started by Cardinal Joseph Bernardin to reconcile polarized groups in the Catholic Church.

At the time of the council, she was a young sister in temporary vows engaged in teaching in Catholic elementary school.

Worth a Life—A Vatican II Story

It was the summer of 1965. In preparation for making final vows in my religious order, the Sisters of St. Joseph of Brentwood, New York, I and sixty classmates were spending two months of extended reflection at our rolling, green, cloistered Motherhouse on Long Island. My heart was very conflicted about whether to make this life-committing decision. The reason for my hesitation was the contrast between the world-denying detachment in spirituality and life-style required by religious life at that time, and my own growing, powerful spiritual inclinations. The trouble was that I was fascinated by this world.

On the one hand, our congregation was living the religious life-style typical of the era: strong top-down authority, strict daily horarium, full habit, restricted human relationships, emphasis on distance from the world and saving one's soul and the souls of others in a church where conciliar renewal had not yet begun. Indeed, the council was a distant event with next to no impact on daily life. On the other hand, the sixties were in mid swing: John F. Kennedy newly dead, Joan Baez and Bob Dylan singing anti-war songs, Martin Luther King dreaming his dream, riots in the cities, LBJ's war on poverty, my own peers in "the outside world" beginning to rebel against the older generation. My sympathies lay with the latter. In contrast to what our vow preparation was teaching, I kept thinking that if God created and loved this world, then shouldn't those of us radically seeking God in religious life be in the forefront of engagement with this world? Wouldn't making final vows box me into a narrow life of perfection when the evolving, struggling world needed to be embraced with the love of God? Wouldn't I be denying the divine call that I felt in my own spirit?

And so I struggled.

One day we were handed, among other materials, a poorly printed pamphlet for personal reading. It was the draft of a conciliar document not yet voted on. Out of curiosity, I took it on my daily walk. Coming to a large, favorite pine tree, I settled in its shade and began to read. The opening words riveted me: "The joys and the hopes, the griefs and the anxieties of the people of this age, especially those who are poor or in any way afflicted, these too are the joys and hopes, the griefs and anxieties of the followers of Christ." Stunned, I read that sentence over and over again. Exactly! And weren't nuns supposed to be followers of Christ? Here was the highest authority in the church challenging the spiritual tradition in which I felt encased, endorsing rather than warning against involvement with the world. But more than that. This document painted a theological vision of humanity created in the image of God, defaced by the evil of sin, but redeemed by Christ and now led in history by the Spirit through the witness of the church. This was a vision I had never before encountered, and it was so beautiful.

All afternoon long I slowly read *Gaudium et Spes*, drinking it in like water in the desert. The sun began to slide down the sky but in a very real way the light was rising. I loved the way the council aimed the message to the "whole of humanity" in a spirit of respect and love. I admired the way it admitted that atheism often arose as a critical reaction to deficiencies in the way believers themselves acted. I thrilled to the idea that the church and the world should be in mutual relationship, each learning from the specific wisdom of the other—the gospel on the one hand, and science, humanities, and technology on the other. I resonated with its analysis of changed conditions in the modern world—new technologies, a new humanistic spirit, the desire for freedom even on the part of women, enormous inequity of material wealth resulting in poverty and hunger, the danger of nuclear weapons—and the impact all of these conditions had on religion, marriage and family, culture, socioeconomic justice, political participation, war and peace, international cooperation: I stirred to the way these issues were addressed in the spirit of the gospel.

Most of all, I reveled in *Gaudium et Spes*'s emphasis on the dignity of the human person. Every human being is created in the image of God. This anthropology grounds the essential equality of all persons, the fierce and repeated call to treat every human person with respect, and the need for an ethic that serves the common good. What ringing words—"with respect to the fundamental rights of the person, every type of discrimination, whether social or cultural, whether based on sex, race, color, social condition, language, or religion, is to be overcome and eradicated as contrary to God's intent" (no. 29).

Just as exciting was the way Jesus Christ gets connected to this struggling humanity, first as the incarnate Word who is truly one of us ("he worked with human hands, he thought with a human mind, acted by human choice, and loved with a human heart," no. 22); and then through his dying and rising as the Savior who transforms our hearts with hope. And wonder of wonders: "All this holds true not only for Christians, but for all persons of good will in whose hearts grace works in an unseen way. For since Christ died for all people, and since the ultimate vocation of human beings is in fact one, we ought to believe that the Holy Spirit in a manner known only to God offers to every person the possibility of being associated with this paschal mystery" (no. 22). The scope of this vision took my breath away.

The whole pastoral constitution was substantial nourishment for my mind and heart. By the time *Gaudium et Spes* concluded with a ringing call for harmony within the church "through the full recognition of lawful diversity" so Christians can then serve the modern world ever more generously and effectively—"let there be unity in what is necessary, freedom in what is unsettled, and charity in any case" (no. 92)—by this time I was possessed with an overriding conviction. This is worth my life.

And so it has proven to be. On that hot summer day, my young, questing spirit intersected with this council document and found its life-long direction. In the decades since then much has changed in myself, my religious community, the church, and the world, but the power of *Gaudium et Spes* to inspire and challenge me has not waned. Many of my decisions in ministry and the direction of my theological scholarship have been made in its light. Its insights have become even more telling as I read through the lens of feminism, applying its principles explicitly to women within the church as well as in society.

Given this personal history, I have met current ecclesiastical efforts to reverse Vatican II's direction with dismay. After almost forty years of living in the spirit of *Gaudium et Spes*, it is spiritually and intellectually impossible for me to return to that narrow-minded and fearful world in which I was originally formed. The respectful, loving intent of *Gaudium et Spes* stands as prophetic witness against those Vatican dicta that are mean-spirited, arrogant, and reactionary. Weaned into my life's commitment by this profoundly humanistic, generous document, I continue to join with others who walk by its light—regardless.

Mary Jo Weaver

Mary Jo Weaver is the oldest of six children, born to Bob and Ann Weaver on December 16, 1942 (missing the feast of St. John of the Cross by two days, but landing on Beethoven's birthday). She received her undergraduate education at St. Mary of the Springs College (now Ohio Dominican), graduating in 1964 with a B.S. in chemistry. After graduation, she worked three years plus for Parke-Davis & Co., in Ann Arbor, Michigan, and began her doctoral work at Notre Dame in 1967. Weaver has two versions of her diploma: one in traditional masculine language, dated June 1972, and (after her complaints) one in feminine language, dated January 1973.

Dr. Weaver describes her academic "trajectory" as quirky: she wrote her dissertation on Philo, but published her first two books on the modernist controversy (late nineteenth-century England), her next two books on American Catholic women and the church, and the next two on rifts in contemporary Catholicism. The book dear to her heart but not on that list is her textbook, Introduction to Christianity, *now in its third edition (1998). Her most recent book is* Cloister and Community: Life within a Carmelite Monastery *(2002).*

Weaver taught for three years at the Pontifical College Josephinum and has been at Indiana University since 1975. Much of her research has been funded by Indiana University and by outside grants (such as the National Endowment for the Humanities and the Indiana Council for the Humanities). But she reserves most of her thanks for the Lilly Endowment, whose generous support led to two edited volumes: Being Right: Conservative Catholics in America, *with Scott Appleby (1995) and* What's Left: Liberal American Catholics *(1999). Weaver has been a strong advocate of women's ordination and has written of homosexual rights in the church.*

At the time of the council, Dr. Weaver was in college, being turned on to the study of scripture (a welcome relief, she reports, from years of a forced march through pre-digested Aquinas).

Lower Case Catholic

Paradoxically, by opening an avenue for me toward a Ph.D. in theology, the Second Vatican Council paved the way to life in a secular university. Put another way, although the council tapped into a carefully nurtured desire to understand the faith in order to become one of its apologists, I have spent my professional life *not* defending Catholicism, but learning to understand it as a lower case word. The council allowed me to train myself for more effective service within the tradition, but gave me the desire to move beyond it, into the very territory I was taught to avoid.

I grew up defending myself for being a Catholic. In my little backwater town in Ohio, residual Klan embers were alive in bullies and bigots. I was beaten up regularly for attending Catholic school, and my parents were not permitted to join the local country club lest the smell of incense distract the duffers. We had been in that town for generations, knew the game (factories that would not hire us, people who would not associate with us), and played our part. That is to say, we were as public and outrageous in our faith as we dared to be (parading around the block during May aided by a loudspeaker as we recited the rosary, for example), thereby reinforcing the worst fears of our neighbors.

When I got bored with the Catholic school students (I graduated in a class of twelve) and wanted to be part of the more glamorous life of the public school kids, I boned up on a little book called (I think) *Forty Questions Most Asked by Protestants*. It did not really help: they were much more interested in french kissing (why a mortal sin) and birth control (why not permitted) than in the questions in the book ("is it true that Catholics chained up Bibles in the Middle Ages?"). But it was a start, and I spent many a slumber party engaged in these issues, while some of my friends were happily making out under blankets in finished basements.

But, if I were somehow part of this world, I was clearly different as well. When everyone else tucked into sleeping bags at dawn, I got on my bike to ride in to church where for several years I was our only organist. Because I was in church constantly, bright and apparently interested in religion (what else was there?), I was an obvious target for convent hustlers. But my wise old mother told me that going to the convent before I finished college would mean that I wouldn't get my B.A. degree until I was forty. "Forget it," she said, "until you're old enough."

Of course, when I was old enough, I was no longer interested. I had survived sixteen years of Catholic education, had a degree in chemistry, and landed, by some perverse providence, in a pharmaceutical company to work on birth control research. Since it was the only job offer I had, whatever moral scruples I may have entertained were trumped by the desire to get out on my own. Besides, when I had argued in an ethics paper that the "population explosion" was real and that birth control might be a moral alternative, I received a C- and a lecture on obedience to church teaching. Making birth control pills was a declaration of independence.

Distressingly, the world of science turned out to be almost as bigoted as my hometown. So, I spent some time defending the church while deconstructing the company prejudice that girls from good Catholic colleges were naturally pliable. My job was interesting but repetitive, rather like being a short order cook with a limited menu. Since it was the mid '60s and the council was in gear, I read some of the new theology books for fun. Louis Bouyer's *Liturgical Piety* changed my life in my senior year of college, Peter Ellis's *The Men and Message of the Old Testament* drew me into the Bible for the first time in my life, and Teilhard de Chardin was magical for me. At the same time, I was reading Betty Friedan and finding that I could *not* defend the Catholic Church where women were concerned. Into this mix of professional boredom, theological turn-on, and early feminism came news of a new doctoral program in theology at Notre Dame. I applied saying that I had no real idea what theology was, but knew I would love it. When I accepted a fellowship, I thought I would learn how to demolish all those lunks I grew up with. I just assumed I would end up in a Catholic college somewhere.

I will pass quietly over my years under the golden dome, saying only that I was not very well trained by today's standards (no theory), but I knew the basics; I loved church history (which they did not offer) and was bewildered by theological discourse. Halfway through my dissertation, I was a finalist for a post-doctoral fellowship at Oxford. I was flown over for an interview and, believe it or not, was greeted with a question about being a "Roman Catholic" (didn't I find it depressing?). I remember (or have invented) a couple of snappy answers to that question (which came up several times). When I did not get the fellowship, I ended up teaching in a seminary where I was hired by the apostolic delegate as M. J. Weaver with a degree in history (not Mary Jo Weaver with a degree in theology). They wanted a Catholic, not a woman, and my three years there taught me about patriarchy and the validity of Weberian leadership types. I pass over this time, too, though often think it might make a good novel.

At Indiana University, where I have been since 1975, I learned to be catholic. I uncoupled myself from the "we-language" that marked my religious conversation and abandoned theology for the academic study of religion. In many ways, it was a baptism by fire. A ghetto Catholic from a small town, a small Catholic college, and Notre Dame was now teaching an introduction to Judaism, Christianity, and Islam. I had never met a Jewish person, knew nothing about Islam, and was teaching more students in one classroom than had comprised the entire student body in my last institution. Most embarrassing for me was my total ignorance of non-Catholic Christianity, something I worked hard to remedy as I taught that course every semester for the next decade.

I was reared in a Catholic ghetto, but shaped in a catholic intellectual environment, a department that accepts the face value of all religious traditions, fosters cross cultural dialogue, and demands that we pay attention to the ecumenical complexities of historical context. An old music hall song chides a runaway woman saying "you'd be out of place in your own home town." That is true for me geographically and intellectually, and I thank the council every day for that escape route. It has given me an angle of vision on myself, my tradition, and American Catholicism that I cannot imagine getting anywhere else.

Mary Catherine Hilkert, O.P.

Mary Catherine Hilkert was born in Akron, Ohio, in 1948 and educated in Catholic elementary and high schools there. She joined the Sisters of St. Dominic of Akron, Ohio (Order of Preachers), in 1966. She received her B.A. degree from the University of Dayton in 1971, with a major in English and a minor in theology. From 1971-1977 she taught religious studies and co-chaired that department at St. Vincent-St. Mary High School in Akron. She subsequently earned an M.A. (1979) and a Ph.D. (1984) in theology from the Catholic University of America.

From 1984-1995, Hilkert was a member of the faculty at Aquinas Institute of Theology in St. Louis. Missouri. Since 1995 she has been associate professor of theology at the University of Notre Dame. She is the author of Speaking with Authority: Catherine of Siena and the Voices of Women Today *(2001),* Naming Grace: Preaching and the Sacramental Imagination *(1997), as well as numerous articles on contemporary theology, spirituality, and preaching. She edited William Hill's* Search for the Absent God *(1992), and with Robert Schreiter coedited* The Praxis of Christian Experience: An Introduction to the Theology of Edward Schillebeeckx *(1989, revised edition forthcoming). A past member of the board of directors of the Catholic Theological Society of America, Hilkert has lectured and preached throughout the United States, as well as in Canada, Ireland, Australia, and South Africa. In 1997 she was awarded the Washington Theological Union's Sophia Award for her theological contributions to ministry.*

During the Second Vatican Council she was a high school student at St. Vincent High School in Akron, Ohio.

The Impact of Vatican II

As I began what I thought would be an easy assignment—to reflect retrospectively on the repercussions or meaning of the council for my work or ministry—I realized that my memories of the council, like all memories, have shifted and taken on new significance at various points in the past forty years. In 1962 I was more concerned about the opening of my high school years than about the new moment unfolding in the history of the church. November 1963 was etched in my mind not because I realized then how profoundly the first conciliar document to be approved, the "Constitution on the Sacred Liturgy," would impact the life and thinking of the church, but because of John F. Kennedy's assassination. That same year I mourned the death of Pope John XXIII with the rest of the world, but with little awareness of how his surprising call for a council to open the windows of the Catholic Church would affect the future of the church as well as my own future.

In religion class during my junior year of high school, we were required to keep a scrapbook of newspaper articles chronicling the developments at the council. I was intrigued by all the interest in the surprising new document, "Schema 13" ("Pastoral Constitution on the Church in the Modern World") and mystified as to why a priest would find it necessary to report on the council under the pseudonym "Xavier Rynne." As I graduated from high school, the war in Vietnam was of far greater concern to me than the council in Rome that closed that year. Several months later I joined a religious congregation—the Akron Dominicans—to explore what was becoming the increasingly murky area of "discerning one's vocation in life." Neither I nor the majority of Dominican sisters throughout the world had any idea at that time that the call of the "Decree on the Appropriate Renewal of the Religious Life" to return to "the spirit of the founder" of the order would involve in many ways a profound shift in our consciousness, life-style, and ministry. Forty years later, we continue to discover what it means to be women who share the charism and mission of the Order of Preachers and to understand religious life as one intense way of living the call to holiness shared by all the baptized.

My novice director in the late 1960s decided that, in addition to scripture and the history of the Order, the most appropriate theological formation we could pursue would be a careful study of the documents of Vatican II. Since the commentaries were not yet written, we were guided in our studies by tapes of talks by Karl Rahner, Edward Schillebeeckx, Yves Congar, Jean Danielou, and other major theologians who helped to shape the vision and documents of the council. With little theological background, we struggled to listen as the major theologians who had helped bishops to formulate contemporary doctrine explained the significance of a turn of a phrase, a debated omission, the placement of a chapter, or the introduction of a whole new document.

Almost forty years later, as I teach students—even doctoral students—who were not born at the time of Vatican II, they look incredulous as yellowed pages fall from my original paperback copy of Abbott's *Documents of Vatican II*. The sense I try to convey to them of the major significance of that ecclesiastical event is one I learned during my graduate studies in the Department of Theology at Catholic University of America in the late 1970s. It wasn't until my systematic study of those documents for our dreaded master's comprehensive examinations that I realized the historic significance of the decrees on religious liberty, or ecumenism, or the relationship of the church to non-Christian religions. In those days the names Karl Rahner, Edward Schillebeeckx, Yves Congar, Hans Küng, Henri de Lubac, Joseph Ratzinger, and Jean Danielou all fit together in my mind as theologians with differing perspectives, all of whom were fostering and interpreting the vision of Vatican II.

From my present vantage point, my memories of the impact of the council on my life and ministry over the last forty years are poignant ones. I can see how my own identity as a baptized woman, a professed member of the Order of Preachers, and a Catholic theologian has been profoundly shaped by the vision of the council. Texts written forty years ago take on new significance and power. At the same time, the stories I studied of the silencing of theologians before the council are now being relived in the lives of colleagues and teachers, whose lives of integrity and commitment to Catholic theology have been a source of inspiration for me and for many others for all these years. Neither the academic community where I first preached in trepidation to a community that included my theological professors and colleagues, nor the theological school where I preached regularly as one of the many theologically trained preachers on the faculty, nor the academic campus where I now teach as a tenured member of the theology faculty, now invite women or lay persons to preach during eucharistic celebrations. Many of the women with whom I studied or whom I later taught no longer find a home in the Roman Catholic Church.

Nevertheless, my deepest memory of the Second Vatican Council is that of a window that was opened quite unexpectedly and can never be closed. The Spirit does indeed breathe freely, forming reluctant prophets like Oscar Romero, drawing women and men into lives of ministry that recent Vatican documents question, developing common ground in some of the most unlikely places, calling all of us to a deeper awareness of our social responsibilities and the vast suffering in our world, and working wonders in communities of believers. In the late 1960s, just years after the council, Cardinal Suenens detected pessimism and a sense of defeat within the church and the broader society and confessed to his own "dark night of hope" during what he called the "winter of the post-Council era." But he also reminded Christians that it is precisely in situations that appear hopeless that genuine hope—a sheer gift of the Spirit—is born. The memory of words from a letter he wrote on Pentecost in 1974 continue to inspire and challenge me: "Who would dare to say that the love and imagination of God were exhausted?"

Robert Blair Kaiser

Robert Blair Kaiser went through ten years in the Society of Jesus, then, three years shy of ordination, left the Jesuits to pursue a career in journalism. He covered Vatican II for Time, *worked on the religion beat for* The New York Times, *and served as journalism chairman at the University of Nevada Reno. Three of his ten published books deal with Vatican II:* Pope, Council and World *(1963) is a report on the council's first session.* The Politics of Sex and Religion *(1985) is a narrative history of the papal birth control commission, and his current* Clerical Error *(2002) is a lights-and-shadows memoir about Vatican II.*

Kaiser won the Overseas Press Club Award in 1963 for the "best magazine reporting of foreign affairs"—for his reporting on the Vatican Council. Editors at three newspapers have nominated him for Pulitzer Prizes, and the book publisher E.P. Dutton nominated him for another Pulitzer for his exhaustive 634-page book on the assassination of Robert F. Kennedy, a work that will be republished next year.

Kaiser's home town is Phoenix, Arizona, where he co-authored a musical comedy, "Jubilee 2000," that celebrates 2000 years of Christian history in 90 minutes of song and dance. This play was produced all over the U.S. and Canada in the Jubilee Year 2000, and has been seen by at least a half million persons.

Kaiser currently covers Rome for The Tablet. *Since the fall of 1999, he has been a contributing editor in Rome for* Newsweek *magazine while writing a book on the future of the church. He has a contract with CBS Television News as an analyst for that network's coverage of the next conclave.*

The Story of Archbishop Thomas Roberts[30]

Early in the first session of Vatican II, I walked into a dim, oversized kind of library room at the Foyer Unitas near the Piazza Navona, and found a slight figure with great bushy eyebrows sitting under a small lamp reading his breviary.

Thomas D'Esterre Roberts was wearing a black cassock speckled with a thin layer of fine cigarette ash; it gave him a slightly raffish look, like Alec Guinness playing Gulley Jimson. He lowered a pair of black horn-rimmed spectacles, looked over the top of them at me, *Time's* correspondent in Rome, with a twinkle in his eye and a wrinkle of his nose, and said, "Are you a Papist?" I burst out laughing.

"Not only am I a Papist," I said, "I was a Jesuit for ten years. Sometimes, I think I am still a Jesuit." His bushy eyebrows worked a bit over that news, but I could tell that this created an instant understanding between us. I only enhanced the good feelings by telling him that I loved his seminal treatise on authority, *Black Popes*.

He wrinkled his nose again. I would soon learn that he always wrinkled his nose, like a rabbit, whenever he was pleased, or about to deliver a zinger. He told me he wasn't even sure he was welcome at this council. He said that in 1960 he had gotten some haughty letters from Archbishop Gerald O'Hara, the Apostolic Delegate in England, and Cardinal Godfrey of Westminster, who told him they'd "delated" *Black Popes* to the Holy Office for "the scandalous material" contained in it. Neither of them had ever bothered telling him how *Black Popes* was "scandalous." I frowned. My guess was that it wasn't just *Black Popes* that caused the trouble. After all, the book had been published more than a decade ago.

My guess was that Roberts had become an aging *enfant terrible*. He was the only bishop in the world who advised Pope Pius XII in 1950 not to define as infallible the dogma of the Assumption of Our Lady. And he had marched with Bertrand Russell in a daring, ban-the-bomb campaign at a time when Catholics didn't march with Protestants (or heathens) in any kind of cause. In a mock serious tone, I asked him how he could urge the Quakers to come to a council to look in on a debate on war and peace and The Bomb when these matters weren't even on the agenda. He wrinkled his nose and said that maybe the presence of the Quakers would help get the question on the agenda.

"Is there anything better I can do here," he said, "than to stop the world from blowing itself up?"

I had no good answer to that. I wondered to myself whether this raffish little Englishman, or even an entire council, could stop the world's leaders from starting a nuclear war if they wanted to. Only time would tell about that. So I changed the subject and asked him how an archbishop, even a Jesuit archbishop, could turn out to be so, well, different.

He said he'd tell me if I would drive him home. Bargain. He lived in a poor convent way out on the Monte del Gallo. On the drive, he told me how he'd just been minding his own business, serving as rector of a small college in Liverpool, when he got the news (from an inquiring newspaper reporter!) that Rome was making him the next archbishop of Bombay, India. He claimed that it wasn't until he had received the holy oils of episcopal consecration that some Vatican functionary discovered he'd tabbed the wrong English Jesuit. By then, of course, it was too late.

I thought to myself that this was a happy accident. Perhaps the Holy Spirit knew what she was doing. In teeming, turbulent, overcrowded, backward Bombay (where Catholics were less than one half of one percent of the population), T. D. Roberts became a very pastoral, very compassionate shepherd who had a surfeit of free time on his hands to do some heavy thinking about the mission of the church in the world. He thought the church had unwisely tied itself to the Latin culture in which it took such solid root, that the missionaries who then branched out from that root did so not only to Christianize Asia and Africa and South America but to Europeanize those continents as well. The missionaries were colonizers for a particular culture as much as witnesses to Christ's coming for all humankind.

Roberts soon realized he would have to abdicate his office. He could see that Gandhi's movement would eventually end with the banishment of the British. So Roberts sent Pope Pius XII a series of letters telling him that the church didn't need an Englishman in Bombay, it needed a native Indian archbishop. The pope did not agree.

Roberts knew that the pope might regret that decision. He saved the situation by a bit of cunning. In 1946, when the Atlee government in England committed itself to Indian independence, he simply got the pope to let him have an Indian auxiliary bishop. Roberts had just the chap in mind for the job, a tall, stately young priest named Valerian Gracias. Then Roberts packed a valise, walked out the door, and told Gracias over his shoulder to run the show—because he was taking a two-year trip around the world via tramp steamer. He ended up in Rome.

"You see?" Roberts told Pius XII. "Now that India has gone independent, you have an Indian in Bombay just when you need him." The pope fixed Roberts with a long, deep, unsmiling stare, then nodded and sighed in French, *Bien*. Gracias would soon become the first native Indian cardinal. As for Roberts, he had schemed himself out of a job. The pope suggested he might return to England where he could preach at the Jesuits' famous church on Farm Street.

When we arrived at Roberts' convent, he was staring ahead through the window of my VW at the macadamed bleakness of the street, with not even a tree or a bush in sight.

"You feel isolated out here?" I asked. He nodded.

Suddenly, I suggested that he might like to come home with me to dinner—that very night. I didn't have to urge him. We drove directly back to Monteverde Vecchio and as we did so Roberts asked me about Mrs. Kaiser. "How can she stand all these—people you bring home?"

"Mary?" I said. "She's got a thing about clerics. She loves 'em."

Mary needed no prompting. She loved Archbishop Roberts. He told a lot of stories, he had a brandy or two, he bounced our little daughter Betsy on his lap, he told some more stories. Mary and I had the same idea almost simultaneously. His Grace was lonely and alone. We had a spare bedroom. Why didn't he stay with us? He pondered that invitation for a millisecond and said he'd be delighted. I moved him in the next day.

With my own council father in residence, so to speak, I had an edge on the other journalists at the council. I began learning things from Roberts that I couldn't get from the official daily briefings at the Press Center. For one thing, each day, he routinely handed me all the secret documents of the council. They were in Latin. But I read Latin rather well. Roberts gave me more than that. Through him, I began to see the council and its changing moods through the eyes of a council father, and from a council father who was also becoming a part of my own family. Each evening, I'd get home to find him preparing for Mass, which he celebrated conversationally, primitively, on a table at one end of our triple living room. "The biggest, most undreamed of thrill of all," Mary wrote home to her family, "is having His Grace say Mass every day in our very own living room. He says Mass facing Betsy and I, with Bob next to him, serving. What a blessing for us."

Afterward, we'd have a cocktail and some dinner, and talk about the council's proceedings, trade rumors and gossip of the day, discuss who'd said what to whom at the two bars behind the main altar at St. Peter's, the Bar Jonah and the Bar Rabbas (where they served brandy and schnapps as well as cafe espresso).

"They turned Ottaviani off today," T. D. reported one evening with a chuckle. "He had gone far beyond the ten-minute item limit. After a warning by the chair, he found he was speaking into a dead microphone."

Ottaviani boycotted the council for a number of days after that, and there was no official accounting for his absence. Then T. D. came home with a story, picked up at the Bar Jonah. "Now they say the reason why Ottaviani hasn't been coming," reported T. D. with a wrinkle of his nose, "is that his chauffeur kept him waiting so long the other morning that he called a passing taxi and told the driver, 'To the Council.'" T. D. paused, then added laconically, with perfect timing, "The cabbie drove him to Trent."

The council sessions lasted until mid-day. Then T. D. would catch a municipal bus home. Sometimes, he'd nap after lunch, then receive an increasing number of visitors around tea time—allies and potential allies in his efforts to get the question of war and peace and The Bomb put on the council's agenda. His own afternoon guest list began to include a steady stream of ban-the-bombers, Czech and Polish and Hungarian bishops who wanted to go back to their governments with a pacifistic statement from the council, members of the United Nations' Food and Agricultural Organization, English civil libertarians, Indian converts in saffron colored saris, Quakers in severe black woolen suits, ex-priests in trouble, seminarians who wanted to know how to disobey their superiors, journalists who wanted to interview him, and artists who wanted to draw him. . . .

Far from being isolated in his resistance to the antediluvian minds of the Roman curia, he found that his venturesome opinions were shared by many others, including some of the best prelates in Christendom. With him, they thought (and said out loud) that the church was overloaded with excess baggage, myth, superstition, and nonsense. With him, they voted on all the important reforms of Vatican II, most of which tended to make the church less Roman—and more Catholic.

Every morning, I'd drive Roberts to the council. He hated the regal trappings of his office, mumbled when he got tangled in his robes as we climbed into my yellow Volkswagen, and made clear his antipathy for humbug whenever he had a chance. One morning, when a pilgrim in St. Peter's Square asked him to bless her rosary, he grimaced and gave it a perfunctory wave. He wore no episcopal ring, and if anyone asked him about it (thinking they might be expected to kiss it), he said with a grin and a wrinkle of his nose that he kept it in his back pocket.

Thomas Groome

Thomas Groome was born on September 30, 1945, in County Kildare, Ireland, the youngest of ten children—nine of whom lived. His father, Terence, was a local politician with a keen commitment to social justice—though he wouldn't have called it that. His mother, Margaret, was a devout Catholic with a deep spirituality—though, he says, she wouldn't have called it that either.

In his time, St. Patrick's Seminary, Carlow, did not confer degrees, so Groome never received a B.A. at the end of his college course or an M.Div. after four years of theology, though he had the equivalent of both. Groome's first earned degree was an M.A. in religious education from Fordham University (1973), followed by a doctorate in theology and education from the joint program of Union Theological Seminary and Columbia Teacher's College (1976).

Since 1976, Groome has taught theology and religious education at Boston College, rising through the ranks to full professor in 1992. His first book was Christian Religious Education: Sharing Our Story and Vision *(1980). With it he introduced a "shared Christian praxis approach" to religious education; essentially this is a participative pedagogy of bringing "life to Faith, and Faith to life." Though he has written a number of books since then,* Christian Religious Education *continues to receive new translations—now in many languages—and to be used widely throughout the world. His most recent publication is entitled* What Makes Us Catholic: Eight Gifts for Life *(2002).*

Much of Groome's writing over the years has been of children's religion curricula. He is the primary author of God With Us *curriculum, grades K to 8 (1984), and of* Coming to Faith, *grades K to 8; the latter has had two major revisions. For almost twenty years, literally millions of U.S. Catholic children in parish programs and parochial schools have received their formal catechesis through these texts—all in the spirit of Vatican II. They are likely Groome's most significant contribution.*

Who Was That Tall Dark Stranger?

I was in a front row seat of the crowded assembly hall. He was a towering figure as I looked up at him, tall, trim, and handsome, with dark, bushy hair. And oh so impeccably dressed. The precise crease in his black suit meant it wasn't the tweed of my culture. His round-collar was the then-modern style, with just a sliver of white showing in front. The peeping cuff-links made for perfection in clerical array. Ah, but more imposing still was his eloquence; he mesmerized us assembled seminarians with the "inside story" from Vatican II.

St. Patrick's, Carlow, is the oldest seminary in the English-speaking world (founded 1793) and is renowned for preparing good pastoral priests. Yet, it has always lived in the shadow of the more elite St. Patrick's, Maynooth—beside Dublin. Famous scholars visiting Ireland rarely ventured this far into the countryside. And now, here was a world-renowned theologian, and a *peritus* no less at Vatican II, holding forth on the stage of our *aula maxima*.

What a night it was! Beyond his imposing stature and eloquence, the stranger's enthusiasm was infectious. Even the stiffs among the faculty seemed caught up in the moment. Everyone was clapping, hurrahing, egging him on, laughing at his jokes. By the end, there was nary a doubt among us but that the whole church would be renewed from top to bottom—or more likely from bottom to top—and soon. And this theological maestro was setting fire in our bellies to go over the hill as front-line troops in the grand *aggiornamento*.

It must have been the fall of 1965 because I was a first year theologian at the time and Vatican II was winding down. Our speaker clearly had first-hand knowledge about the council and could range across its many documents. Most memorable, however, were his comments about the "Decree on Ecumenism." As to the present day in Ireland, this topic can be politically loaded. But he was so persuasive. Of course Protestants are "brothers and sisters in faith," members by baptism of the same "Body of Christ." Who could disagree? Beyond that, surely God's love and saving will are universal. We'd heard of "baptism of desire" already but this theological pimpernel was saying much more, about dialogue and being open to learn from people of non-Christian faiths. What a novel notion!

The Irish newspapers were fairly extensive in their coverage of Vatican II, and our seminary profs would make cautious comments occasionally about what was "going on over there." But that memorable night and speaker amounted to my first existential awareness that a deep-down turning point was unfolding for the Catholic Church—and in our time. How exciting!

As I recall, it was about the same time that the seminary abandoned its great standard text-books. For as long as anyone could remember, we used a Nolden manual for moral theology, and texts by Ott and Tanquerey for dogma. Upon "crossing the wall" from philosophy to theology, one could pick up a set of these for a few shillings—maybe tenth hand and with invaluable cheat notes in the margins—and be well equipped for the next four years. But no more.

Pa Brophy, the dogma professor—and who came to epitomize the spirit of the council on our seminary faculty—introduced an array of modern texts, including a work by Charles Davis, then making headlines. Lar Ryan, the moral prof and later bishop of Kildare and Leighlin, dropped Nolden with its emphasis on preparing priests to hear confessions and taught us moral theology as the ethics of Christian living. And the whisper of "optional celibacy" for priests began to waft about, a topic of more than passing interest to a seminary full of testosterone-laden Irish lads. Ah, what a heady time it was!

Let me offer a brief retrospect on what Vatican II caused in my area of alleged expertise—religious education. Two particular catalysts come to mind.

First, remember that Trent had overwhelmingly favored a definition of faith as belief in the official teachings of the church. Thereafter, the mode of catechesis became a question and answer catechism that summarized the beliefs for children to memorize. Indeed, the success of Luther's *Short Catechism* also prompted Catholics to embrace this tool, but Trent gave the catechism its theological warrant by emphasizing faith as belief. It was precisely on this score that Vatican II put a cat among the catechetical pigeons.

In sum, the council proposed an understanding of Christian faith that includes "right belief" (orthodoxy) but likewise "right action" (orthopraxis) and "right worship." Catholics relearned from Vatican II that their faith must engage their heads, hearts, and hands, permeating every nook and cranny of their lives. Reclaiming a wholistic faith required a more wholistic approach to catechesis, one that would help people to integrate "life" and "faith" as a "living faith" in the midst of the world. Though the catechetical renewal encouraged by the council may have had its aberrations, in general and by God's grace it "continues to bear very welcome fruit" (*General Directory for Catechesis,* no. 24).

Second and closely related, the council revived a radical theology of baptism with major consequences for the church's educating in faith. By radical I mean a return to the roots, reclaiming baptism as a call to transformation of life after "the way" of Jesus. It confers great rights and responsibilities to participate in the church's function of continuing the mission of Jesus in the world. With baptism—not just with vows or holy orders—comes "the call of the whole Church to holiness" (*Lumen Gentium,* Ch. 5). In sum, Vatican II was a catalyst for Catholics to become active agents in their faith rather than passive dependents.

The spin-offs for catechetical education were myriad: a huge increase of lay leadership in catechetical education, greater numbers and a higher level of training among volunteers, increased parental participation in the faith education of children, awareness that faith must be integrated into daily life and lived for God's reign in the world, a new emphasis on adult religious education and on Christian faith as a life-long journey into holiness of life. The list could go on!

And that tall dark stranger? It was the young Gregory Baum. Little did I imagine as a "first divine" in Carlow seminary that some fifteen years later he would write me a cherished note of appreciation after I published my first book. Like the council, Gregory has "matured" since I looked up at him on stage at St. Patrick's, Carlow. But I still cling to the hopes that he and the council engendered in our young hearts back then, that the church can ever renew itself as an effective symbol—a sacrament—of God's reign in the world. And whenever I hear people debating about the true spirit of the council, I still think of Gregory Baum—then and now.

Notes

Preface

1. Max DePree, *Leadership is an Art* (New York: Dell Publishing, 1989), pp. 81-82.

Part One: The Council in Context

1. Material used in this introductory chapter was previously published in *St. Anthony Messenger*, vol. 104 (December, 1996): 50-51; vol. 106 (April, 1999): 50-51; vol. 109 (August, 2001): 50-51. I am indebted to the editors and authors of the first three volumes of *History of Vatican II*, ed. by Giuseppe Alberigo; English version ed. by Joseph A. Komonchak (Maryknoll: Orbis Books, 1995-).

2. In making reference to "fathers," mention must also be made of "mothers" of the council. Women were there. A good place to start is *Guests in Their Own House: The Women of Vatican II* (New York: Crossroad, 1996) by Carmel Elizabeth McEnroy.

3. For more on this, see *History of Vatican II*, 1:60-72. In Chapter 2, "The Antepreparatory Phase: The Slow Emergence from Inertia," Fouilloux asks the question whether or not the church was ready for a council.

4. For more on the reaction to the council both within and outside the church, see Giuseppe Alberigo, "The Announcement of the Council: From the Security of the Fortress to the Lure of the Quest," in *History of Vatican II*, 1:1-54. As the footnote on page 1 of the book shows, this title from the newspaper *La Croix* first appeared on January 30, 1959.

5. See J. Oscar Beozzo, "The External Climate," in *History of Vatican II*, 1:357-404.

6. Alberigo, "The Announcement," in *History of Vatican II*, 1:18-26. Here Alberigo examines in greater detail the episcopal responses, sharing one aside that Cardinal Spellman (New York) felt that the council was "destined for certain failure."

7. See Pope John's Opening Address in *The Documents of Vatican II*, ed. by Walter M. Abbott, trans. by Joseph Gallagher (New York: Guild Press, 1966), p. 716.

8. See Peter Hebblewaithe, *Pope John XXIII: Shepherd of the Modern World* (New York: Doubleday, 1985), p. 414.

9. See *History of Vatican II*, 1:33-44.

10. See *History of Vatican II*, 1:44-49.

11. These comments are found in Murphy's book review of *History of Vatican II, Vol. I: Announcing and Preparing Vatican Council II* in *Commonweal* (September 13, 1996), p. 34.

12. See *History of Vatican II*, 1:109-166.

13. See *The Documents of Vatican II*, pp. 712-713.

14. For more on the pope's opening address, see Andrea Riccardi, Chapter I, "The Tumultuous Opening Days of the Council," in *History of Vatican II*, 2:14-18.

15. For more background on this, see *History of Vatican II*, 2:26-32.

16. This and other stories and anecdotes can be found in *A Book of Catholic Anecdotes* by John Deedy (Allen, TX: Thomas More, 1997), p. 195.

17. The four volumes were *Letters from Vatican City* (1963), *The Second Session* (1964), *The Third Session* (1965), and *The Fourth Session* (1966), all published by Farrar, Straus & Giroux of New York. These reflections were reprinted in 1999 by Orbis Books under the title *Vatican Council II*.

18. This excerpt is taken in modified form from Xavier Rynne, *Vatican Council II* (Maryknoll: Orbis Books, 1999).

19. Richard Hooker as quoted in Samuel Johnson, *Dictionary of the English Language*, Preface (1755).

20. This reflection is an excerpt from the new introduction to the Transaction Edition of Michael Novak's *The Open Church* (Transaction Books: New Brunswick, NJ, 2001).

21. Leon-Joseph Suenens, *Memories and Hopes* (Dublin: Veritas Publications, 1991), p. 334.

22. John XXIII, "Opening Speech to the Council" (October 11, 1962), in *The Documents of Vatican II*, pp. 712-13.

23. Quoted in Xavier Rynne (pseud.), *The Second Session*, p. 6.

Part Two: Vatican II and the Liturgy

1. Mark S. Massa, *Catholics and American Culture: Fulton Sheen, Dorothy Day, and the Notre Dame Football Team* (New York: Crossroad, 1999), p. 149.

2. For Jungmann's reflections on the "Constitution on the Sacred Liturgy," see *Commentary on the Documents of Vatican II*, 5 vols., ed. by Herbert Vorgrimler (New York: Herder and Herder, 1966), 1:1-88.

3. See Daniel P. Grigassy, O.F.M., "The Liturgical Movement" in *The New Dictionary of Theology*, ed. by Joseph A. Komonchak, Mary Collins, and Dermot A. Lane (Collegeville: The Liturgical Press), pp. 586-91; and Mark Searle, "Liturgical Movement," in *The HarperCollins Encyclopedia of Catholicism*, ed. by Richard P. McBrien (New York: HarperCollins, 1995), pp. 783-85. Lengthier studies of the liturgical movement include: Marcel Metzger, *History of the Liturgy: The Major Stages*, trans. by Madeleine Beaumont (Collegeville: The Liturgical Press, 1999) and J.D. Crichton, *Light in the Darkness: Fore-Runners of the Liturgical Movement* (Collegeville: The Liturgical Press, 1996). An American perspective on the movement can be found in Keith F. Pecklers, *The Unread Vision: The Liturgical Movement in the United States of America: 1926-1955* (Collegeville: The Liturgical Press, 1998).

4. Fr. Diekmann's comments can be found in an interview ("Vatican II: there's been nothing like it in a 1,000 years") with the editors of *U.S. Catholic* (November, 1991):14-23.

5. Diekmann expands on this point in "The Constitution on the Sacred Liturgy," in *Vatican II: An Interfaith Appraisal*, ed. by John H. Miller, C.S.C. (Notre Dame: University of Notre Dame Press, 1966), p. 19.

6. I heard this example during a talk given by Untener entitled, "The Reforms of Vatican II: How Have We Done? Where Are We Going?" The recording was made and sponsored by The Emmaus Center for Music, Prayer, and Ministry in St. Paul, MN. The tape is distributed by St. Anthony Messenger Press (Cincinnati, 1996).

7. "The Constitution on the Sacred Liturgy," no. 50, in *Vatican Council II: The Basic Sixteen Documents,* ed. by Austin Flannery, O.P. (Northport, NY: Costello Publishing Co., 1996), pp. 135-36.

8. Diekmann, "The Constitution," in *Vatican II: An Interfaith Appraisal*, p. 23.

9. Cited by Diekmann, "The Constitution," in *Vatican II: An Interfaith Appraisal*, p. 23.

10. Arthur Jones, *New Catholics for a New Century: The U.S. Church Today and Where It's Headed* (Allen, TX: Thomas More Publishing, 2000), pp. 65-66.

11. This reflection appears in modified form in *Vatican II in Plain English: The Council* (Allen, TX: Thomas More, 1997).

12. Bernard Botte, *From Silence to Participation. An Insider's View of Liturgical Renewal,* trans. by John Sullivan, O.C.D. (Washington, D.C., The Pastoral Press, 1988), p. 170.

Part Three: What It Means To Be Church

1. See Vatican I, "Dogmatic Constitution on the Church of Christ" (1870) in Norman P. Tanner, ed. *Decrees of the Ecumenical Councils* (London: Sheed & Ward; Washington: Georgetown University Press, 1990), 2 vols., 2:811-12. Heinrich Denzinger et al., eds. *Enchiridion Symbolorum, Definitionum et Declarationum de Rebus Fidei et Morum* (Freiburg: Herder & Herder, 29th ed.), 1821.

2. See Tanner, 2:814-15; Denzinger, 1831.

3. See Tanner, 2:816; Denzinger, 1839.

4. In a schema on the Supreme Pastor, which was distributed but not discussed at Vatican I, we read: "The Church of Christ is not a society consisting of equal members, as though all the faithful who form part of it had the same rights. It is, on the contrary, an unequal (hierarchical) society in that some of the faithful are clergy and others are laity. It is above all such a society because there is in the church a power that is divinely instituted which some have received in order to sanctify, teach and govern and which others have not received." J.D. Mansi, *Sacrorum conciliorum nova et amplissima collectio,* 53 vols. (Florence, Venice, Paris, Leipzig: 1759-1927), 51:543. Cited by Yves Congar, "Moving Towards a Pilgrim Church," in *Vatican II Revisited By Those Who Were There* (Minneapolis: Winston Press, 1986), p. 133. The understanding of the church as an unequal society, in which the duty of the faithful is "to allow themselves to be led, and, like a docile flock, to follow the Pastors" is repeated by Pope Pius X in his encyclical *Vehementer nos* (1906). See Claudia Carlen, ed., *The Papal Encyclicals* (New York: McGrath, 1981), 3:47-48

5. See Xavier Rynne (pseud.), *Letters from Vatican City. Vatican Council II (First Session): Background and Debates* (New York: Farrar, Straus & Company, 1963), pp. 215-219, 222-231. Giuseppe Ruggieri, "Beyond an Ecclesiology of Polemics: The Debate on the Church," in *History of Vatican II,* 2:330-40. Gérard Philips, "History of the Constitution," in *Commentary on the Documents of Vatican II,* ed. by Herbert Vorgrimler, 5 vols. (New York: Crossroad, 1989), 1:109.

6. See Giuseppe Alberigo's summary of the state of the question in 1963-64: "Conclusion: The New Shape of the Council," in *History of Vatican II*, 3:491-498.

7. See Rynne (pseud.), *Letters from Vatican City*, p. 215.

8. Francis X. Murphy observed at the time that Chapter 2 of the Consitution, dealing with the church as the people of God, was "actually the heart of the Council's break-away from a scholastic approach to the theology of the Church. It described the mystery of the Church in biblical terms adapted to the existentialist world in which the Church now finds itself." Xavier Rynne (pseud.), *The Third Session: The Debates and Decrees of Vatican Council II, September 14 to November 21, 1964* (New York: Farrar, Straus & Giroux, 1965), p. 14.

9. "Though they differ essentially and not only in degree, the common priesthood of the faithful and the ministerial or hierarchical priesthood are none the less interrelated; each in its own way shares in the one priesthood of Christ." (no. 10) And: "The holy people of God shares also in Christ's prophetic office: it spreads abroad a living witness to him, especially by a life of faith and love and by offering to God a sacrifice of praise, the fruit of lips confessing his name (see Heb 13:15)." (no. 12) Austin Flannery, ed., *Vatican Council II: The Basic Sixteen Documents* (Northport, NY: Costello Publishing, 1996), pp. 14 and 16.

10. *Lumen Gentium*, no. 12, in Flannery, *Vatican Council II*, pp. 16-17.

11. In the original draft, the Council "teaches and solemnly professes that there is only one true Church of Jesus Christ, namely the one we celebrate in the creed as one, holy, catholic, and apostolic . . . which, after his resurrection, he entrusted to St. Peter and his successors, the Roman pontiffs, to be governed; therefore only the Catholic Roman has a right to be called the Church." Quoted by Giuseppe Ruggieri, "Beyond an Ecclesiology of Polemics: The Debate on the Church," in *History of Vatican II*, 2:286.

12. *Lumen Gentium*, no. 8. Flannery, *Vatican Council II*, p. 9.

13. *Lumen Gentium*, no. 15, in Flannery, *Vatican Council II*, pp. 20-21.

14. *Lumen Gentium*, no. 16, in Flannery, *Vatican Council II*, p. 22.

15. Already during the first session of the council (beginning in October, 1962), as the assembled bishops discussed their first topic, the liturgy, the question about the extent of the power of bishops to legislate liturgical requirements in their different nations became an issue. See Xavier Rynne (pseud.), *Letters from Vatican City*, pp. 97-98.

16. So even in the earliest phase of preparation for the council, known as the antepreparatory phase, the pope intervened so that the bishops around the world would have the opportunity to identify the items to be discussed at the council, rather than being presented with an agenda prepared by the Antepreparatory Commission and being asked for their reaction. At its May 26, 1959 meeting, the Antepreparatory Commission received from their president, Domenico Cardinal Tardini, a draft of a letter to the bishops and a questionnaire intended to guide their responses. In it, the defense of certain doctrinal and moral truths against modern errors and the return of "dissident brothers and sisters to the Roman Church" were identified as agenda items for the council. But at the meeting of the full commission on June 30, 1959, in the presence of Pope John, the procedure for consulting the bishops was completely changed. There would be no questionnaire, but only a simple letter in which the bishops would be asked to communicate with "complete freedom and honesty" the critiques and suggestions that their pastoral concern directs them to offer as possible points of discussion at the future council. See É. Fouilloux, "The Antepreparatory Phase: The Slow Emergence from Inertia (January, 1959-October, 1962)" in *History of Vatican II*, 1: 92-94.

17. Cited in Xavier Rynne (pseud.), *The Third Session*, p. 251. Archbishop Dino Staffa, Secretary of the Congregation of Seminaries, was especially energetic in working against the adoption of the doctrine of collegiality. The critics of collegiality argued that the doctrine was opposed to Vatican I and would, therefore, have the effect of suggesting that Vatican I was mistaken, thereby completely undermining the authority of the pope and opening the door to claims that the church was mistaken on other issues as well. See pp. 242-245.

18. See *Lumen Gentium*, "The Explanatory Note," in Flannery, *Vatican Council II*, pp. 92-95.

19. See Paul VI's Opening Address, cited in Rynne (pseud.), *The Third Session*, pp. 287-296; here p. 290. The pope declared that the council's deliberations on this subject "will certainly be what distinguishes this solemn and historic synod in the memory of future ages," p. 290. He further emphasized the need to coordinate this council's declarations on the subject with the teaching of Vatican I:

"The fathers of the first Vatican Council defined and proclaimed the truly unique and supreme powers conferred by Christ on Peter and handed on to his successors. This recognition has appeared to some as having limited the authority of bishops, the successors of the apostles, and as having rendered superfluous and prevented the convocation of a subsequent Ecumenical Council, which, however, according to canon law has supreme authority over the entire church.

"The present ecumenical synod is certainly going to confirm the doctrine of the previous one regarding the prerogatives of the Roman Pontiff. But it will also have as its principal objective the task of describing and honoring the prerogatives of the episcopate. . . .

"Let us repeat as our own those well-known words which our distant and saintly predecessor of immortal memory, Gregory the Great, wrote to Eulogius, Bishop of Alexandria: 'My honor is the honor of the universal church. My honor is the strength of my brothers. I am thus truly honored when the honor due to each and every one of them is not denied to them.'

"The integrity of Catholic truth now calls for a clarification consonant with the doctrine of papacy which will place in its splendid light the role and mandate of the episcopate," pp. 291-92.

20. *Lumen Gentium*, no. 22, in Flannery, *Vatican Council II*, pp. 30-31.

21. Avery Dulles, "Introduction to the Dogmatic Constitution on the Church," in *The Documents of Vatican II*, ed. by Walter M. Abbott (New York: Guild Press, 1966), p. 10. Cardinal Léger of Montreal regarded the document on the church as the hinge of the entire council. See Rynne (pseud.), *Letters from Vatican City*, p. 222. And Pope Paul VI believed that it would be the crowning achievement that "distinguishes this solemn and historic synod in the memory of future ages." See his Opening Address for the Third Session (September 14, 1964), in Rynne, *The Third Session*, p. 290.

22. This story is an excerpt in modified form of the speech Örsy gave in 1999 at the Catholic Theological Society of America annual meeting, when he was awarded the John Courtney Murray Award.

23. See "Detour: The Commission on Birth Control," *U.S. Catholic* (September 1995), p. 12. The *U.S. Catholic* article is an excerpt from Robert McClory, *Turning Point* (New York: Crossroad, 1995).

24. See Chapter 4 of *Lumen Gentium*, especially nos. 33-35, in Flannery, *Vatican Council II*, pp. 51-54.

Part Four: Revelation, Scripture, and Tradition

1. See R.A.F. MacKenzie, "Introduction to Dei Verbum," in Abbott, *The Documents of Vatican II*, p. 107. Murphy, writing pseudonymously under the name Xavier Rynne, concurred: "There can be little doubt that the Constitution on Divine Revelation will be regarded as the most important document promulgated by the Council after the Constitution on the Church. Together with *Lumen Gentium*, it enshrined and consecrated the new biblical approach to theology which has become one of the hallmarks of Vatican II." Rynne, *The Fourth Session: The Debates and Decrees of Vatican Council II, September 14 to December 8, 1965* (New York: Farrar, Straus and Giroux, 1966), p. 184.

2. Giuseppe Ruggieri, "The First Doctrinal Clash," in *History of Vatican II*, 2: 233. See also: Joseph Ratzinger, "Dogmatic Constitution on Divine Revelation, Origin and Background," in *Commentary on the Documents of Vatican II*, 3:155-67; Donald Senior, "Dogmatic Constitution on Divine Revelation," in *Vatican II and Its Documents: An Americal Reappraisal*, ed. by Timothy E. O'Connell (Wilmington: Glazier, 1986), pp. 122-140.

3. See Xavier Rynne (pseud.), *Letters from Vatican City*, pp. 140-141. Ruggieri, "Doctrinal Clash," *History of Vatican II*, 2:235.

4. Congar in *Informations Catholiques Internationales*, December 1, 1962, p. 2; cited in Rynne (psued.), *Letters from Vatican City*, p. 141.

5. In his *Disquisitio*, Rahner outlined four principal criticisms of the schema on revelation. First, the schema was too long and attempted to settle theological issues that were still controverted. Second, the text lacked a pastoral orientation. Third, the text also lacked an ecumenical spirit. Fourth, the schema improperly placed all of its statements on the same dogmatic level. See Ruggieri, "Doctrinal Clash," *History of Vatican II*, 2:237-240. Concerning Rahner's influence, see also p. 260.

6. Ruggieri, "Doctrinal Clash," *History of Vatican II*, 2:240.

7. See Rynne, *Letters from Vatican City*, pp. 141-143; Ruggieri, "Doctrinal Clash," *History of Vatican II*, 2:250-251.

8. Liénart, as quoted in Rynne, *Letters from Vatican City*, p. 143.

9. "It can be said that during the week of discussion of *De fontibus* the Council took possession of its purpose in the terms in which *Gaudet Mater Ecclesia* [John XXIII's Opening Address on October 11, 1962] had described it. It was the decisive phase of a process that was clearly articulated in Bea's intervention on November 14: (a) The Pope has given the Council a pastoral purpose; (b) the Council has already made this purpose its own in its opening 'Message;' and (c) the need now is consciously to ratify this purpose by rejecting a schema that runs counter to it. The clarity of Bea's vision of the real issue should not allow us to forget how passionate this debate was." Ruggieri, "Doctrinal Clash," *History of Vatican II*, 2:253. See also Rynne (pseud.), *Letters from Vatican City*, p. 149. In his diary entry for November 14, 1962, John XXIII wrote: "That disputes will arise can be foreseen. On the one hand, the draft [the preparatory schema] does not take into account the specific intentions of the Pope in his official discourses. On the other hand, a good eight cardinals, relying on these discourses, have discredited the main point of the draft. May the Lord help us and make us one." See Ruggieri, p. 256.

10. The Rules of Procedure constituted an Appendix to the document *Motu Proprio Appropinquante Concilio* (August 6, 1962). The text can be found in *La Documentation*

Catholique (October 7, 1962), p. 1231. Concerning whether the schema had papal approval, see Ruggieri, "Doctrinal Clash," *History of Vatican II*, 2:163, note #80.

11. Bishop Charue of Namur, Belgium, for example, rejected the suggestion that modernism needed to be condemned in the conciliar document: "It is not up to the Council to do the work of the Holy Office, or of theologians, but it is up to the Council not to set the stage for another Galileo incident! Our Council should imitate that of Jerusalem, and not put unbearable burdens on those outside the Church or the faith. The fact that the Church can house men of diverse opinions and attitudes gives us hope for the future." Cited by H. Fesquet, *Le Monde* (21 November 1962); Rynne (pseud.), *Letters from Vatican City*, p. 158.

12. See Rynne, *Letters from Vatican City*, pp. 161-163; Ruggieri, "Doctrinal Clash," *History of Vatican II*, 2:258-259.

13. See Rynne (pseud.), *Letters from Vatican City*, pp. 164-166; Ruggieri, "Doctrinal Clash," *History of Vatican II*, 2:262-263.

14. Rynne (pseud.), *Letters from Vatican City*, p. 167.

15. König as quoted in Xavier Rynne (pseud.), *The Third Session*, p. 44.

16. Butler stated: "We do not want the childish comfort of averting our gaze from the truth, but a truly critical scholarship which will enable us to enter into dialogue with non-Catholic scholars." Quoted in Rynne (pseud.), *The Third Session*, p. 47.

17. See Rynne (pseud.), *The Fourth Session*, pp. 187-196.

18. "Dogmatic Constitution on Divine Revelation" (*Dei Verbum*), no. 9 in Flannery, *Vatican Council II*, p. 103.

19. See Abbot Christopher Butler, "The Constitution on Divine Revelation," in *Vatican II: An Interfaith Appraisal*, p. 49.

20. *Dei Verbum*, no. 11 in Flannery, *Vatican Council II*, p. 105.

21. See the study Reid has done jointly with Leslie J. Hoppe, O.F.M., *Preaching from the Scriptures. New Directions in Preparing Preachers* (Pulaski, WI: Franciscan Printing, 1998).

22. See Heinrich Denzinger et al., eds. *Enchiridion Symbolorum, Definitionum et Declarationum de Rebus Fidei et Morum* (Freiburg: Herder & Herder, 29th ed.), 4214.

23. Denzinger, *Enchiridion*, 3886.

24. Karl Rahner, "Scripture and Theology," in *Theological Investigations*, vol. 6 (Baltimore: Helicon Press, 1969), p. 93. "Bible. B. Theology," in *Sacramentum Mundi*, 6 vols. (New York: Herder and Herder, 1968-70), 1:171-78, especially 176-77.

25. See Denzinger, *Enchiridion*, 4226.

26. See *Acta Apostolicae Sedis* 56 (1964), 712-18; Denzinger, *Enchiridion*, 4402-7.

27. See Denzinger, *Enchiridion*, 4404-06.

Part Five: Ecumenism and Interreligious Dialogue

1. Pius XI as cited in Williston Walker et al., *A History of the Christian Church*, 4th ed. (New York: Charles Scribner's Sons, 1985), p. 686.

2. See Rynne (pseud.), *Letters from Vatican City*, p. 44.

3. Rynne (pseud.), *Letters from Vatican City*, p. 77.

4. See Rynne (pseud.), *Letters from Vatican City*, pp. 190-191.

5. See Claude Soetens, "The Ecumenical Commitment of the Catholic Church," in *History of*

Vatican II, 3: 258-259, 264-266. Rynne (pseud.), *The Second Session*, pp. 216-217.

6. The Spanish cardinal de Arriba y Castro, for example, stated that the promotion of dialogue with other Christians seemed to contradict current church law, which forbade the publication or reading of books containing "heresy." From his perspective, "ecumenism" meant simply the right of the Catholic Church to engage in proselytization. Arriba y Castro proclaimed: "It should not be forgotten that only the Catholic Church has the right and duty to evangelize." Cited in Rynne (pseud.), *The Second Session*, p. 238. See also pp. 250, 264, and 274.

7. Soetens, "The Ecumenical Commitment," *History of Vatican II*, 3:263. Cardinal Ritter of St. Louis, for example, declared that the schema marked the end of the Counter-Reformation and gave substantial impetus to the unity of Christians. Ritter declared that the text should clearly acknowledge the validity of the sacraments of the Oriental Churches and should avoid any expressions offensive to Protestants. He added that there was no legitimate reason for denying the use of the term "church" to the religious groups that originated after the sixteenth century. See Rynne (pseud.), *The Second Session*, p. 237. See also pp. 251 and 263.

8. "The emendations were sent to Cardinal Bea as 'suggestions,' but in view of the lateness of the hour—it is said that they were communicated the previous evening when it was no longer possible to discuss them in a full meeting of the Secretariat and the final decision as to whether to accept or reject them had to be made by the cardinal with some of his aides—there can be little doubt that the papal suggestions were the equivalent of an 'order.' To have refused them would have jeopardized the whole decree." Rynne (pseud.), *The Third Session*, p. 264.

9. See Rynne (pseud.), *The Third Session*, p. 265.

10. "Decree on Ecumenism," in Flannery, *Vatican Council II*, pp. 502-503.

11. Cited by Walter Abbott in The *Documents of Vatican II* (New York: Guild Press, 1966), p. 338.

12. See Fourth Lateran Council, *Constitutions*, section 1 ("On the Catholic Faith"), in Norman P. Tanner, ed., *Decrees of the Ecumenical Councils*, 2 vols. (Washington: Georgetown University Press, 1990), 1:230. For the Council of Florence, see Tanner, *Decrees*, 1:578.

13. The Catholic Church's Holy Office rejected Feeney's claim that only Catholics could be saved by distinguishing between those who "really" belong to the church by means of explicit faith and actual baptism and those who "belong" to the church "by desire," that is, those people of good will who would join the church if they knew it to be the one, true Church of Christ. See "Feeney" in *The Harper Collins Encyclopedia of Catholicism*, ed. by Richard P. McBrien (San Francisco: Harper, 1995), p. 522.

14. See Francis A. Sullivan, *Salvation Outside the Church? Tracing the History of the Catholic Response* (New York: Paulist Press, 1992), pp. 3-6.

15. "Introduction" to *Nostra Aetate* in *The Documents of Vatican II*, ed. by Walter M. Abbott, p. 656.

16. See Rynne (pseud.), *The Second Session*, pp. 235, 239.

17. Bea said: "The Secretariat to which the care of promoting Christian Unity is given undertook the question treating the Jews not on its own initiative, but by reason of the express command of the Supreme Pontiff, Pope John XXIII of happy memory. This was given verbally to the President of the Secretariat." Quoted in Rynne (pseud.), *The Second Session*, p. 218. See also pp. 222-223.

18. See Rynne (pseud.), *The Second Session*, pp. 221, 222.

19. "Different reasons were alleged for this move: because the Pope [i.e., Paul VI] was anx-

ious not to compromise the reception he might receive in Jordan and Jerusalem on his intended pilgrimage; because of sharp Arab protests against the document made directly to the Vatican Secretariat of State through diplomatic channels; because of misgivings on theological grounds by some of the Pope's advisers, perhaps shared by Pope Paul; because of pressure exercised by the minority in the Council." Rynne (pseud.), *The Third Session*, p. 33.

20. *Nostra Aetate*, no. 4, in Flannery, *Vatican Council II*, p. 573.

21. *Nostra Aetate*, no. 2, in Flannery, *Vatican Council II*, p. 571.

22. It is important to read these statements together with the statements concerning Islam and Judaism in the "Dogmatic Constitution on the Church" (*Lumen Gentium*), no. 16, where the possibility of salvation for those who have not received the gospel is affirmed.

23. For an excellent history of the development of Catholic thinking on the issue of salvation outside the church, see Francis A. Sullivan, *Salvation Outside the Church?*

24. See Sullivan, *Salvation Outside the Church?*, pp. 70-73. This idea that some people might justifiably reject Christian faith because of the poor witness of Christians is picked up at Vatican II. See the "Pastoral Constitution on the Church in the Modern World" (*Gaudium et spes*), no. 19.

25. Sullivan, *Salvation Outside the Church?*, p. 98.

26. *Lumen Gentium*, no. 13, in Flannery, *Vatican Council II*, p. 19.

27. *Lumen Gentium*, no. 16, in Flannery, *Vatican Council II*, p. 22. See also *Gaudium et spes*, no. 22.

28. Editors' note: After acknowledging that the church was late in recognizing the principle of religious liberty, Murray continued: "In any event, the document is a significant event in the history of the Church. It was, of course, the most controversial document of the whole Council, largely because it raised with sharp emphasis the issue that lay continually below the surface of all the conciliar debates—the issue of the development of doctrine. The notion of development, not the notion of religious freedom, was the real sticking point for many of those who opposed the Declaration even to the end." Cited in Abbott, *Documents of Vatican II*, p. 673.

29. *Dignitatis Humanae*, no. 4, in Flannery, *Vatican II*, pp. 555-556; see alternative translation in Abbott, *Documents of Vatican II*, p. 682.

30. *Dignitatis Humanae*, no. 7, in Flannery, *Vatican II*, p. 558; see alternative translation in Abbott, *Documents of Vatican II*, p. 687.

31. Gerald M. Costello, op-ed piece, "[A Vatican Council Footnote:] The Cardinal Stepped In," *Catholic New York*, Oct. 10, 1982, 11.

32. Donald Pelotte, S.S.S., *John Courtney Murray: Theologian in Conflict* (New York and Ramsey, N.J.: Paulist, 1976), p. 82.

33. Costello, "The Cardinal Stepped In."

34. Bernard Häring, *My Witness for the Church*, trans. Leonard Swidler (New York and Mahwah, NJ: Paulist, 1992), p. 576.

35. Pietro Pavan, "Ecumenism and Vatican II's Declaration on Religious Freedom," in *Religious Freedom: 1965 and 1975. A Symposium on a Historic Document*, ed. Walter J. Burghardt, S.J. (Woodstock Studies 1: New York and Ramsey, NJ: Paulist, 1976), pp. 7-38, at p. 12.

36. Pavan, p. 10.

37. *Nostra Aetate*, no. 2 in Flannery, *Vatican II*, p. 571; alternative translation in Abbott, *Documents of Vatican II*, p. 663.

Part Six: World Issues and Social Justice

1. *Gaudium et spes*, no. 1, in Flannery, *Vatican II*, p. 163.

2. Jay P. Dolan, *The American Catholic Experience: A History from Colonial Times to the Present* (Garden City, NJ: Doubleday, 1985), p. 228.

3. As quoted by Justo Gonzalez in *The Story of Christianity: The Reformation to the Present Day* (New York: Harper & Row, 1985), p. 298.

4. See Donal Dorr, *Option for the Poor: A Hundred Years of Catholic Social Teaching*, revised and expanded edition (Maryknoll: Orbis Books, 1992); John A. Coleman, ed., *One Hundred Years of Catholic Social Thought: Celebration and Challenge* (Maryknoll: Orbis Books, 1991); and Michael Walsh and Brian Davies, eds., *Proclaiming Justice and Peace: Papal Documents from Rerum Novarum through Centesimus Annus*, revised and expanded edition (Mystic, CT: Twenty-Third Publications, 1991).

5. See Michael J. Schultheis, Edward P. De Berri, and Peter J. Henriot, *Our Best Kept Secret: The Rich Heritage of Catholic Social Teaching* (Washington: Center of Concern, 1987).

6. See Campion's Introduction to the "Pastoral Constitution on the Church in the Modern World," in Abbott, *Documents of Vatican II* , p. 183.

7. For this conversation and the remarks of Suenens concerning the plan for the Council, see his article, "A Plan for the Whole Council," in *Vatican II Revisited by those who were there*, ed. by Alberic Stacpoole (Minneapolis, MN: Winston Press, 1986), pp. 88-105.

8. Leon-Joseph Cardinal Suenens, *Memories and Hopes*, trans. by Elena French (Dublin: Veritas Publications, 1992), p. 78.

9. See Suenens, "A Plan for the Whole Council," in Stacpoole, *Vatican II Revisited*, p. 88.

10. Suenens, *Memories and Hopes*, p. 78.

11. Suenens, *Memories and Hopes*, pp. 97-98.

12. Quote from Pope John XXIII's September 11, 1962 radio address, cited in *History of Vatican II*, 2:437.

13. See Charles Moeller's "History of the Constitution," in *Commentary on the Documents of Vatican II*, 5:10-11.

14. Alberigo, *History of Vatican II*, 2: 200-203.

15. Vorgrimler, *Commentary on the Documents of Vatican II*, 5:10-11.

16. Suenens, *Memories and Hopes*, p. 86.

17. Suenens, *Memories and Hopes*, p. 87.

18. For those desiring more information than this brief introduction can provide, see *Commentary on the Documents of Vatican II*, ed. by Herbert Vorgrimler (New York: Herder and Herder, 1969), Volume V. This whole volume is devoted to the "Pastoral Constitution on the Church." Two other sources, though much shorter in their overview, include: "The Church in the Modern World" by Enda McDonagh in *Contemporary Catholic Theology: A Reader*, ed. Michael A. Hayes and Liam Gearon (New York: Continuum, 1998) and "The Constitution on the Church in the Modern World" by Bishop Mark G. McGrath, C.S.C. in *Vatican II: An Interfaith Appraisal*, ed. John H. Miller, C.S.C. (Notre Dame, IN: University of Notre Dame Press, 1966), 397-412.

19. Alberigo, *History of Vatican II*, 2:412.

20. Joseph Ratzinger, *The Theological Highlights of Vatican II* (New York: Paulist Press, 1966), p. 148.

21. Vorgrimler, *Commentary on the Documents of Vatican II*, 5:3.

22. Miller, *Vatican II: An Interfaith Appraisal*, p. 296. For more on the story of the Birth Control Commission, see Robert Blair Kaiser, *The Politics of Sex and Religion* (Kansas City: Leaven, 1985).

23. See Häring's article, "Marriage and the Family" in *Vatican II: An Interfaith Appraisal*, p. 439.

24. See Charles Moeller, "Man, the Church and Society" in *Vatican II: An Interfaith Appraisal*, p. 417.

25. McDonagh, "The Church in the Modern World," in *Contemporary Catholic Theology*, p. 306.

26. McGrath, "The Constitution on the Church in the Modern World, " in *Vatican II: An Interfaith Appraisal*, p. 397.

27. McDonagh, "The Church in the Modern World," in *Contemporary Catholic Theology*, pp. 300-301.

28. *Gaudium et spes*, no. 29, in Flannery, *Vatican Council II*, p. 194.; alternative translation in Abbott, *The Documents of Vatican II*, pp. 227-28.

29. *Lumen Gentium*, no. 32, in Flannery, *Vatican Council II*, pp. 49-50; alternative translation in Abbott, *Documents of Vatican II*, p. 58.

30. This story is excerpted from Kaiser's book *Clerical Error* (New York: Continuum Books, 2002).

Of Related Interest...

Church Emerging from Vatican II
A Popular Approach to Contemporary Catholicism
Dennis M. Doyle

Explains what it means to be a believing, practicing Catholic today in terms of Vatican II ecclesiology and theology.

0-89622-507-0, 368 pp, $19.95 (C-86)

Catholic Customs and Traditions
A Popular Guide
Greg Dues

From Candlemas, to the Easter candle, through relics, Mary, the saints, indulgences, the rosary, mystagogia, laying on of hands, and more, the author traces the vast riches of the traditions, customs, and rituals of Roman Catholics.

0-89622-515-1, 224 pp, $12.95 (C-14)

Pilgrim Church
A Popular History of Catholic Christianity
William J. Bausch

A delightful discovery for people who want to know how the church came to be and grew through the centuries.

0-89622-395-7, 480 pp, $24.95 (B-52)

A New Look at the Sacraments
William J. Bausch

Traces the history and development of the seven sacraments from a pastoral perspective.

0-89622-174-1, 300 pp, $14.95 (B-48)

Exploring Catholic Theology
God, Jesus, Church, and Sacraments
Brennan Hill

Using Scripture. history, and the thoughts past and present, Dr. Brennan Hill presents the basic theological teachings that underlie Catholic beliefs. He also addresses many common questions, objections, and misconceptions about these core teachings. Included are extensive footnotes, discussion notes at the end of each chapter, suggested readings, and a comprehensive index.

0-89622-661-1, 400 pp, $19.95 (M-44)

TWENTY-THIRD PUBLICATIONS
185 WILLOW STREET • PO BOX 180 • MYSTIC, CT 06355
TEL: 1-800-321-0411 • FAX: 1-800-572-0788
E-MAIL: ttpubs@aol.com • www.twentythirdpublications.com